MIKE SWARTZ
MARCH 2014

The Black Book
of the American Left

The Black Book of the American Left

The Collected Conservative Writings
of David Horowitz

Volume 1
My Life and Times

Second Thoughts Books

ENCOUNTER BOOKS
New York • London

First American edition published in 2013 by Encounter Books, an activity of Encounter for Culture and Education, Inc., a nonprofit, tax exempt corporation.

Encounter Books website address: www.encounterbooks.com

Manufactured in the United States and printed on acid-free paper. The paper used in this publication meets the minimum requirements of ANSI/NISO Z39.48 1992 (R 1997) *(Permanence of Paper)*.

FIRST AMERICAN EDITION

LIBRARY OF CONGRESS CATALOGING-IN-PUBLICATION DATA

Horowitz, David, 1939–
    The black book of the American left : the collected conservative
writings of David Horowitz / by David Horowitz.
    volumes   cm.
    Includes bibliographical references and index.
    ISBN 978-1-59403-694-1 (hardback)—ISBN 978-1-59403-695-8
(ebook)
    1. Socialism—United States. 2. Conservatism—United States.
3. New Left—United States—History.   4. Horowitz, David, 1939–
Political and social views.   I. Title.
HX86.H788 2013
335.00973   2013000496

10   9   8   7   6   5   4   3   2   1

Acknowledgments

The essays and articles in *The Black Book of the American Left* and the project itself would not have been possible without the David Horowitz Freedom Center and the dedicated individuals who staff it. Foremost among these are Mike Finch, who is the operating head of the Center, its fundraiser, and an informed counselor in all we do, and Peter Collier who has been my literary collaborator and friend for nearly fifty years. Mike Bauer gathered and helped to edit all the articles contained in these volumes, and John Perazzo and Elizabeth Ruiz helped with the research on many of them. Finally, I wish to acknowledge the love and support of my wife April through the years of writing and editing these volumes, and to thank her for being there for me.

Contents

Preface to
The Black Book of the American Left

The idea for these volumes came about as the result of a self-inventory undertaken to map the development of my political views over the last thirty years. This inquiry involved a survey of all the articles and essays I had written as a conservative—since the day Peter Collier and I published a cover story in the *Washington Post Magazine* announcing our "second thoughts" about the left and our departure from its ranks. These writings, which were assembled with the indispensable help of Mike Bauer, added up to more than 690 articles and essays, and a million and a half words. Some were lengthy considerations of "big" issues, others reactions to current events, and some were polemical responses to political opponents. But when I had looked over this body of work, I realized that virtually everything I had written was really about one subject: the American left.

The ancient Greek poet Archilochus was the author of a philosophical fragment that became the focus of a famous essay by the writer Isaiah Berlin, which he called "The Hedgehog and the Fox." In his fragment Archilochus observed, "The fox knows many things, but the hedgehog knows one big thing." For whatever reason, in the many years I have been a writer I have never been a fox. It is true that my subjects have been varied, and I have even authored two volumes of philosophical reflections about mortality and life. But the primary focus of my work—even of those thoughts on mortality and existence—has remained one big thing: the nature, deeds and fortunes of the political left.

The first part of my life was spent as a member of the "New Left" and its Communist predecessor, in which my family had roots. After the consequences of those commitments became clear to me in the mid-1970s, I came to know the left as an adversary; and if sheer volume were the measure, as its principal intellectual antagonist. Some have seen an obsession in my efforts to define the left and analyze what it intends. In a sense that is true; I had left the left, but the left had not left me. For better or worse, I have been condemned to spend the rest of my days attempting to understand how it pursues the agendas from which I have separated myself, and why.

When I was beginning this quest nearly three decades ago, I paid a visit to the New York intellectual, Norman Podhoretz, who had had his own second thoughts a decade earlier, though not from so radical a vantage as mine. Podhoretz asked me why I was spending my time worrying about an isolated community on the fringes of politics. I should focus, he said, on liberals not leftists. This advice reflected what seemed an accurate description of the political landscape at the time. Many would have seconded his judgment when the walls of Communism came tumbling down shortly thereafter. But the progressive faith is just that, a *faith*, and despite the exceptions of individual cases no fact on the ground will dispel it.

When Podhoretz and I met, progressives and radicals had already escaped the political ghettos to which my parents' generation had been reasonably confined. The massive defeat they suffered in the fall of the Marxist states they helped create had the ironic, unforeseen effect of freeing them from the burden of defending them. This allowed them in the next decade to emerge as a major force in American life. In the wake of the Communist collapse, this left has become a very big thing—so big that by 2008 it was the dominant force in America's academic and media cultures, had elected an American president, and was in a position to shape America's future. Because of its post-Communist metastasis, what Norman Podhoretz once saw as a parochial interest in a fringe cause has become an effort to understand the dominant development in America's political culture over the last fifty years. That is the subject of these volumes.

The essays contained herein describe the left as I have known it; first from the inside as one of its "theorists," and then as a nemesis confronting it with the real-world consequences of its actions. In all these writings I was driven by two urgencies: a desire to persuade those still on the left of the destructive consequences of the ideas and causes they promoted; and second, the frustration I experienced with those conservatives who failed to understand the malignancy of the forces mobilized against them. Most conservatives habitually referred to leftists who were determined enemies of America's social contract as "liberals." In calling them liberals, conservatives failed to appreciate the Marxist foundations and religious dimensions of the radical faith or the hatreds it inspired. And they failed to appreciate the left's brutal imposture in stealing the identity of the intellectually pragmatic, patriotic, anti-totalitarian "Cold War liberals" whose influence in American political life they began killing off in 1972 with the McGovern *coup* inside the Democratic Party.[1]

When this syllabus of my conservative writings was finally assembled and I had read their contents through, I realized that even though they would take up multiple volumes they added up to a single book, which my colleague Peter Collier quickly christened the "The Black Book of the American Left" (a flattering allusion to *The Black Book of Communism*, the authoritative 1997 work by several European academics outlining the terror and catastrophe created by communist states.) Contained in these volumes is a diary, written over more than half a century, that describes one man's encounters with a movement which, in the words of its most prominent figure, Barack Obama, is seeking to

---

[1]One consequence of this was the large number of conservatives who voted in 2008 for Barack Obama, a man whose political outlook was shaped in the same radical crucible as mine—first Communist, then New Left. "Exit Polls Reveal Conservatives Abandoned McCain." *Newsmax*, November 9, 2008, http://www.newsmax.com/InsiderReport/Conservatives-Abandoned/2009/12/14/id/342127. On Obama's career in the radical left, see Stanley Kurtz, *Radical-in-Chief*.

"fundamentally" transform the United States of America. The diary records the progress of that transformation, documenting the changes of a shape-shifting movement that constantly morphs itself in order to conceal its abiding identity and mission, which, as these pages will make clear, is ultimately one of destruction.

It is almost a certainty that no other "book" will be written like this one, since it can only have been the work of someone born into the left and condemned Ahab-like to pursue it in an attempt to comprehend it. Yet this is not so much a project of monomania, as my adversaries will undoubtedly suggest, but of discovery; an attempt not only to understand a movement, but to explore its roots in individual lives, including my own. While I hope this book may be useful to those fighting to defend individual freedom and free markets, I do not deceive myself into believing that I have finally set the harpoon into the leviathan, a feat that is ultimately not possible. Progressivism is fundamentally a religious faith, which meets the same eternal human needs traditional faiths do, and for that reason will be with us always. In the last analysis, the progressive faith is a Gnosticism that can only be held at bay, never finally beaten back to earth.

My Life and Times

The essays included in this, the first of nine volumes on the American left—a tenth will feature a comprehensive bibliography and index—are shaped by a biographical perspective, drawn directly from my life-experiences in that left.[1] They contain reflections first on the political path my life took, and then on the course pursued by others who shared that path but did not have second thoughts that prompted them to leave it.

Because the left is a religious movement that engages an individual identity at the deepest levels, there can never be a separation between the personal and the political. Members of the faith know very well the implications of doubt: to leave the progressive faith is to invite expulsion from its utopia and the fellowship of its community, and forever after to be shunned as a person morally unfit for decent company. This is a daunting prospect that discourages challenges to its orthodoxy and keeps its adherents in line. This reality makes the narrative of one who departed its ranks not only a deeply personal document but also a political text.

Part I

In December 1974, my life was forever altered when members of the Black Panther Party murdered a bookkeeper named Betty Van Patter whom I had recruited to keep accounts for a Panther school

---

[1]See my autobiography, *Radical Son* (1997). Several shorter autobiographical testimonies that can be found in other books I have written: *Destructive Generation* (1989), *The Politics of Bad Faith* (1998), *The End of Time* (2005), *A Cracking of the Heart* (2009) and *A Point in Time* (2011).

I had helped to create. The tragedy threw me into a personal crisis, creating an ideological turmoil that was compounded five months later by the bloodbath in Southeast Asia following the Communist victory in Vietnam. The state of distress into which I was thrown by these events was such that for more than a decade I did not engage in any political activities. During this period I took time to reflect on the beliefs that had guided me and then betrayed me, and I tried to figure out how I was going to function without them. In 1979, I had dinner in Berkeley with the leftwing author E. L. Doctorow, whose novel about the Rosenbergs had referenced one of my books. I told him of my concerns about the left, and he suggested I write them up for *The Nation* on whose board he sat. The result was an article I called "Left Illusions," which *The Nation* retitled "A Radical's Disenchantment." It put my doubts before a community with whom I still identified but was getting ready to leave, though I was still reluctant to concede that, even to myself.

My formal departure came in 1985 with the publication of our divorce-notice in *The Washington Post*. The following year I wrote "Why I Am No Longer a Leftist," a more personal explanation of the events behind my turn. It was published in another progressive venue, *The Village Voice*, and is included as the second chapter in this volume. The decision to write the article was a particularly difficult one because it was the first public statement I had made about the murder. In publishing it I was concerned first of all about the safety of my family since the killers were still at large (as they are today). The fear was great enough that I did not name the individuals I believed responsible. This was something I would eventually do seven years later in a lengthy autobiographical article "Black Murder, Inc.," which is included as chapter five in the present text.

My intention in publishing "Why I Am No Longer a Leftist" in a leftwing paper like the *Voice* was to encourage its readers to have second thoughts and to warn them about the dangers of failing to have them. What I elicited instead was an anathema upon myself— an excommunication from the progressive community. The anathema was pronounced in the form of an article that appeared in the same paper shortly afterward called, "The Intellectual Life and the Renegade Horowitz." It made clear that my words were not going to be taken as an attempt to retrieve a bitterly earned truth about what we leftists had done, but as the betrayal of a noble cause by a person who had gone over to the dark side. The author was the socialist writer Paul Berman; he began by praising me as an intellectual leader among New Leftists in the Sixties and concluded by damning me as one who now consorted with monsters, in particular with a homicidal member of the Nicaraguan *contras* whose *nom de guerre* was *Suicida.* This was, in point of fact, an individual I had never heard of, and whom the *contras* themselves had executed for his crimes, which were indeed heinous. This kind of reckless assault on my character was to prove typical of the left's responses to my work in years to come.

A year after the *Voice* article appeared, Peter Collier and I organized a "Second Thoughts Conference" in Washington to which we invited others who had taken steps along the path we had chosen. Two years later we held another Second Thoughts event in Cracow, Poland, just months before the collapse of the Communist regime. The speech I gave, "Reality and Dream," whose text is included as chapter three in this volume, was an effort to tell my story and summarize the case against socialism for an audience whose members were still prisoners of the Soviet occupation.

While focusing on the left, I also felt the need to define the new "conservative" outlook at which I had arrived. The article "My Conservatism" is a statement of the views I had developed, along with the reasons I did not regard this new perspective as parallel to the one I had abandoned but different in its very nature. I addressed the same subject in *The Politics of Bad Faith,* which was published in 1998, and which contains the fullest statement of the rationale for my political change.

The event that forced me to look at the reality of what I and my comrades had done is the subject of the memoir "Black Murder,

Inc." At the time the crime was committed, the Black Panther Party was regarded as a progressive vanguard and its leader Huey Newton was being compared in *The New York Times* to Martin Luther and Mahatma Gandhi. Even today, in respected academic texts like Henry Louis Gates's *African American National Biography*, the Party is portrayed as a noble vanguard, victimized by a racist government. This is a reflection not of the facts but of the way the left dominates and has corrupted the academic culture—the subject of the sixth volume of *The American Left*, titled *The Left in the University*.

After the publication of the *Post* and *Village Voice* articles, liberal venues were for all intents and purposes closed to me as a "renegade" from their ranks. "Black Murder, Inc." first appeared in a publication that Peter Collier and I had created, called *Heterodoxy*. We published it on the front page with a "Wanted" poster of Elaine Brown, the Panther most directly responsible for the murder, although I have no doubt that it was Huey Newton who ordered the execution from his exile in Cuba.[2] One of the most unpleasant responses of the left to the article was to attempt to place the blame for Betty's death on me. "Letter to the Past" is my reply to one of these accusations made by a lifelong friend of mine who had remained on the left and was obviously a friend no more. Our exchange reflects the raw emotions I felt at the time.

In retrospect, it is clear to me that the failure of the political culture and major media to take note of the Panthers' crimes and be horrified by them, indeed the support the perpetrators received from the progressive ranks, was a small but ominous sign of the profound change that the Sixties left had worked on the American political landscape. The resurfacing in the 1990s of a violent radical like Weatherman leader Bill Ayers as the intimate political ally of a future American president is a parallel phenomenon. It indicates just how far the influence of the left has reached.[3]

---

[2]My reasons for concluding this are laid out in *Radical Son*, pp. 221–250.
[3]Cf. Stanley Kurtz, Radical-in-Chief

Progressives are necessarily forced to choose between the future they desire and the reality they inhabit. The primary moral obligation of a revolutionary is to destroy the existing social and political framework in order to prepare the revolutionary future; and radicals perceive America as the principal defender of the capitalism they hate all over the world. Consequently, a radical politics generally leads to uncertain loyalties to country and community. Yet leftists have succeeded in making the issue of their loyalties the most taboo of political subjects, deploying blanket charges of "McCarthyism" and "witch-hunt" as a way of silencing their critics. As someone who experienced the conflict between principles and country directly, I have inevitably made them a focus of my work. "Treason of the Heart," an article written to promote my autobiography *Radical Son*, includes the accounts of three episodes, described in the book, which dramatize this conflict.[4]

Having rejected the left, I quickly discovered that the political center where I expected to find a home had vanished, while outlets for my work that I had expected to be available had shut their doors to me. "A Political Romance" was written at the request of an editor at *The New York Times Sunday Magazine*, who wanted a piece for the weekly "Lives" feature located at the back of the issue. I undertook the assignment as a challenge; another attempt to sum up in succinct fashion the hard lessons I had learned. But when I submitted the article, the editor rejected it by saying that it wasn't the "type" of piece *The Times* had in mind for the feature.

I was skeptical of this explanation, and suspected that what the editor really didn't like about the article was its political conclusion rejecting the left. This was borne out a few weeks later when the "Lives" page featured another piece, which was also about the left and was written as though it had been commissioned in reply to mine. The author was a leftist who admitted to some second

---

[4] This is a prominent theme of the essays contained in Volume 5 of this series, *9/11 and the "War on Terror."*

thoughts about what she and her comrades had done in the Sixties but, in contrast to me, resolved not to abandon what she still regarded as a noble cause. This episode provided a particularly dispiriting indication of the media environment in which I was now operating. Despite my quarantine as a conservative, I was still interested in engaging younger leftists, hoping I might help them avoid the painful lessons I had been forced to learn. "Think Twice" is an open letter to young people who protested against an American response to 9/11 within two weeks of the attacks.

Almost a decade after publishing *Radical Son*, I again turned inward in a series of books that I regard as my best writing. They include *The End of Time* and *A Point in Time*, along with the memoir I wrote about my daughter Sarah, *A Cracking of the Heart*. Those reflections articulated the themes that have animated my life's work. The "End of Time" in this volume is a presentation I made to promote the book. It consists of excerpted passages interspersed with commentary, and provides a glimpse of how I came to connect the personal with the political in the autumn of my career. "What My Daughter Taught Me" describes the dialogue I had with Sarah before her untimely death about the way in which human beings might make the world "a better place." My daughter Sarah was a compassionate soul and our discussions were the kind of dialogue I missed on the infrequent occasions when liberals bothered to address my work.

The most unpleasant aspect of my political odyssey has been the relentless, often malicious distortion of the positions I have taken by those who disagree with my political conclusions. Three of the last four articles in Part I deal with this phenomenon. The first, "Getting This Conservative Wrong," is my response to an academic historian named Kevin Mattson, who profiled me in a book called *Rebels All!* as the exemplar of a "post-modern conservatism," ascribing to me views I simply did not hold. This was typical of the responses to my work by critics from the left who rarely engaged my ideas in an intellectual manner but picked at them hoping to find ways to discredit their bearer. The only real interest they showed in my work, or that of other conservatives, was to make it a symbol of something to despise and suppress. "Something We Did" is my response to a caricature of me in an Off-Broadway play about the Weathermen terrorists called *Something You Did*. The intention of the play was to exculpate the guilty and indict those who attempted to hold them accountable. Like Kevin Mattson, the playwright had no interest in defending, let alone correcting, his distorted views when I confronted him with the facts.

Another example of this syndrome is described in "Who I Am," which is my response to a cover story that appeared in *The Tablet*, an online magazine for Jewish progressives. *The Tablet*'s editors had assigned a very young leftist the task of doing my portrait. The piece he finally produced, "David Horowitz Is Homeless," was an attempt to portray me as a hapless figure whose fortunes were declining as he approached the end of his life, where he found himself lost between the warring camps of left and right, unable to find a home in either. "Who I Am" is my attempt to put the facts back in place. *The Tablet* declined to publish it, but this self-portrait provides a reasonable facsimile of my state of being in what was then my seventy-third year.

Peter Collier has been my friend for fifty years. He was my collaborator at *Ramparts* and in the launching of my literary career with three dynastic biographies we co-authored about the Rockefeller, Kennedy and Ford familes—all *New York Times* best-sellers, *The Kennedys* reaching the top of that list. Peter was also my confidant and partner in the joint transition we made from left to right, organizing the "Second Thoughts" conference with me, co-authoring our *démarche* in *The Washington Post* and co-writing *Destructive Generation*, which we published in 1989. Peter has also been my collaborator in guiding the David Horowitz Freedom Center, although he took a ten-year hiatus to create Encounter Books, an independent publishing company. During that time, he continued to edit our magazine, *Heterodoxy*. "Peter and Me," an introduction I wrote to a talk he gave at the Center's Wednesday

Morning Club about his biography of Jeane Kirkpatrick, is my tribute to a valued friend and colleague and the impact he has had on me.

Part II

The essays that make up the second part of this volume begin with "Goodbye to All That," our swansong to the left. The article was published by *The Washington Post* under the title "Lefties for Reagan" and was our formal "coming-out" as conservatives, although it was based on second thoughts that had been gestating since the mid-Seventies.

The next two essays, "My Vietnam Lessons" and *"Semper Fidel,"* belong to this genre, and are attempts I made to confront our radical cohort with the harsh realities of what we had actually done. Vietnam was the defining issue of our generation but the events that unfolded proved that those of us who were active in the anti-war movement had been wrong on every critical point, and that our actions had tragic consequences for the people we claimed to be defending. My decision to vote for Ronald Reagan and join the conservative cause was also inspired by events in Nicaragua where Castro Marxists had seized power through a political *coup.* *"Semper* Fidel," originally titled "A Speech to My Former Comrades on the Left," was about those events. It was given at a conference organized by Berkeley radicals who probably didn't realize what they were in for, and who shut off my microphone before I could finish.

Following the appearance of our *Post* article, Peter and I were repeatedly forced to defend our conservative views. "Keepers of the Flame" is one of these defenses, written following our return from a trip to Nicaragua and in response to a review of *Destructive Generation* that appeared in *The New Republic.* The essay reflects our continuing effort to understand what had happened to us—not only why we weren't welcomed into what we thought would be the political center, but also why our anti-Communist politics were treated with such hostility by the liberal press. The review that provoked our response was written by Paul Berman who insinuated that the sins we described in *Destructive Generation* were basically our own, and did not reflect the general behaviors or attitudes of the left.

This attempt to revise the past was a common tack of the leftists we now faced. In "Carl Bernstein's Communist Problem and Mine," I drew on my personal experiences to expose the misrepresentations in the memoir this Watergate reporter had written about his Communist childhood. The article has even more resonance today than it did when I wrote it because it describes, from the inside, the milieu in which the 44th president of the United States also grew up, along with his chief advisors David Axelrod and Valerie Jarrett.[5]

A series of attacks on the political right by the writer Michael Lind provided me with an opportunity to describe what a political conversion actually entails and also to correct the distorted picture of the right that was becoming commonplace among its leftist opponents. I responded to Lind's defamation of conservatives in an article called "Political Cross-Dresser."

Time and again as I attempted to describe my experiences as a radical, I encountered the resistance put up by leftists to any candor on the subject, their inability to face up to the past, and their penchant for rewriting it instead. "Still Lying After All These Years" and "Repressed Memory Syndrome" are efforts to address this resistance to historical truth. I am not referring here to differences in interpretation of what happened, but to the deliberate suppression of facts or inversion of facts in the service of a political cause.

The article "Fidel, Pinochet and Me" is another attempt to confront my former comrades with the results to which our political advocacies had led. In this article, I compare the achievements of Chile's dictator Augusto Pinochet, whom progressives loathed, to those of Cuba's dictator Castro, whom they adored and whose

---

[5]http://discoverthenetworks.org/individualProfile.asp?indid=1511

excesses they excused. Comparing those histories provided a measure of progressives' disconnect from reality in the service of a destructive illusion, and of their blindness to the human consequences of their ideas and actions. Shortly after publishing the article, I found myself on a radio show with Christopher Hitchens who at the time was one of the radical harassers of the terminally-ill Pinochet, calling for his arrest and extradition for crimes he had committed as Chile's dictator decades before. When I pointed out that Pinochet's dictatorship was no worse for Chileans than Castro's was for Cubans, and arguably a lot better, Christopher burst out on air: "How dare you, how *dare* you!" I was taken aback by this fervor but replied in as amicable a tone as I could muster: "Christopher, aren't we getting a little old for 'how-dare-yous'?" This was the first time Christopher and I had spoken in nearly twenty years and it was to his credit that the next time we did we became friends.[6]

It was a continuing source of fascination to me that progressives, who had been so demonstrably on the wrong side of history during the Cold War, were able to maintain their air of superiority when it was over, while simultaneously marginalizing conservatives in the academic and literary cultures they dominated. The essay "Marginalizing Conservative Ideas" is another facet of my ongoing effort to identify the differences between the two perspectives that lead to such different outcomes.

In the two articles "Can There Be A Decent Left" and "The Left and the Constitution," I analyze the nature of the left by engaging the ideas of two of its more intellectually interesting figures, Michael Walzer and Hendrik Hertzberg. Regrettably, neither one responded to these overtures, a not uncommon occurrence. The nature of the left is also the subject of the three essays on "Neo-Communism," which were written after the onset of the Iraq War—an American intervention vigorously opposed by

---

[6]See "Defending Christopher" and note, Volume 2; also "The Two Christophers" in David Horowitz, *Radicals: Portraits of a Destructive Passion.*

almost the entire progressive spectrum, with notable but rare exceptions such as Hitchens and Paul Berman. (The latter was steadily moving from his earlier positions and was no longer an antagonist of mine.) That war proved to be a defining political crossroads, and I used the occasion to articulate my understanding of what the "post-Communist" left shared with its Communist precursors. The continuities of the left by now had become a central theme of my work.

"Neo-Communism," a term I chose to characterize the left, failed to catch on, as I had suspected it would. This was a credit to leftists' success in embargoing attempts to link them to their Communist predecessors by associating their critics with problematic figures like Senator Joseph McCarthy. The very use of the word "communist" is taken to be evidence of "McCarthyism." But the effect of accepting the preferred euphemisms, such as "progressive" and "liberal" (a term applied by *The New York Times* even to card-carrying Communists like Angela Davis) has had the dual effect of obscuring their agendas and burying the lessons of their past. The second volume of this series, *Progressives*, returns to these issues.

The chapter "Discover The Networks" is the defense of an online encyclopedia of the left I created by that name, and a further attempt of mine to provide a taxonomy of the species.[7] "Keeping an Eye on the Domestic Threat" is a further explication of this database, and thus another inquiry into the nature of the faith.

Part III

The essays in this section, "Slander as a Political Discourse," address several attempts to distort the facts of my life in order to discredit my ideas and neutralize my criticisms of the left and its deeds. It includes an exchange provoked by Sidney Blumenthal's libel suit against Matt Drudge, which throws light on the techniques leftists employ to defame and then quarantine critics, and

[7]http://www.discoverthenetworks.org/

reflects the particularly low state of political discourse at the time. I knew John Judis, the author of one of these attacks, when he was an editor of *Socialist Revolution*. Later he became an editor of *The New Republic*, and was able to write a fairly objective biography of William F. Buckley. The fact that he would advocate a boycott of the magazine Peter and I published is just one indication of the determination of progressives to create a wall of silence around our work and prevent us from reaching the next generation with what we had learned.

Part IV

This volume concludes with the texts of two talks I gave on auto-biographical themes. The first was given over the fierce objections of my leftwing classmates to my 50th class reunion at Columbia College. In it I attempted to weigh the changes that had taken place over the course of the half-century since we had graduated, and explain the conservative viewpoint to an audience that remained steeped in the presumptions of a progressive culture. The second is a speech I gave at the annual dinner of the Zionist Organization of America, which provided me an opportunity to reflect on my identity as a Jew, my attitudes towards Israel and America, and to the war against them.

PART I

Reflections From My Life

I

Left Illusions

For most of my adult and professional life, I regarded myself as a man of the left. The identification was stronger than just politics. Ever since marching in my first May Day parade down New York's Eighth Avenue 30 years ago, I had looked on myself as a soldier in an international class-struggle that would one day liberate all humanity from poverty, oppression, racism and war. It was a romantic conception to be sure, but then revolution as conceived in the Marxist and socialist canons *is* a romantic conception; it promises the fulfillment of hopes that are as old as mankind; it posits a break with the whole burdened progress of human history—freedom from the chains that have bound master and slave, lord and peasant, capitalist and proletariat from time immemorial.

Not long after the end of the Vietnam War, I found myself unable to maintain any longer the necessary belief in the Marxist promise. Along with many other veterans of the 1960s struggles, I ceased to be politically active. It was a characteristic and somewhat unique feature of our radical generation, as distinct from previous ones, that we did not then join the conservative forces of the *status quo*. Instead, politics itself became suspect. We turned inward—not, I would say, out of narcissism but out of a recognition in some ways threatening to our radical ideas that failure (like

---

This article was published in the December 8, 1979 issue of *The Nation* as "A Radical's Disenchantment"—a title provided by the editors. It turned out to be my farewell to the left. (See *Radical Son*, pp. 305–7.)

15

success) is never a matter merely of "the objective circumstances" but has a root in the acting self.

Few of us, I think, felt at ease with the political limbo in which we found ourselves. It was as though the radicalism we shared was in some deep, perhaps unanalyzable sense a matter of character rather than of commitment. It was as though giving up the vision of fundamental change meant giving up the better part of oneself. So we continued to feel a connection to the left that was something more than sentimental, while our sense of loss led to conflicts whose appearance was sometimes less than fraternal. Such feelings, I believe, were an unspoken but significant element in the controversy over Joan Baez's open letter to the Vietnamese, and in the Ronald Radosh-Sol Stern article on the Rosenbergs in *The New Republic*.[1]

Antonio Gramsci once described the revolutionary temperament as a pessimism of the intellect and an optimism of the will. For the veterans of my radical generation, the balance was tipped when we sustained what seemed like irreparable damage to our sense of historical possibility. It was not even so much the feeling that the left would not be able to change society; it was rather the sense that, in crucial ways, the left could not change itself.

Above all, the left seems trapped in its romantic vision. In spite of the defeats to its radical expectations, it is unable to summon the dispassion to look at itself critically. Despite the disasters of

---

[1] Baez had written an "Appeal to the Conscience of North Vietnam" to protest the post-peace repression in Vietnam. Even though the ad blamed the United States for its role in the war, she was denounced as a CIA agent by Tom Hayden and Jane Fonda for her efforts (*Radical Son* pp. 302–3). Later I appeared on a television talk-show with Baez to discuss the Vietnam War. During the discussion she peremptorily dismissed my views, saying, "I don't trust someone who's had second thoughts." Stern and Radosh had published an article, based on FBI files released under the Freedom of Information Act, suggesting that Julius Rosenberg was indeed a Soviet spy. There was an uproar in the left and the two of them came under vitriolic attack from their (now) ex-friends. My role in the genesis of this article and the subsequent book by Radosh and Joyce Milton (*The Rosenberg File*) is described in *Radical Son*, pp. 300–302.

20th-century revolutions, the viability of the revolutionary goals remains largely unexamined and unquestioned. Even worse, radical commitments to justice and other social values continue to be dominated by a moral and political double standard. The left's indignation seems exclusively reserved for outrages that confirm the Marxist diagnosis of capitalist society. Thus there is protest against murder and repression in Nicaragua but not Cambodia, in Chile but not Tibet, South Africa but not Uganda, Israel but not Libya or Iraq. Political support is mustered for oppressed minorities in Western countries but not in Russia or the People's Republic of China, while a Third World country that declares itself "Marxist" puts itself—by the very act—beyond reproach. In the same vein, almost any "liberation movement" is embraced as just that, though it may be as unmistakably atavistic and clerically fascist on first sight as the Ayatollah Khomeini's in Iran.[2]

This moral and political myopia is compounded by the left's inability to accept responsibility for its own acts and commitments. Unpalatable results like the outcome of the Revolution in Russia are regarded as "irrelevant"—and dismissed—as though the left in America and elsewhere played no role in them, and as though they have had no impact on the world the left set out to change. Or they are analyzed as anomalies—and dismissed—as though there were in fact a standard of achieved revolution by which the left could have confidence in its program and in its understanding of the historical process.

Recently the shock of events in Indochina—mass murder committed by Cambodia's Communists, the invasion and unacknowledged occupation of Cambodia by Vietnam, the invasion of Vietnam by China—has produced new and promising responses among radicals still committed to the socialist cause.[3] Paul Sweezy, the dean of America's independent Marxists, wrote in

---

[2]The *Nation's* Richard Falk was one of the outspoken promoters of the idea that the Ayatollah's revolution would be a "liberation" for Iran.
[3]This was obviously wishful thinking.

Monthly Review this June of "a deep crisis in Marxian theory" because not one of the existing "socialist" societies behaves the way Marx and "most Marxists ... until quite recently ... thought they would." Classes haven't been eliminated; nor, he observes, is there any visible intention to eliminate them. The state, far from disappearing, has grown more powerful, and Marxist regimes "go to war not only in self-defense but to impose their will on other countries—even ones that are also assumed to be socialist."

The current dimensions of the left's intellectual crisis are more readily grasped in a writer like Noam Chomsky, who, as an anarchist, has never had illusions about existing "socialisms" and has no attachment, intellectual or visceral, to pristine Marxism. Chomsky's intellectual integrity and moral courage, to my mind, set a standard for political intellectuals.[4] Yet in a manner that is not only characteristic of the non-Trotskyist left but seems endemic to its political stance, Chomsky refuses to devote his tenacious intelligence to a systematic scrutiny of "socialist" regimes or even anti-Western regimes of the Third World.

Thus, in a passage from his new book *Language and Responsibility,* Chomsky criticizes the absence of socialist journalists in the mass media and comments: "In a sense, we have over here the 'mirror image' of the Soviet Union, where all the people who write in *Pravda* represent the position they call 'socialism'—in fact, a certain variety of highly authoritarian state socialism." Chomsky attributes this conformity to "ideological homogeneity" among the U.S. intelligentsia and to the fact that the mass media are capitalist institutions. Chomsky then offers examples of press conformity in connection with the Vietnam War and concludes: "It is notable that despite the extensive and well-known record of Government lies during the period of the Vietnam War, the press, with

---

[4]Chomsky's extreme adverse reaction to this reference, which is described in *Radical Son* (he wrote me two six-page single-spaced, vituperative and personally abusive letters in response), caused me to begin a reassessment of his character. For my second thoughts on Chomsky, see the articles in Volume Two of this series, *Progressives.*

fair consistency, remained remarkably obedient, and quite willing to accept the Government's assumptions, framework of thinking, and interpretation of what was happening."

The questions I find myself asking, when I read these words just now, are: By what standard does Chomsky judge the obedience of the American press remarkable? Is there a national press that is not obedient in the sense described? Does Chomsky mean that the American press was remarkably *more* obedient to its government during the Vietnam War than other national presses would have been in similar circumstances? Looking back at those events from the present historical juncture, one would be inclined to say exactly the reverse. Not only did the American press provide much of the documentation on which the antiwar movement's indictment of the American war effort was based—including the My Lai atrocities—but in *defiance* of its government and at the risk of prosecution for espionage and treason, it published the classified documents known as the "Pentagon Papers," which provided a good deal of the tangible record of official lies to which Chomsky refers.[5]

This is not to say that Chomsky's characterization of press subservience is wrong but rather to put the criticism in perspective. Within the framework of ideological conformity and institutional obedience that Chomsky rightly deplores, a body of dissent developed during the 1960s which has continued to influence the conduct of America foreign policy and the structure of international relations in the present decade. Who would have thought ten years ago that the anti-American revolution in Iran, the linchpin of America's imperial interests in the Middle East, would not trigger an immediate American military intervention? Who would have believed that the 25,000 military "advisors" in Africa's civil conflicts in the 1970s would be Cubans rather than Americans?

---

[5]Chomsky ignored this obvious criticism and went on to elaborate the same preposterous thesis in his most famous book, *Manufactured Consent*, co-authored with Edward S. Herman.

Consider, too, for a moment, Chomsky's misleading comparison of the Soviet and American presses as "mirror images." In fact, the ignorance imposed on the Soviet public by government-controlled media and official censorship is mind-boggling by Western standards. At a bare minimum, the information necessary to carry on a public debate over government policies in areas such as foreign policy and defense is not available to the Soviet citizen (who would be forbidden to use it, if it were). Censorship is carried to such an extreme that the Soviet citizen may be uninformed about such noncontroversial threats to his wellbeing as natural disasters, man-made catastrophes or even military provocations by the United States. When Washington mined Haiphong Harbor and dared Russian vessels to challenge the blockade, a crisis—compared at the time to the 1962 confrontation over Cuban missiles—ensued. For twenty days during this crisis, the Soviet people were not informed that the mining had taken place. (The purpose of the blackout was to allow the Soviet leadership to capitulate to the American threat without domestic consequences.)

Why bring this up? Why dwell on the negative features of the Soviet system (or of other Communist states) which in any case are widely reported in the American media? What is the relevance? These are questions the apologists of the left raise when they are confronted by the Soviet case. Unfortunately, the consequences of ignoring the flaws of practical Communism are far-ranging and real. To begin with, the credibility of the left's critique is gravely undermined. Chomsky's article is a good example. The American press does not look inordinately servile when compared with its real-world counterparts—and especially its socialist opposites. Only when measured against its own standards and the ideals of a democratic society does it seem so. Yet it is Chomsky who raises the Soviet comparison, precisely because the United States and the Soviet Union *are* in an adversary relationship—a political fact of prime importance that the left often prefers to ignore, when it suits their purposes—and he does so in a misleading way. The result is that his argument is vitiated, or at least seriously weakened, for anyone who has not internalized the special expectations of the left that a future socialist press would be really independent, critical and accurate.

Latent in Chomsky's critique is a comforting illusion: namely, that the left's failure to sustain itself as a political force with a radical alternative social vision is due to the absence of socialist journalists in the capitalist media, rather than to its own deficiencies—the failure of the left's ideals in practice; its moral inconsistency; its inability to formulate and fight for realistic programs; in short, the fact that it cannot command moral and political authority among its constituencies.

The blind-spot toward the Soviet Union provides a good instance of the left's lack of political realism. The Soviet Union is one of the two predominant military powers in the world. That alone makes it a crucial subject of any contemporary political analysis that claims to be comprehensive. Radicals often seem to think that Western policy can be explained independently of Soviet behavior by reference to the imperatives of the system, the requirements of the "disaccumulation crisis," etc. This was always a weakness in the radical perspective; but now, as a result of the continuing development of Soviet power in the last decade, it has passed a critical point and has become crippling.

During the 1950s, and even in the 1960s, the Soviet Union was significantly weaker militarily than the United States. The celebrated "missile gap" was all on the other side. Hence, whatever Soviet intentions, Washington's influence on the dynamics of the arms race and the cold war was preponderant. This is no longer the case. The Soviet Union has now achieved nuclear parity with the United States for the first time since the onset of the atomic era. This profoundly affects, among other things, the Soviet ability to intervene in political and military conflicts outside its borders. The political pendulum has also swung in its favor. In an earlier day, John Foster Dulles used to attack the nonaligned states for "immoral" neutrality. At the recent conference of nonaligned countries in Havana, the policy of Washington's representatives was to *keep* the participants neutral (i.e. not aligned with the Soviet bloc).

These changes and the trend they represent make a realistic analysis of Soviet policies crucial for any political movement. Yet in a special issue of *The Nation* concerned with the problem of military interventions (June 9), only one of ten articles was even partially devoted to the Soviet Union.[6] That article, by Michael Klare, employed a comparative analysis of U.S. and Soviet military forces to *discount* the impression that the Soviet Union is now or intends to become an interventionist power.

Klare achieved this feat in two ways: by defining "interventionist forces" in such a restrictive manner as to exclude the Soviet invasion of Czechoslovakia and the occupation forces it maintains there; and by describing Soviet intervention in the Middle East, Africa, and Asia as "aid" to "beleaguered allies"—in short, by taking a page from the apologists for American intervention. When Klare was compelled under his own ground-rules to admit that some Soviet missions had the look of interventionist forces, he quickly denied the implication, saying, ". . . but it is important to remember that the units involved are seen by Moscow as being 'on loan' from their normal, defensive mission, and so would be recalled the moment they were needed at home." So, presumably, would the U.S. "advisers" that began America's involvement in Vietnam, if they had been needed at home.

Failure to appreciate the world role of a major power—the depressing history of leftist apologias for that power aside—would be serious enough. But the Soviet Union, despite all the qualifying circumstances of its origins and development, is the country in which the revolutionary socialist solution—state ownership of the means of production—has been tested and found wanting. For this reason, far more than for the others, it requires radical attention.

---

[6]Another, by Gareth Porter, however, did admirably deal with Vietnam's invasion of Cambodia.

The point was forcefully made a few years ago by the Polish philosopher Leszek Kolakowski:

> Why the problems of the real and the only existing Communism, which Leftist ideologies put aside so easily ("all right, this was done in exceptional circumstances, we won't imitate these patterns, we will do it better" etc.), are crucial for socialist thought is because the experiences of the "new alternative society" have shown very convincingly that the only universal medicine these people have for social evils—state ownership of the means of production—is not only perfectly compatible with all disasters of the capitalist world, with exploitation, imperialism, pollution, misery, economic waste, national hatred and national oppression, but that it adds to them a series of disasters of its own: inefficiency, lack of economic incentives and, above all, the unrestricted role of the omnipotent bureaucracy, a concentration of power never known before in human history.

Can the left take a really hard look at itself—the consequences of its failures, the credibility of its critiques, the viability of its goals? Can it begin to shed the arrogant cloak of self-righteousness that elevates it above its own history and makes it impervious to the lessons of experience?

In a previous essay, Kolakowski wrote that the left was defined by its "negation" of existing social reality. But not only this: "It is also defined by the direction of this negation, in fact by the nature of its utopia." Today, the left's utopia itself is in question. That is the real meaning of the crisis of Marxism. Paradoxically, the way for the left to begin to regain its utopia, to fashion a new, more adequate vision of radical commitment and radical change, is to take a firmer grip on the ground under its feet.

2

Why I Am
No Longer a Leftist

My life as a leftist began with a May Day Parade in 1948, when I was nine years old, and lasted for more than twenty-five years until December 1974, when a murder committed by my political comrades brought my radical career to an end. My parents had joined the Communist Party along with many other idealistic Americans in the 1930s, before I was born. Just as today's leftists believe that the seeds of justice have been planted by the Marxist Sandinistas in Nicaragua, my parents and their radical friends saw them blooming in Soviet Russia, which many of them visited during Stalin's purges. Not even the testimony of a Bolshevik legend like the exiled Trotsky could persuade them that they were deceived about the "new society" they thought they saw under construction in the socialist state. Confident that their own ideals were pure, my parents and their political friends dismissed Trotsky and others whose experience had caused them to know better, smearing them as "counter-revolutionaries," "anti-Soviets" and "renegades."

Twenty years later, when my parents had reached middle age, their arrogance betrayed them and took away their self-respect. In 1956 power shifted in the Kremlin, and my parents along with the rest of the progressive left discovered that the socialist future they had served all their lives was a monstrous lie. They had thought they were fighting for social justice, for the powerless and the poor.

---

*This article appeared in *The Village Voice*, September 30, 1986.

But in reality they had served a gang of cynical despots who had slaughtered more peasants, caused more hunger and human misery, and killed more leftists like themselves than all the capitalist governments since the beginning of time.

After Stalin's death, it was the confrontation with this reality, and not Senator Joe McCarthy's famous crusade, which demoralized and destroyed the old Communist guard in America. I was seventeen at the time, and at the funeral of the Old Left I swore to myself I would not repeat my parents' fate. I would never be loyal to a movement based on a lie or be complicit in political crimes; I would never support a cause that required the suppression of its own truths, whether by self-censorship or firing squads or political smears. But my youth prevented me from comprehending what the catastrophe had revealed. I continued to believe in the fantasy of the socialist future. When a New Left began to emerge a few years later, I was ready to believe that it was a fresh beginning and eager to assist at its birth.

For a long time I was able to keep the promises I had made. As an activist and writer in the movement of the Sixties, I never endorsed what I knew to be a lie or concealed what I knew to be a crime. I never stigmatized a dissenting view as morally beyond the pale. At the same time, however, I closed my eyes to evidence that would have shown me the left had not really changed at all. Like the rest of my radical comrades, I welcomed Castro's triumph in Cuba, which he proclaimed a revolution of "bread without terror" and "neither red nor black but Cuban olive green." When Castro established his own dictatorship and *gulag* and joined the Soviet axis, I too blamed his dereliction on the anti-Communist phobia of the United States, and I averted my eyes from the truth.

A decade later, when the Vietnam War came to an end, there was a massive exodus from the New Left by those who had joined its ranks to avoid military service. I stayed. I had never been eligible for the draft and had joined the movement in order to serve the progressive ideal.

In 1974 I began a new project with the Black Panther Party, which the New Left had identified in the Sixties as the "vanguard of the revolution." I raised the funds to create a "Community Learning Center" for the Panthers in the heart of the East Oakland ghetto. The Center provided schooling and free meals to 150 children, and community services to an even larger number of adults. The following year the woman I had hired as a bookkeeper for the Center was kidnapped, sexually tormented, and then brutally murdered by my Black Panther comrades.

When I first discovered what had happened, I was paralyzed with fear, a fear that grew as I learned about other murders and violent crimes the Panthers had committed—all without retribution from the law. At the time, the left saw the Panthers as a persecuted vanguard, victimized by racist police because of their role in the liberation struggle. The Panthers' leader had found refuge from several criminal indictments in Castro's Cuba; the Party's spokesmen appeared regularly at progressive rallies to agitate against capitalist "repression" at home. In the eyes of the left, the Panthers were what they always had been: an embodiment of the progressive idea. To defend them against the "fascist" attacks of the police was a radical's first responsibility and task.

In reality the Panthers were a criminal gang that preyed on the black ghetto itself. With the weapons they had justified as necessary for "self-defense" against "racist authority," they pursued various avenues of criminal violence which included extortion, drug-trafficking and murder. Not all the murders they committed had a monetary rationale. Some were merely gratuitous, as when they killed a leader of the Black Students Union at Grove Street College in Oakland because he had inadvertently insulted one of their enforcers. The Oakland police were aware of the Panthers' criminal activities; but were rendered powerless to stop them by the nationwide network of liberal and radical Panther supporters who sprang to their defense.

With community fronts like the school I had created, with lobbyists in the state house and activists in the streets, with million-dollar defense funds and high-powered attorneys, with civil liberties organizations ready with lawsuits and witnesses ready to perjure themselves, the New Left provided the Panthers with an Achilles Shield that protected them from the law. All the celebrated "Cointelpro" programs of the Nixon White House and the anti-subversive campaigns of the FBI, all the alleged wiretaps and infiltrations of the Panther organization, could not provide the means to sustain a single legal conviction against the Panthers for their crimes, or prevent the 20 or more murders they committed, including that of the woman I had hired. During a decade of radical protest as reckless in its charges as it was indiscriminate in its targets, the left had made civil authority in America so weak that the law could not punish ordinary criminal acts when committed by its progressive vanguard.

Because of what I knew, I myself now lived in fear of the Panther terror. In my fear, it became impossible for me not to connect these events with the nightmares of the radical past. Just as Stalin had used the idealism and loyalty of my parents' generation to commit his crimes in the Thirties, so the Panthers had used my generation's idealism in the Sixties. My political odyssey had come full circle. When I was beginning, I had promised myself that I would never be silent when confronted by such misdeeds; that I would fight within the left for the same justice as the left demanded of the world outside. But now I discovered that I could not keep my promise and remain a part of the movement I had served. Because a progressive vanguard had committed the crime, my duty as a progressive was to defend the criminal. As a result, the left suddenly became a hostile terrain for me. I had already been threatened by the Panthers to keep silent about what I knew. The facts I knew would not be conclusive evidence in a court of law; but they posed a threat to the Panthers' political shield. If their criminal acts were exposed to the left, the Panthers might lose their protection and support.

But even if I told what I knew, the Panthers might have little to fear. The whole history of the radical past, from Trotsky on, warned that my individual truth would have little effect on the attitude of the left. Confronted by such a truth, the left would seek first to ignore and then to discredit it, because it was damaging to the progressive cause.

At the murdered woman's funeral, I had approached her daughter, who was 18 and a radical like me. On the way to the graveside, I told her that I was convinced the Panthers had killed her mother. The daughter's grief for her mother was great, but so was the solidarity she felt for black people who were oppressed and for their revolutionary vanguard. When later she was asked publicly about the tragedy, she said that as far as she was concerned the Panthers were above suspicion. To suggest the contrary was racist.[1]

What the daughter of the murdered woman did was "politically correct." I knew at the time that if I were to step forward and publicly accuse the Panthers of the crime, I would be denounced by my own community in the name of the values we shared. All my previous life of dedication and commitment to the radical cause overnight would count for nothing. My own comrades would stigmatize me as a "racist," shun me as a "renegade" and expel me from their ranks.

My dedication to the progressive cause had made me self-righteous and arrogant and blind. Now a cruel and irreversible crime had humbled me and restored my sight. I had started out with others of my generation confident that we were wiser than our parents and would avoid their radical fate. But all our wisdom had been vanity. I could no longer feel superior to the generation that had been silent during the years of Stalin's slaughters. The Stalinists and the Panthers may have operated on stages vastly different in scale, but ultimately their achievements were the same. Stalin and the Panthers were ruthless exploiters of the radical dream; just like our forbears, my comrades and I were credulous idealists who had served a criminal lie.

---

[1]Years later Betty's daughter, Tamara Baltar, came to the conclusion that the Panthers had murdered her mother. With the help of friends, she hired a private detective who had worked regularly for leftwing defense attorneys to investigate the case. His report concluded that the Panthers were responsible for the murder of Betty Van Patter.

Through this microcosm I saw what I had failed to see 18 years before, at the time of "de-Stalinization," when the New Left was born. The problem of the left was not Stalin or "Stalinism." The problem was the left itself.

Although the Panther vanguard was isolated and small, its leaders were able to rob and kill without incurring the penalty of law. They were able to do so because the left had made the Panthers a law unto themselves—the same way the left had made Stalin a law unto himself—the same way the left makes Fidel Castro and the Sandinista *comandantes* laws unto themselves.

By crowning the criminals with the halo of humanity's hope, the left shields them from judgment for their criminal deeds. Thus in the name of revolutionary justice, the left defends revolutionary injustice; in the name of human liberation, the left creates a new world of oppression.

The lesson I had learned for my pain turned out to be modest and simple: the best intentions can lead to the worst results. I had believed in the left because of the good it had promised. Now I learned to judge it by the evil it had done.

3

Reality and Dream

I was born fifty years ago in 1939, just before the Germans invaded Poland. This is my first trip to your country, and it has been inspiring to me to see that although you have been occupied for half a century you have not been defeated.

The members of my family were socialists for more than a hundred years, first in Moravia and the Ukraine, then in New York and Berkeley; first as socialists; then as Communists; and then as New-Left Marxists. My grandparents came to New York to escape persecution as Jews in the Pale of Settlement. My grandfather was a tailor. He lived with other Jews in poverty on the Lower East Side and earned three dollars a week. He was so poor that sometimes he had to sleep under his sewing-machine in the factory where he worked. Compared to czarist Russia from which he had fled, America was a new world. He was still poor, but he had arrived in a land of opportunities provided by its free-market economy and political democracy; a land where people could grow rich beyond their wildest dreams.

That was my grandfather's reality. Like many others who arrived in America, my grandfather also had a dream. His dream, however, was not a dream of riches. It was a dream he shared with other members of the international left: the dream of a socialist future, a world of planned economy and economic equality, of material abundance and social justice. In 1917, my grandfather

This is from a talk delivered at the Second Thoughts Conference in Krakow, Poland, May 4–7, 1989, just before Poland became free. http://archive.frontpagemag.com/Printable.aspx?ArtId=21734

thought he saw his dream become reality in Bolshevik Russia. By this time he also had a son. Like the children of other immigrant families, his son studied and worked hard to take advantage of the opportunities provided by America's freedom. He became a high-school teacher and married a colleague and also had a son.

By this time my father was no longer poor like his father but middle-class. He and my mother could afford culture, travel, an automobile, and a grand piano. In 1949, with their schoolteachers' salaries, they bought a six-room house on credit for $18,000. In 1986, when my father died, the house belonged to him as his property. It was worth $200,000. That was my father's reality: riches and freedom beyond his father's wildest dreams.

But like his father, my father had his heart set on a dream beyond the freedom and wealth that America had made possible for him. Just as his father had been a socialist, my father was a Communist. He supported the "social experiment" that Lenin and Stalin had begun in Soviet Russia. All his life he dreamed the Communist future, and he transmitted that dream to his son.

In 1956, events occurred in Moscow and in Eastern Europe that almost made me give up the dream I had inherited as a birthright. In 1956 the head of the Soviet Communist Party, Nikita Khrushchev, gave his secret speech on the crimes of Stalin and thus drew aside a veil that had concealed from the faithful the grim reality of the socialist future. Soviet tanks thundered across the border to crush the brave forces of the Hungarian revolution and to discourage the hopeful beginnings of the Polish October.

Instead of being awakened by these events, I joined a new generation that hoped to revive the humanist spirit of the dream itself. I was inspired to join the New Left by a Polish Marxist named Isaac Deutscher, who was my teacher. It was Deutscher who devised the theory out of which we hoped to revive the socialist dream.

According to Deutscher, the Stalinist state that had murdered millions and erected an edifice of totalitarian lies was a deformation of the socialist ideal that socialists themselves would overcome. The socialist revolution had taken place in the backward environment of czarist Russia. Stalinism was a form of "primitive socialist accumulation" produced by the cultural backwardness of that environment and the political necessities of building an industrial economic base.

In 1956, when Khrushchev launched the process of de-Stalinization, Deutscher saw it as a prelude to the humanist future of which we all had dreamed. The socialist "economic base"—infinitely superior in rationality and productive potential to its capitalist competitor—had already been created. Socialist accumulation had been completed; the socialist superstructure would follow in due course. Socialist abundance would produce socialist democracy.

When we heard words like these, New Leftists all over the world became new believers in the socialist cause. Stalinism had been terrible, but the terror was over. The socialist economic base had been built in Russia. To complete the dream, all that was required was political democracy. In the New Left in the Sixties, we had a saying: "The first socialist revolution will take place in the Soviet Union." Some leftists are still saying it today.

For 17 years, I waited in vain for the democratic revolution to come to Soviet Russia to complete the socialist dream. But it did not come. Oh, there was a spring in Prague. But Soviet tanks again rolled across the border to crush it. Five years later, another Polish Marxist—now ex-Marxist—stepped forward to explain why socialism would never be realized except in a totalitarian state. In 1956, Leszek Kolakowski had been a leader of the Polish October. In 1968, Kolakowski had been a defender of the Prague spring. Now, in 1973, at a conference in England, he summed up a hundred years of critiques of socialism that history had repeatedly confirmed. The effort to transform natural inequalities into social equality could only lead to greater, more brutal inequality; the socialist effort to transform individual diversity into social unity could only lead to the totalitarian state.

Deutscher had been wrong. There would never be a socialist political democracy erected on a socialist economic base. Socialism was an impossible—and therefore destructive—dream.

But if Kolakowski was right, the future of peoples who lived under socialism was dark indeed. The totalitarian empire could not reform, but it could expand. Aided by dreamers all over the world, the expansion of that empire seemed likely, even inevitable—until now, the era of *glasnost.* Now, instead of a continuing expansion, we see Communism everywhere in retreat. Now its believers are fewer and fewer, and the terrain itself is beginning to shrink. Who among us expected this? A year and a half ago, I participated in an international panel in Paris that discussed the question: Is Communism reversible? No member of the panel thought it was. This year, if a similar panel were held, the question would be: Can Communism save itself? Who would be so bold to say that it can?

Why were we so wrong? Because all of us, Kolakowski included, had our roots in the intellectual traditions of the socialist left. Experience had taught us all to be anti-Communist, but our critique of socialism was based on political theory and political considerations. We knew that totalitarianism was evil, but we thought that socialism worked. We were wrong. It does not work.

While we were wrong, others all along had been right. All those years, outside the socialist tradition, there had been voices crying in the wilderness saying that not only would socialism bring tyranny and suffering, it would not work. Seventy-seven years ago, five years after the Bolshevik triumph, Ludwig von Mises wrote a book on socialism that predicted the catastrophe we see before us. Socialist economy, he argued, was economic irrationality, and socialist planning a prescription for chaos. Only a capitalist market could provide a system of rational allocations and rational accounts. Only private property and the profit-motive could unleash the forces of individual initiative and human creativity to produce real and expanding wealth—not only for the rich but for society as a whole.

Ludwig von Mises, Friedrich von Hayek, and the other liberal theorists of a free-market economy who warned of this outcome are the true prophets of the reality we see before us—of socialist bankruptcy and Communist retreat. Glastnostian democracy has not completed and cannot complete the socialist dream; it can only expose this dream as a nightmare from which Communism cannot wake up. The only way to wake up is to give up the dream. In 1989, according to Soviet economists, the average Soviet citizen had a daily ration of meat that was smaller than the daily intake of the average Russian in 1913 under the czar. Socialism makes men poor beyond their wildest dreams. The average Polish citizen is poorer today, in 1989, than my poor grandfather was in America fifty years ago, when I was born.

The law of socialist economy is this: from each according to his exploitability, to the *nomenklatura* according to its greed. Not only does the socialist economy not produce wealth at the rate a free economy does; the socialist economy consumes wealth. It consumes the natural wealth of the nation and also the wealth it accumulated in the past. Every Communist revolution begins as a rape of the present and continues as a cannibalization of the past. Every Communist Party is the colonizer of its own country, and the Soviet empire is the colonizer of them all. That is the law of socialist distribution: from each nation according to its exploitability, to the empire according to its greed.

But a system that lives by cannibalism, which consumes more wealth than it produces, is sooner or later destined to die. And that is what is happening before our eyes.

For myself, the family tradition of socialist dreams is over. Socialism is no longer a dream of the revolutionary future. It is only a nightmare of the past. But for you, the nightmare is not a dream. It is a reality that is still happening. My dream for the people of socialist Poland is that someday soon you will wake up from your nightmare, and be free.

4

My Conservatism

I was recently invited to address the question "Are We Conservatives?" before an audience at the Heritage Foundation. The very posing of the question tells us something about contemporary conservatism. I could no more have put the question "Are We Progressives?" to a comparable gathering of the left than I could ask a crowd of citizens "Are we Americans?" To raise such an issue to those audiences would be to question an identity and the foundations of a faith.

Conservatism, then, is not an ideology in the sense that liberalism is, or the various forms of radicalism are. It is not an "identity politics" whose primary concern is to situate its adherents in the camp of moral humanity and thus to confer on them the stamp of History's approval. Conservatism does not have a party line. It is possible for conservatives to question virtually any position held by other conservatives including, evidently, the notion that they are conservatives at all, without risking excommunication, expulsion, or even a raised eyebrow.

Conservatives do sometimes claim religious principles as the basis for their convictions. But it is not a religious commitment that makes them conservatives. There are radicals and liberals who have similar commitments and make similar claims. What makes an outlook "conservative' is that it is rooted in an attitude about the *past* rather than in expectations of the future. The first principles of conservatism are propositions about human nature

This was published in *Heterodoxy* magazine, January 1993.

and the way human beings behave in a social context; about limits, and what limits make possible. This practicality, this attention to experience, to workable arrangements, explains why the conservative community can be liberal and tolerant toward its members in ways that the progressive left cannot.

In contrast to the conservative outlook, liberal and radical ideologies are about the future, about desired outcomes. The first principles of the left are the principles of politically constructing a "better world." Throughout the modern era, the progressive future has been premised on a social contract that would make all of society's members equal—or at least provide them with equal starting-points.

Since ideologies of the left are commitments to an imagined future, to question them is to provoke a moral rather than an empirical response: *Are you for or against the equality of human beings?* To dissent from the progressive viewpoint is not a failure to assess relevant facts but an unwillingness to embrace a liberated future. It is, therefore, to *will* the imperfections and injustices of the present order. In the current cant of the left, it is to be "racist, sexist, classist," a defender of the *status quo*.

That is why not only radicals, but even those who call themselves liberals, are instinctively intolerant towards the conservative position. For progressives, the future is not a maze of human uncertainties and unintended consequences. It is a moral choice. To achieve the socially just future requires only that enough people decide to will it. Consequently, it is perfectly consistent for progressives to consider themselves morally and intellectually enlightened, while dismissing their opponents as morally repulsive reactionaries, unworthy of the community of other human beings.

While the politics of the left is derived from assumptions about the future, its partisans are careful to construct a view of history that validates their claims: history as a narrative of progressively expanding human rights. Thus the revolutions of the 18th century institutionalized *civil* rights of free speech and religion, and a government of laws for white property-holding males. The 19th century extended the rights of suffrage and the *political* base of freedom, ending slavery and establishing the equality of individual males as participants in the political process. The 20th century's task, and now the task of the 21st is to extend the same rights to women and other minorities, while adding *social* and *economic* rights to education, health-care, material wellbeing, and equality. This is the revolution for "social justice," which, of course, is the socialist revolution that has failed, but that the left will not give up.

Modern, or post-modern, or better still post-Communist conservatism begins with the recognition that this agenda and the progressive paradigm that underpins it are bankrupt. They have been definitively refuted by the catastrophes of Marxism, which demonstrate that the quest for social justice, pressed to its logical conclusion, leads inexorably to the totalitarian result. The reason is this: to propose a solution that is utopian, in other words impossible, is to propose a solution that requires coercion and requires absolute coercion. Who wills the end wills the means.

Post-Communist conservatism, then, begins with the principle that is written in the blood of these social experiments. "It is just not true," as Hayek wrote in *The Constitution of Liberty*, "that human beings are born equal; ... if we treat them equally, the result must be inequality in their actual position; ... [thus] the only way to place them in an equal position would be to treat them differently. *Equality before the law and material equality are, therefore, not only different but in conflict with each other.*" (my emphasis)

In other words, the rights historically claimed by the left are self-contradicting and self-defeating. The regime of social justice, of which the left dreams, is a regime that by its very nature must crush individual freedom. It is not a question of choosing the right (while avoiding the wrong) political means in order to achieve the desired ends. The means are contained in the ends. The leftist revolution must crush freedom *in order* to achieve the social justice that it seeks. It is therefore unable to achieve even that justice. This is the totalitarian circle that cannot be squared. Socialism is not bread without freedom, as some maintain; it is neither freedom nor bread. The shades of the victims, in the endless cemetery of 20th-century revolutions, cry out from their still-fresh graves: *the liberated future is a destructive illusion.* To heed this cry is the beginning of a conservative point of view.

The conservative vision does not exclude compromise; nor should it condemn every attempt, however moderate, to square the circle of political liberty and social welfare. A conservative view does not require that all aspects of the welfare state be rejected in favor of free-market principles. After all, conservatives are (or should be) the first to recognize the intractable nature of the human condition. The perfectly free society is as untenable as the perfectly just society, and for the same reason. We would have to rip out our all-too-human hearts in order to achieve it.

The Hayekian paradox—the point from which contemporary conservatism begins—is an understanding shared by the architects of the American republic. It is no accident, as Marxists would say, that *Federalist #10* describes the Constitutional arrangement as a design to thwart the projects of the left—"a rage for paper money, for an abolition of debts, for an equal division of property, or for any other improper or wicked project." A conservative is thus a conserver of the framework of the American Constitution.

But are we really conservatives? Well, yes and no. The principles of the American founding are, of course, those of classical liberalism. The fathers of modern conservatism—Locke, Burke, Madison—were classical liberals, anti-Tory architects and defenders of the great liberal revolutions of their time. But while modern radicals have failed in their efforts to expropriate the means of material production, they have succeeded in appropriating enough of the means of cultural production to hijack the term "liberal" for their own anti-liberal agenda, and to keep it there.

The radical wolves in sheep's clothing fall into two categories. First are the Crypto-Marxists, calling themselves radical feminists, post-structuralists, post-modernists, or merely progressives, whose agendas remain totalitarian. Then come the Fellow-Travelling Liberals, who acknowledge the bankruptcy of socialism and make a grudging commitment to free markets, but who still do not want to give up the agenda of "social justice"—the idea that government can arrive at a standard of what is just, and that the state can implement such a standard without destroying economic and political freedom.

The liberal ascendancy that dominates the current horizon is a popular front of these two groups. Their victories are visible all around us. Under the banner of expanding rights, they have transformed the idea of America from a covenant to secure liberties to a claim for entitlements. They have expanded the powers of the state and constricted the realm of freedom. They have eroded the private economy and stifled individual initiative. Through race-based legislation and the concept of group rights, they have subverted the neutrality of the law and the very idea of a national identity.

So ingrained have the premises of the Old Left become in their new "liberal" clothing that in post-Cold War America, conservatives are now the counterculture. That is why we must think in other-than-conservative terms when confronting the challenges that face us. We must think of ourselves as heirs to Locke and Burke and Madison, who faced a similar challenge from the leftists of their time. And with them we must proclaim:

We are the revolutionaries demanding a universalist standard of one right, one law, one nation for all;

We are the champions of tolerance, the opponents of group privilege, and of communal division;

We are the proponents of a common ground that is color-blind, gender-equitable and ethnically inclusive—a government of laws that is neutral between its citizens, and limited in scope;

We are the advocates of society as against the state, the seekers of a dramatic reduction in the burdens of taxation, and of redress from the injustices of government intervention;

We are the defenders of free markets against the destructive claims of the socialist agenda; and

We are the conservers of the Constitutional covenant against the forces of modern tyranny and the totalitarian state.

5

Black Murder Inc.

A book arrived this month that sent a chill into my marrow. The author's face on the dust jacket was different from the one I remembered. Its hair was cropped in a severe feminist do, its skin pulled tight from an apparent lift, its eyes artificially lit to give off a benign sparkle. But I could still see the menace I knew so well underneath. It was a holograph of the darkest period in my life.

I first met her in June 1974, in a dorm room at Mills College, an elite private school for women in Oakland. The meeting had been arranged by Huey Newton, leader of the Black Panther Party and icon of the New Left. For almost a year before that I had been working with Newton, developing a school complex in the East Oakland ghetto. I had named it the Oakland Community Learning Center and was the head of its Planning Committee.

The unusual venue of my first meeting with Elaine Brown was the result of the Panthers' odd disciplinary notions. They were actually Huey's notions because (as I came to understand later) the Party was an absolutist state where the leader's word was law. Huey had sentenced Elaine to Mills as a kind of exile and house arrest. "I sent her to Mills," he explained to me, "because she hates it there."[1]

This article was published in *Heterodoxy Magazine,* March 1993
[1] I never asked or learned what connection allowed him to simply place her in this exclusive private institution.

Elaine was a strikingly attractive woman, light-skinned like Huey, but with a more fluid verbal style that developed an edge when she was angry. I had been warned by my friends in the Party that she was also crazy and dangerous. A festering inner rage erupted constantly and without warning wherever she went. At such times, the edge in her voice would grow steel-hard and could slice a target like a machete.

I will never forget standing next to Elaine, as I did months later in growing horror, as she threatened KQED-TV host Bill Schechner over the telephone. "I will kill you motherfucker," she promised him in her machete voice, if he went through with plans to interview the former Panther Chairman, Bobby Seale. Seale had gone into hiding after Huey expelled him from the Party in August. As I learned long afterwards, Seale had been whipped—literally—and then personally sodomized by Huey with such violence that he had to have his anus surgically repaired by a Pacific Heights doctor who was a political supporter of the Panthers. A Party member told me later, "You have to understand, it had nothing to do with sex. It was about power." But in the Panther world, as I also came to learn, nothing was about anything except power.

That day at Mills, however, Elaine used her verbal facility as an instrument of seduction, softening me with stories of her rough youth in the North Philly ghetto and her double life at the Philadelphia conservatory of music. Her narrative dramatized the wounding personal dilemmas imposed by racial and class injustice, inevitably winning my sympathy and support.

Elaine had the two characteristics necessary for Panther leadership. She could move easily in the elegant outer world of the Party's wealthy liberal supporters, but she could also function in the violent world of the street gang, which was the Party's internal milieu. Elaine was being punished in her Mills exile by Huey, because even by his standards her temper was explosive and therefore a liability. Within three months of our meeting, however, his own out-of-control behavior, had forced him to make her supreme.

The summer of 1974 was disastrous for Newton. Reports had appeared in the press placing him at the scene of a drive-by shooting at an "after hours" club. He was indicted for pistol-whipping a middle-aged black tailor named Preston Callins with a .357 magnum, for brawling with two police officers in an Oakland bar, and for murdering a 17-year-old prostitute named Kathleen Smith. When the day arrived for his arraignment in this last matter, Huey failed to show. Assisted by the Panthers' Hollywood patrons, he had fled to Cuba.

With Huey gone, Elaine took the reins of the Party. I was already shaken by Huey's flight and by the dark ambiguities that preceded it. As a "politically conscious" radical, however, I understood the racist character of the media and the repressive forces that wanted to see the Panthers destroyed. I did not believe, therefore, all the charges against Huey. Although disturbed by them, I was unable to draw the obvious conclusion and leave.

My involvement with the Black Panther Party had begun in early 1973. I had gone to Los Angeles with Peter Collier to raise money for *Ramparts*, the flagship magazine of the New Left, which he and I co-edited. One of our marks was Bert Schneider, the producer of *Easy Rider*, the breakthrough film of the Sixties, which had brought the counter-cultural rebellion into the American mainstream. Schneider gave *Ramparts* $5,000, and then turned around and asked us to meet his friend Huey Newton.

At the time, Newton was engaged in a life and death feud with Black Panther Eldridge Cleaver. Cleaver had fled to Algiers after a shoot-out with Bay Area police. (Eldridge has since admitted that he ambushed them). Schneider wanted us to take Eldridge's name off the *Ramparts* masthead where he was still listed as "International Editor."

Huey's attraction to the Left had always been his persona as "Minister of Defense" of the Black Panther Party, his challenge to revolutionary wannabees to live up to their rhetoric and "pick up the gun." Huey had done just that in his own celebrated confrontation with the law that had left Officer John Frey dead with a bullet wound in his back. Everybody in the Left seemed to believe that Huey had killed Frey, but we wanted to believe as well that Huey—as a victim of racism—was also innocent. Peter's and my engagement with the Panthers was more social than political, since *Ramparts* had helped the Party become a national franchise. I was put off by their military style, but now a change in the times prompted the two of us, and especially me, to be interested in the meeting.

By the early 70s, it was clear that the Movement had flamed out. As soon as Nixon signaled the end of the military draft, the anti-war demonstrations stopped and the protestors disappeared, marooning hardcore activists like myself. I felt a need to do something to fill the vacancy. Huey Newton was really alone among Movement figures in recognizing the change in the *zeitgeist* and making the most of it. In a dramatic announcement, he declared the time had come to "put away the gun" and, instead, to "serve the people," which seemed sensible enough to me.

Our meeting took place in Huey's penthouse eyrie, 25 floors above Lake Oakland. In its intra-party polemics, the Eldridge faction had condemned Huey for "selling out the armed struggle," and made much of Huey's lavish lifestyle. But the apartment itself was sparely furnished and I was ready to accept Schneider's explanation that it was necessary for "security." (A TV screen allowed Huey to view entrants to the building, 25 floors below). Not only J. Edgar Hoover's infamous agents but also the disgruntled Cleaver elements might very well want to see Huey dead. There had been several killings already. One of Huey's East Coast loyalists, Sam Napier, had been shot and doused with gasoline, and set on fire.

Somehow, because of Huey's sober pronouncements and his apparent victory in the intra-party struggle I regarded this reality as part of the past, and no longer threatening. Unlike Elaine, Huey was able to keep his street passions in check in the presence of white intellectuals he intended to make use of. In all the time I worked with him, I never saw him abuse another individual, verbally or otherwise. I never saw him angry or heard him utter a threat. I never saw a gun drawn. When I opposed him on important political issues, as I did at our very first meeting, I found him respectful of my differences, a seduction I could not resist. (My partner, Peter, was more cautious and politically aloof and, as events were to prove, wiser than I.)

After the meeting, I offered to help Huey with the Party's community projects and to raise money for the Panther school. Huey wanted to buy a Baptist church facility in the East Oakland ghetto with an auditorium, cafeteria and 35 classrooms. In the next months, I raised more than $100,000 to purchase the buildings on 61st Avenue and East 14th Street. The $63,000 down payment was the largest check I had ever seen, let alone signed. The new Oakland Community Learning Center was administered by a Planning Committee, which was composed of Panthers whom Huey had specially selected to work with me. Neither Bobby Seale, nor Elaine Brown, nor any other Panther leaders were among them.

The Learning Center began with more than 100 Panther children. Its instruction was enriched by educationalists like Herbert Kohl whom I brought in to help. I took Kohl to see Huey in the penthouse eyrie, but the meeting went badly. Within days, Huey's spies had reported that Kohl (who was street smart in ways I was not) was telling people that Huey was using cocaine. When I confronted Herb, he said: "He's sniffing. He was sniffing when we were up there."

I had not been part of the Sixties drug culture and was so unfamiliar with cocaine at that time, that I had no idea whether Kohl was right. Huey's runny nose, his ability to stay alert despite the fifth of Courvoisier he daily consumed, the sleepless nights at Schneider's Beverly Hills home where once Bert and his girlfriend Candice Bergen had gone to bed Huey talked endlessly to me about politics and the millions of dollars the Party had squandered on bail—all these were tell-tale signs I could not read. I assumed the innocent possibility that Huey was "sniffing" because he had a cold, which is what I told Kohl, who probably thought I was shining him on. After the incident, Huey banished Kohl from the penthouse, but let him continue to help on the Learning Center.

The Center was operated by a front I had created called the Educational Opportunities Corporation, a California tax-exempt 501(c)(3). It was imperative—or so I thought—to keep the books of the school in order and to file appropriate tax reports so that hostile authorities would not be given a pretext to shut us down. This proved to be only another aspect of my politically induced innocence. Long after I had gone, too, I watched the Center operate illegally, without filing proper tax reports, while Huey and Elaine were diverting large sums of money (received as government grants) to themselves and their gunmen to keep them in fancy cars and clothes and, when necessary, out of jail. Unable to conceive such a possibility for a Party all leftists knew was targeted for destruction by J. Edgar Hoover, I engaged the services of our bookkeeper at *Ramparts*, Betty Van Patter, to keep the Learning Center accounts.

Virtually my entire relationship with Huey and the Party was through the activities of the school. In the months following the purchase of the building on East 14th, it became apparent to me that things were not proceeding as planned. In particular, it was still exclusively a Party operation. I had never been enthusiastic about the Party as such, which seemed to me merely an ideological sect whose time had passed. I had conveyed these views to Huey at the outset of our relationship and he had pretended to agree. He had even promised that if we purchased the facility and built an educational center, it would gradually be turned over to the East Oakland community and not become just another Party institution.

Six months had gone by, however, and there were only Panthers in attendance. The impoverished black community around the school remained aloof, as did the black intellectuals like Berkeley sociology professor Troy Duster, whom I periodically approached to help out with the operation, and who would come up to the penthouse to see Huey, but afterwards never follow through or come back. Adding to my dismay was the fact that the school head, Brenda Bay, had been replaced by Ericka Huggins, a prominent Party figure and in my view an individual who was mentally unbalanced. (It did not improve my dim view of Ericka, when I saw her punish a child by commanding the 9 year old to write 1,000 times, "I am privileged to attend the Black Panther Party's Learning Center because ...") My concerns about the school came to a head on May 19, 1974, which was Malcolm X's birthday.

A "Malcolm X Day" celebration was held in the school auditorium, which I attended. One after another, Bobby Seale, Elaine Brown, and other Panthers mounted the podium to proclaim the Party as "the only true continuator of the legacy of Malcolm." Looking around at the familiar faces of the Panthers in the hall, I felt depressed and even betrayed. Huey had assured me that the Center would not become the power base for a sect, and had even excluded Bobby and Elaine from its operation to make me a believer. And yet now I could see that's all that it was.

At the next Planning Committee meeting in Huey's apartment, I braced myself and launched into a passionate complaint. On a day that all black Oakland should have been at the Center, I said, the occasion had been turned into a sectarian promotion for the Black Panther Party. My outburst was met by a tense silence from the others at the table. But Huey seemed unfazed and even to lend some support to what I had said. This duplicitous impression of yielding was almost a performance art with him.

Elaine had a similar talent for seduction when it fitted her agenda. In our first encounter at Mills, she had strategically brought the Malcolm X incident into our conversation. In her most disarming manner, she related how, after the meeting, Ericka Huggins had reported to her and other members of the Party that, "David Horowitz said that the Malcolm X Day celebration was too black."

It was a shrewd gambit, reminding me of my precarious position in the Panther environment, while at the same time making her appear as a friend and potential protector. She had her reasons to ingratiate herself with me then, because she knew that somehow I had Huey's ear, and she wanted desperately to end her exile. A month later, Huey kicked Bobby out of the Party and her wish was granted. She became the new Party chairman. A month after that, Huey was gone to Cuba.

When Huey left, all the Panthers whom Huey had assigned to work with me—all the members of the Planning Committee except Ericka—fled too. They left, suddenly, without warning, in the middle of the night. A week earlier, which was the last time I saw them, they had worried about Elaine's new ascendance. When I asked why they were afraid of Elaine, they said, "She's crazy." Now they had disappeared, and I had no way of contacting them to question them further.

Although I had been warned about Elaine's dark side, at this point I had only seen benign aspects myself. Now, as she took charge of the Party, she revealed another dimension of her personality that was even more attractive.

Where Huey had pretty much ignored the Learning Center after its creation, Elaine threw herself into its every detail, from curriculum to hygiene. She ordered it scrubbed from top to bottom, got proper supplies for the children, and made the Center's needs a visible priority. Soon, the first real community event was held on its premises. It was a teen dance attended by 500 youths from the neighborhood. I could not have asked for a more concrete sign that things were going to be different. And these efforts were ongoing. Eventually Elaine would recruit Oakland dignitaries to the board of the Center, like Mayor Lionel Wilson and Robert Shetterly the president and chairman of the Oakland Council for Economic Development. How could I not support her efforts in behalf of a project that had seemed so worthy and to which I had dedicated so much effort?

There were other seductive aspects to her leadership as well. The Black Panther Party—the most male dominated organization of the Left—was suddenly being led by an articulate, take-charge

woman. And not just one woman. Elaine's right and left hands in
the Party organization—Joan Kelley and Phyllis Jackson—were
also female, as was its treasurer Gwen Goodloe.[2] With Huey gone
under a dark cloud, Elaine and the Center were facing formidable
obstacles. My social and racial privilege always afforded me a way
out of these difficulties (as my leftist conscience was constantly
reproving me). How could I face myself, if I abandoned their ship
now?

So I stayed. And when the Party's treasurer, Gwen Goodloe,
fled a week later, and Elaine became desperate over who would
manage its finances, I suggested a solution. Betty Van Patter, who
was already doing the books for the Learning Center, might be of
help in handling the general accounts. This was to be my last act
of assistance to the Party. The crises of the fall had piled on one
another in such swift succession, that I was unable to assess the
toll they were taking. But in November, an event occurred that
pushed me over the edge.

There had been a second teen dance, and this time there was a
shooting. A Panther named Deacon was dead. His assailant, a
black youth of 16, was in the county hospital. When I phoned
Elaine to ask what had happened, she exploded in the kind of violent outpouring I was now becoming used to, blaming the disaster
on "the police and the CIA." This stock paranoia was really all I
needed to hear to tell me things were not what they had seemed
and were terribly wrong. (Years later, I learned from Panthers who
had fled and were now in contact with me that the shooting had
been over drugs, which the Party was dealing from the school.)

When I walked into the school auditorium where Deacon lay in
state (there is really no other term for the scene in front of me), I
suddenly saw the real Party to which I had closed my eyes to for so

---

[2]Many years later Gwen Goodloe contacted me. She was then working as
an executive in the finance department of Hughes Aircraft, a defense con-
tractor. How did you get your clearance, I asked her? "I told them the
truth," she said.

long. Of course, the children were there, as were their parents and teachers, but dominating them and everything else physically and symbolically was the honor guard of Panther soldiers in black berets, shotguns alarmingly on display. Added to this spectacle, mingling with the mourners, there were the unmistakable gangster types, whose presence had suddenly become apparent to me after Elaine took over the Party: "Big Bob," Perkins, Aaron, Ricardo, Larry. They were fitted in shades and Bogarts and pinstripe suits, as though waiting for action on the set of a B crime movie. In their menacing faces there was no reflection of political complexity such as Huey was so adept at projecting, or of the benevolent community efforts like the breakfast for children programs that the Center provided.

Underneath all the political rhetoric and social uplift, I suddenly realized was the stark reality of the gang. I remember a voice silently beating my head, as I sat there during the service, tears streaming down my face: "What are you doing here, David?" it screamed at me. It was my turn to flee.

Betty did not attend the funeral, and if she had would not have been able to see what I saw. Moreover, she and I had never had the kind of relationship that inspired confidences between us. As my employee, she never really approved of the way Peter and I ran *Ramparts.* For whatever reasons—perhaps a streak of feminist militancy—she didn't trust me.

Just as a precaution, I had warned Betty even before Deacon's funeral not to get involved in any part of the Party or its functioning that she didn't feel comfortable with. But Betty kept her own counsel. In one of our few phone conversations, I mentioned the shooting at the dance. She did not take my remark further.

Later it became obvious that I hadn't really known Betty. I had counted to some extent on her middle class scruples to keep her from any danger zones she encountered in Panther territory. But this too was an illusion. She had passions that prompted her to want a deeper involvement in what she also perceived as their struggle against oppression.

There was another reason I did not express my growing fears to Betty. The more fear I had the more I realized that it would not be okay for me to voice such criticism, having been so close to the operation. To badmouth the Party would be tantamount to treason. I had a wife and four children, who lived in neighboring Berkeley, and I would not be able to protect them or myself from Elaine's wrath.

There were other considerations in my silence, too. What I had seen at the funeral, what I knew from hearsay and from the press were only blips on a radar screen that was highly personal, dependent on my own experience to read. I had begun to know the Panther reality, at least enough to have a healthy fear of Elaine. But how could I convey this knowledge to someone who had not been privy to the same things I had? How could I do it in such a way that they would believe me and not endanger me? Before fleeing, my Panther friends had tried to warn me about Huey through similar signs, and I had failed to understand. My ignorance was dangerous to them and to myself. Finally, only the police had ever accused the Panthers of actual crimes. Everyone I knew and respected on the left—and beyond the left—regarded the police allegations against the Panthers as malicious libels by a racist power structure bent on holding down and eliminating militant black leadership. It was one of the most powerful liberal myths of the times.

One Friday night, a month or so after Deacon's funeral, a black man walked into the Berkeley Square, a neighborhood bar that Betty frequented, and handed her a note. Betty, who seemed to know the messenger, read the note and left shortly afterwards. She was never seen alive again.

On the following Monday, I received an anxious phone call from Tammy Van Patter, Betty's 18-year-old daughter, who had also worked for me at *Ramparts*. She told me her mother was missing and asked for my help. I phoned Elaine, but got Joan Kelley instead. Joan told me that Elaine had had a fight with Betty on Thursday and fired her. (Later, Elaine lied to investigating police, telling them she had fired Betty the previous Friday and hadn't seen her for a week before she disappeared.)

When Elaine returned my call, she immediately launched into a tirade against Betty, calling her an "idiot" who believed in astrology, and who "wanted to know too much." She said that Betty was employed by a bookkeeping firm with offices in the Philippines, and was probably working for the C.I.A. Then Elaine turned on me for recommending that Betty be hired in the first place. She noted that I was "bawling" at Deacon's funeral and had not "come around for a long time." Perhaps I was scared by the dangers the Party faced, she suggested. Then she asked why was I so concerned about this white woman who was crazy, when all those brothers had been gunned down by the police? White people didn't seem to care that much when it was black people dying. I didn't answer her back.

A week later, when Betty still had not turned up, I called Elaine one more time, and was subjected to another torrent of abuse culminating in a threat only thinly veiled: "If you were run over by a car or something, David, I would be very upset, because people would say I did it."

I was visited in my home by the Berkeley police. They told me they were convinced the Panthers had taken Betty hostage and had probably already killed her. From her daughter Tammy I learned that the very small circle of Betty's friends and acquaintances had all been questioned since her disappearance, and none had seen her for some time. She had left her credit cards and birth control pills at home, and thus could not have been going on an unexpected trip when she left the Berkeley Square with the mysterious messenger. Just to the rendezvous to which she had been summoned.

Betty was found on January 13, 1975, five weeks after she had disappeared, when her water-logged body washed up on the western shore of San Francisco Bay. Her head had been bashed in by a blunt instrument and police estimated that she had been in the water for seventeen days. She was 42 years old.

By this time, everything I knew about Betty's disappearance led to the conclusion that the Panthers had killed her. Everything I knew about the Party and the way it worked led me to believe that Elaine Brown had given the order to have her killed. Betty's murder shattered my life and changed it forever. But even as I sank into a long period of depression and remorse, Elaine's star began to rise in Oakland's political firmament. A white woman who worked for the Black Panther Party had been murdered, but—despite our rhetoric about police conspiracies and racist oppression—there seemed to be no consequences for Elaine or her Party.

The press made nothing of it. When Peter Collier approached Marilyn Baker, a Pulitzer Prize winning reporter for Channel 5 with the story, she said she "wouldn't touch it unless a black reporter did it first." No black reporter did. Betty's friends in the Bay Area progressive community, who generally were alert to every injustice, even in lands so remote they could not locate them on a map, kept their silence about this one in their own backyard. Peter also went to the police who told him: "You guys have been cutting our balls off for the last ten years. You destroy the police and then you expect them to solve the murders of your friends."

While the investigation of Betty's death continued, Elaine ran for the Oakland City Council and garnered 44 percent of the vote. The following year, under her leadership, the Party provided the political machine that elected Oakland's first black mayor, Lionel Wilson. Elaine herself secured the endorsement of Governor Jerry Brown and was a Jerry Brown delegate to the Democratic Convention in 1976. (Before making his run, Brown phoned Elaine to find out what kind of support the Party could provide him.) Tony Cline, a Panther lawyer and confidante of Elaine, was also a college roommate of the Governor and became a member of his cabinet. Using her leverage in Sacramento, Elaine was able to get approval for an extension of the Grove-Shafter Freeway, which had been blocked by environmentalists. On the basis of this achievement, she began negotiations with the head of Oakland's Council for Economic Development to control 10,000 new city jobs that the freeway would create.

In all these successes, the Learning Center was her showpiece. Capitalizing on liberal concerns for Oakland's inner city poor, she obtained contributions and grants for the school, and bought herself a red Mercedes. The Party's political influence climbed to its zenith. It was an all-American nightmare.

While Elaine's power grew to alarming proportions, I intensified my private investigations into the Panther reality that had previously eluded me. I had to confront my blindness and understand the events that had led to such an irreversible crossroads in my life, and ended Betty's. I interrogated everyone I could trust who had been around the Panthers about the dark side of their operations, seeking answers to the questions of Betty's death.

I discovered the existence of the Panther "Squad"—an enforcer group that Huey had organized inside the Party to maintain discipline and carry out criminal activities in the East Oakland community.[3] I learned of beatings, arson, extortion and murders. The Learning Center itself had been used as the pretext for a shakedown operation of after-hours clubs which were required to "donate" weekly sums and whose owners were gunned down when they refused.

I learned about the personalities in the Squad, and about their involvement in Betty's murder. One of them, Robert Heard, was known as "Big Bob" because he was 6'8" and weighed 400 pounds.[4] Big Bob told friends, whom I talked to, that the Squad had killed Betty and more than a dozen other people, in the brief period between 1972 and 1976. The other victims were all black, and

---

[3]Many years after the publication of "Black Murder Inc.," a member of the Squad, whom the police believed to be Betty's probable killer, Flores Forbes, described its criminal activities, in particular its shakedowns of the afterhours clubs, while omitting the murders it committed in the course of the shakedowns, in a memoir called *Will You Die With Me?*, July, 2006

[4]After the Party disintegrated in the mid-Seventies, Heard continued his criminal career and was eventually convicted of a non-Panther related homicide.

included the Vice President of the Black Student Union at Grove Street College, whose misfortune was to have inadvertently insulted a member of the Squad.

Betty's children commissioned Hal Lipset, a private eye with connections to the Left (and to the Panthers themselves who had employed him during Huey's trials) to investigate the case. Lipset confirmed the police conclusion that the Panthers had killed Betty. They also tried to get the case against the Panthers re-opened, but without success.

In the summer of 1977, unable to stomach exile any longer, Huey suddenly returned from Cuba. He was given a welcome by the local Left, culminating in a ceremony and "citizenship award" presented by Democratic Assemblyman Tom Bates, husband of Berkeley's radical mayor, Loni Hancock.

Not everyone was ready to turn a blind eye to the Panther reality. The minute Huey stepped off the plane, Alameda Country prosecutors began preparing to try him for the murder of Kathleen Smith, the 17-year-old prostitute he had killed three years earlier.

Huey made preparations too. One day before the preliminary trial hearings were to begin in Oakland, Squad member Flores Forbes and another Panther gunmen tried to break into a house in the nearby city of Richmond, where they expected to find the prosecution's eye-witness, Crystal Gray, and assassinate her.[5] But it was the wrong door, since Gray lived in an apartment in the back. The owner of the front apartment, a black bookkeeper, picked up her .38 and fired at the intruders. A gun battle ensued in which Forbes inadvertently killed his partner. Forbes was also wounded.

Forbes fled the scene to seek the assistance of another Panther, named Nelson Malloy, who was not a Squad member and had only just joined the Party. Fearing that the innocent Malloy might link him to the assassination attempt, Huey ordered a hit team to follow Malloy and Forbes to Las Vegas, where they had fled. The

---

[5]The assassination attempt is described in Flores Forbes' book, *Will You Die With Me?* In the book Forbes claims, implausibly, that this plot was his own initiative, unauthorized by Newton.

assassins found them and shot Malloy in the head and buried him in a shallow roadside grave in the Nevada desert. Miraculously he was discovered by tourists who heard his moans and rescued him, although he remained paralyzed from the neck down for the rest of his life.

Shortly after the Richmond incident, Elaine herself was gone. The Squad members had never really accommodated themselves to being ruled by a woman. When Huey returned, tensions between Elaine and the Squad reached a head, and Huey came down on the side of his gunmen. Elaine left for Los Angeles, never to return.

The botched assassination attempt on the prosecution witness, together with the headlines about Malloy's burial in the desert, destroyed the alliances that Elaine had so carefully built. Lionel Wilson, and the head of Clorox along with the other Oakland dignitaries resigned from the Learning Center board. With its power diminished and its sinister reality in part revealed, the Panther Party had been de-clawed. I began to breathe more easily.

But I was still unable to write or make public what I had come to know about the Party and its role in Betty's murder. I had given some of the information to radical journalist Kate Coleman who wrote a courageous story for the magazine *New Times*. It was called "The Party's Over" and it helped speed the Panther decline. But I could not be a witness myself. I was no longer worried about being denounced as a racist or government agent by my friends on the Left if I accused the Panthers of murdering Betty. During the five years since Betty's death, my politics had begun to change. But there remained a residue of physical fear. Huey was alive in Oakland, and armed, and obviously crazy, and dangerous. I now realized how powerless the law in fact was. Huey seemed untouchable. He had managed to beat his murder rap with the help of testimony by friends ready to perjure themselves for the cause. The pistol-whipping case had been dropped, too. After being threatened and bribed, the tailor Preston Callins retracted his charges. For me, caution seemed to be the prudent course.

Then, in 1980, an event took place that provided me with an occasion to relieve myself of a portion of my burden. It provided a story that was parallel in many respects to what I had been through. It would afford me the opportunity to speak about things that had been unspeakable until now. In May 1980, Fay Stender, an attorney who had defended Black Panther George Jackson, took her own life in Hong Kong. She had withdrawn to this remote city away from family and friends, in order to kill herself after a member of Jackson's prison gang had shot and paralyzed her the year before. She had stayed alive just long enough to act as a witness for the prosecution in the trial of her assailant.

Peter Collier and I wrote her story, calling it "Requiem for A Radical."[6] In it, we recounted the details of her life and death, and were able to lift a part of the veil that had obscured the criminal underside of the Black Panther Party. We described the army of thugs that had been trained in the Santa Cruz Mountains to free Jackson from his San Quentin cell. We described the killing fields in those same mountains where the Panthers had buried the corpses of Fred Bennett and others who had violated their Party codes. We were also able to write honestly about Jackson himself, whom the Left had made into a romantic legend and who, like Huey, was a criminal psychopath. Obscured by the love letters Jackson had written in the book *Soledad Brother,* which Fay Stender had edited, was the murderer who had boasted of killing a dozen men in prison and whose revolutionary plan was to poison the water system of Chicago where he had grown up.

When our story appeared in *New West* magazine, I learned through mutual friends that Bert Schneider, Huey's Hollywood patron, was unhappy with the account Peter and I had written. Although I sensed that Bert was aware of the Party's criminal activities, including Betty's murder, I was not as afraid of him as I was of Huey, and I decided to go and see him. I did so on a principle taken from the Godfather movies, that you should get near to your

---

[6]A chapter in *Destructive Generation,* 1989

enemies and find out what they have in mind for you. The Fay Stender story was not a direct hit on Huey or Bert and their reactions might tell me something I needed to know. Perhaps the past was not as alive for them as I imagined. Perhaps I did not have so much to fear.

Bert had an estate on a hill above Benedict Canyon in Beverly Hills. I called my name through the security gate and was admitted into the main house. Bert appeared, wearing a bathrobe, and in a quiet rage. He was angrier than I had ever seen him. "You endangered my life," he hissed at me.

I didn't have the slightest idea what he was talking about. He directed me to a passage in our Fay Stender article about Jackson's attempted escape from San Quentin prison (an episode in which the Panther and his comrades slit the throats of three prison guards they had tied up, before Jackson himself was killed): "The abortive escape left a thicket of unanswered questions behind.... Had Jackson been set up? If so, was it by the Cleaver faction of the Black Panther Party? Or by Newton, fearful of Jackson's charismatic competition?"

Joe Durden Smith's book *Who Killed George Jackson?* had described Bert as being in close contact with Huey during the escape attempt. Perhaps he was referring to that. Even so, I still could not understand why Bert was so agitated. I was already focusing, however, on something else Bert had said that had far greater significance for me. In defending his reaction to the article he had admitted, "Huey isn't as angry as I am." It was the opening I was looking for. I told him I would like to see Huey, and a lunch was arranged.

When I arrived at Norman's, the North Berkeley restaurant that Huey had chosen, he was already there, sunk into one of the vinyl divans, his eyes liverish and his skin pallid, drunker than I had ever seen him. He was so drunk, in fact, that when the lunch was over he asked me to drive him back to the two-story house that Bert had bought for him in the Oakland Hills, and left his own car outside the restaurant. When we arrived, he invited me in. I was a little nervous about accepting but decided to go anyway. The decor—piled carpets, leather couches and glass-topped end tables—was familiar. Only the African decorative masks that had been mounted on the beige walls seemed a new touch.

As we settled ourselves in Huey's living room, the conversation we had begun at lunch continued. Huey told me about a project he had dreamed up to produce *Porgy and Bess* as a musical set in contemporary Harlem, starring Stevie Wonder and Mick Jagger. It was a bizarre idea but not out of character for Huey, whose final fight with Bobby Seale had begun with a quarrel over who should play the lead role in a film Huey wanted to make. Huey even showed me the treatment he had prepared in Braille for Stevie Wonder, while complaining that the people around the singer had badmouthed him and killed the deal. When he said this, his face contorted in a grimace that was truly demonic.

Then, just as suddenly, he relaxed and fell into a distant silence. After a minute, he looked directly at me and said: "Elaine killed Betty." And then, just as abruptly, he added a caveat whose cynical bravado was also typical, as though he was teaching me, once again, how the world really worked: "But if you write that, I'll deny it." Until that moment I had thought Elaine was solely responsible for the order to kill Betty. But now I realized that Huey had collaborated with her and probably given the order himself. It was the accusation against Elaine that provided the clue. He might have said, "David, I'm sorry about Betty. It should never have happened, but I was in Cuba and couldn't stop it." But he didn't. He chose instead to point a finger at Elaine, as the one alone responsible. It had a false ring. It was uncharacteristically disloyal. Why point the finger at anyone, unless he wanted to deflect attention from himself? I went home and contacted several ex-Panthers, who were living on the East Coast. I asked them how Elaine, as a woman, had been able to run the Party and control the Squad. The answer was the same in each case: Elaine had not really run the Party while Huey was in Cuba. Huey had run it. He was in daily contact with Elaine by phone. The Squad stayed loyal to Elaine out of fear of Huey. The same sources told me that the fate of Betty had been debated for a week. Elaine had provided Huey with the reasons for killing Betty; Huey had made the final decision.

In 1989, fourteen years after Betty disappeared, Huey was gunned down by a drug dealer he had burned. It was a few blocks away from where Huey had killed the 17-year-old prostitute Kathleen Smith. It might have been poetic, but it was not justice. He should have died sooner; he should have suffered more. On the other hand, if I had learned anything through all this, it was not to expect justice in this world, and to be grateful for that which did occur, however belated and insufficient.

Huey's death allowed Peter and me to write his story and to describe the Panther reality I had uncovered. (We called it "Baddest" and published it as a new chapter in the paperback edition of our book *Destructive Generation*.) By now, we had become identified with the political right (although "libertarian irregulars" might better describe our second thoughts). What we wrote about the Panthers' crimes, therefore, was either dismissed or simply ignored by an intellectual culture that was dominated by the left. Even though Huey's final days had tainted the Panthers' legacy, their glories were still fondly recalled in all the Sixties nostalgia that continued to appear on public television, in the historical monographs of politically correct academics and even in the pages of the popular press. The Panther crime wave was of no importance to anyone outside the small circle of their abandoned victims.

Then, in an irony of fate, Elaine Brown emerged from obscurity early this year to reopen the vexed questions of the Panther legacy. She had been living in a kind of semi-retirement with a wealthy French industrialist in Paris. Now she was back in America seeking to capitalize on the collective failure of memory with a self-promoting autobiography called *A Taste of Power*. It was published by a major New York publisher, with all the fanfare of a major New York offering.

With her usual adroitness, Elaine had managed to sugarcoat her career as a political gangster by presenting herself as a feminist heroine and victim. "What Elaine Brown writes is so astonishing," croons novelist Alice Walker from the dust jacket of the book, "at times it is even difficult to believe she survived it. And yet she did, bringing us that amazing light of the black woman's magical resilience, in the gloominess of our bitter despair." "A stunning picture of a black woman's coming of age in America," concurs the Kirkus Reviews. "Put it on the shelf beside *The Autobiography of Malcolm X.*" To the *Los Angeles Times'* Carolyn See, it is "beautiful, touching, ... astonishing. ... Movie makers, where are you?" (In fact, Suzanne DePasse, producer of *Lonesome Dove,* who appears to have been the guiding spirit behind the book is planning a major motion picture of Elaine's life.[7]) *Time* magazine's review invokes Che Guevara's claim that "the true revolutionary is guided by great feelings of love," and comments: "In the end, Brown discovers, love is the most demanding political act of all."

A full-spread *New York Times Magazine* profile of Elaine ("A Black Panther's Long Journey"), treated her as a new feminist heroine and prompted View and Style sections of newspapers in major cities across the nation to follow suit. Elaine, who reportedly received a $450,000 advance from Pantheon Books, has been touring the book circuit, doing radio and television shows from coast to coast, including a segment of the *MacNeil/Lehrer NewsHour,* where she appeared on a panel chaired by Charlayne Hunter Gault as an authority on black America. ("I hate this country," she later told the *Los Angeles Times.* "There's a point at which you're black in this country, poor, a woman, and you realize how powerless you are." In contrast, Elaine once told me privately: "The poorest black in Oakland is richer than 90 percent of the world's population.") At Cody's Books in Berkeley, two hundred radical nostalgists came to hear her, flanked by her "bodyguard," Huey's old gunman, Flores Forbes, who had served his four years on a second degree murder charge for the Richmond killing and was now prospering in his new career as an urban planner.

[7]Mercifully, this never came to pass.

I read Elaine's book. Jaded though I am, I was still amazed by its reception. The only accurate review seemed to come from the Bloods and Crips who flocked as fans to her Los Angeles appearance, recognizing that she was a gangster like them. *A Taste of Power* is, in its bloody prose, and despite the falsehoods designed to protect the guilty, the self-revelation of a sociopath, of the Elaine I had come to know.

"I felt justified in trying to slap the life out of her,"—this is the way Elaine introduces an incident in which she attempted to retrieve some poems from a radical lawyer named Elaine Wenders. The poems had been written by Johnny Spain, a Panther who participated in George Jackson's murderous attempt to escape from San Quentin. Elaine describes how she entered Wenders' office, flanked by Joan Kelley and another female lieutenant, slapped Wenders' face and proceeded to tear the room apart, emptying desk-drawers and files onto the floor, slapping the terrified and now weeping lawyer again, and finally issuing an ultimatum: "I gave her twenty-four hours to deliver the poems to me, lest her office be blown off the map."

Because Wenders worked in the office of Charles Garry, Huey's personal attorney, Elaine's thuggery produced some mild repercussions. She was called to the penthouse for a "reprimand" by Huey, who laughingly told her she was a "terrorist." The reprimand apparently still stings and Elaine even now feels compelled to justify the violence that others seemed to consider merely impolitic: "It is impossible to summarize the biological response to an act of will in a life of submission. It would be to capture the deliciousness of chocolate, the arousing aroma of a man or a perfume, the feel of water to the dry throat. What I had begun to experience was the sensation of personal freedom, like the tremor before orgasm. The Black Panther Party had awakened that thirst in me. And it had given me the power to satisfy it."

The thirst for violence is a prominent feature of this self-portrait: "It is a sensuous thing to know that at one's will an enemy can be struck down," Elaine continues. In another passage she provides one of many instances in her book of this pleasure. Here, it is a revenge exacted, after she becomes head of the Party, on a former Panther lover named Steve, who had beaten her years before. Steve is lured to a meeting where he finds himself looking down the barrel of a shotgun. While Elaine's enforcer, Larry Henson, holds Steve at gunpoint, Elaine unleashes four members of the Squad, including the 400 pound Robert Heard, on her victim: "Four men were upon him now ... Steve struggled for survival under the many feet stomping him.... Their punishment became unmerciful. When he tried to protect his body by taking the fetal position, his head became the object of their feet. The floor was rumbling, as though a platoon of pneumatic drills were breaking through its foundation. Blood was everywhere. Steve's face disappeared."

The taste for violence is as pervasive in Elaine's account, as is the appetite to justify it in the name of the revolutionary cause. She describes the scene in Huey's apartment just after he had pistol-whipped the middle-aged black tailor Preston Callins with a .357 Magnum. (Callins required brain surgery to repair the damage): "Callins's blood now stained the penthouse ceilings and carpets and walls and plants, and [Huey's wife's] clothes, even the fluffy blue-and-white towels in the bathroom." This is Elaine's reaction to the scene: "While I noted Huey's irreverent attitude about the whole affair, it occurred to me how little I, too, actually cared about Callins. He was neither a man nor a victim to me. I had come to believe everything would balance out in the revolutionary end. I also knew that being concerned about Callins was too costly, particularly in terms of my position in the Party. Yes, I thought, f—k Callins."

Elaine deals with Betty's murder in these pages, too. "I had fired Betty Van Patter shortly after hiring her. She had come to work for the Party at the behest of David Horowitz, who had been editor of *Ramparts* magazine and a onetime close friend of Eldridge Cleaver. He was also nominally on the board of our school.... She was having trouble finding work because of her arrest record...." This is false on every significant count. Betty had no arrest record that Elaine or I knew about. I was one of three legal incorporators of the Learning Center and, as I have already described, the head of its Planning Committee not "nominally on the board." Finally, I had met Eldridge Cleaver only once, in my capacity as a fledgling editor at *Ramparts*. (Elaine's purpose in establishing this particular falsehood is clearly to link Betty to a possible plot: "I began wondering where Betty Van Patter might have really come from.... I began re-evaluating Horowitz and his old Eldridge alliance...").

Elaine continues: "Immediately Betty began asking Norma, and every other Panther with whom she had contact, about the sources of our cash, or the exact nature of this or that expenditure. Her job was to order and balance our books and records, not to investigate them. I ordered her to cease her interrogations." She continued. "I knew that I had made a mistake in hiring her.... Moreover, I had learned after hiring her that Betty's arrest record was a prison record—on charges related to drug trafficking. Her prison record would weaken our position in any appearance we might have to make before a government body inquiring into our finances. Given her actions and her record, she was not, to say the least, an asset. I fired Betty without notice."

Betty had no prison record for drug trafficking or anything else.

"While it was true that I had come to dislike Betty Van Patter," Elaine concludes, "I had fired her, not killed her."

Yet, the very structure of Elaine's defense is self-incriminating. The accurate recollections that Betty, who was indeed scrupulous, had made normal bookkeeping inquiries that Elaine found suspicious and dangerous, provides a plausible motive to silence her. The assertions that Betty was a criminal, possibly involved in a Cleaver plot, are false and can only be intended to indict the victim. Why deflect guilt to the victim or anyone else, unless one is guilty oneself?

Violence was not restricted to the Panthers' dealings with their enemies, but was an integral part of the Party's internal life as well. In what must be one of the sickest aspects of the entire

Panther story, this party of liberators enforced discipline on the black "brothers and sisters" inside the organization with bull-whips, the very symbol of the slave past. In a scene that combines both the absurdity and pathology of the Party's daily routine, Elaine describes her own punishment under the Panther lash. She is ordered to strip to the waist by Chairman Bobby Seale and then subjected to ten strokes because she had missed an editorial deadline on the Black Panther newspaper.

A *Taste of Power* inadvertently provides another service by describing how the Panthers originally grew out of criminal street gangs, and how the gang mentality remained the core of the Party's sense of itself even during the heyday of its political glory. Elaine writes with authority, having come into the Party through the Slausons, a forerunner of the Bloods and the Crips. The Slausons were enrolled en masse in the Party in 1967 by their leader, gang-ster Al "Bunchy" Carter, the so-called "Mayor of Watts." Carter's enforcer, Frank Diggs, is one of Elaine's first Party heroes: "Frank Diggs, Captain Franco, was reputedly leader of the Panther under-ground. He had spent twelve years in Sing Sing Prison in New York on robbery and murder charges." Captain Franco describes to Elaine and Ericka Huggins his revolutionary philosophy: "Other than making love to a Sister, downing a pig is the greatest feeling in the world. Have you ever seen a pig shot with a .45 automatic, Sister Elaine?...Well, it's a magnificent sight." To Elaine, then a newly initiated Panther, this is revolutionary truth: "In time, I began to see the dark reality of the revolution according to Franco, the revolution that was not some mystical battle of glory in some distant land of time. At the deepest level, there was blood, nothing but blood, unsanitized by political polemic. That was where Franco worked, in the vanguard of the vanguard ..." The vanguard of the vanguard.

The Panthers were—just as the police and other Panther detractors said at the time—a criminal army led by gangsters and murderers at war with society and with its thin blue line of civic protectors. When Elaine took over the Party, even she was "stunned by the magnitude of the party's weaponry.... There were literally thousands of weapons. There were large numbers of AR-18 short automatic rifles,. 308 scoped rifles, 30-30 Winchesters, .375 magnum and other big-game rifles, .30 caliber Garands, M-15s and M-16s and other assorted automatic and semi-automatic rifles, Thompson submachine guns, M-59 Santa Fe Troopers, Boys .55 caliber anti-tank guns, M-60 fully automatic machine guns, innumerable shotguns, and M-79 grenade launchers.... There were caches of crossbows and arrows, grenades and miscellaneous explosive materials and devices."

I remember vividly an episode in the mid-70s, when one of the Panther arms caches, a house on 29th Street in East Oakland, was raided by the police and 1,000 weapons including machine guns, grenade launchers and anti-tank guns were uncovered. Party attorney Charles Garry held a press conference at which he claimed that the weapons were planted by the police and that the 29th Street house was a dormitory for teachers at the Panther school (which it also, in fact, was, as well as a dormitory for children in the Panther school). Then Garry denounced the police raid as just one more repressive act in the ongoing government conspiracy to discredit the Panthers and destroy militant black leadership.

Of course, all right thinking progressives rallied to the Panthers' support. And right thinking progressives are still rallying. How to explain the spectacle attending the reception of Elaine's book? After all, this is not pre-*glasnost* Russia, where crimes were made to disappear into a politically controlled void. The story of the Panthers' crimes is—thanks to our efforts—now not unknown. But it is either uninteresting or unbelievable to a progressive culture that still regards white racism as the primary cause of all ills in black America, and militant thugs like the Panthers as mere victims of political repression.

The existence of a Murder Incorporated in the heart of the American Left is something the Left really doesn't want to know or think about. Such knowledge would refute its most cherished self-understandings and beliefs. It would undermine the sense of righteous

indignation that is the crucial starting point of a progressive attitude. It would explode the myths on which the attitude depends.

In the last two decades, for example, a vast literature has been
produced on the "repression of the Panthers" by the FBI The
"Cointelpro" program to destabilize militant organizations and
J. Edgar Hoover's infamous memo about the dangers of a "black
messiah" are more familiar to today's college students probably
than the operations of the KGB or the text of Magna Carta. In *A
Taste of Power*, Elaine Brown constantly invokes the FBI specter
(as she did while leader of the Party) to justify Panther outrages
and make them "understandable" as the hyper-reflexes of a necessary paranoia, produced by the pervasive government threat. A
variation of this myth is the basic underpinning of the radical
mind-set. Like Oliver Stone's fantasies of a military-industrial conspiracy behind the murder of J.F.K., it justifies the radical's limitless rage against America itself.

On the other hand, even in left-approved accounts, like
William O'Reilly's *Racial Matters*, the actual "Cointelpro" program, never amounted to much more than a series of inept
attempts to discredit and divide the Panthers by writing forged letters in their leaders' names. (According to O'Reilly's documents,
FBI agents even suspended their campaign when they realized how
murderous the Panthers actually were, and that their own intelligence pranks might cause real deaths.) Familiarity with the Panthers' reality, suggests a far different question from the only one
that progressives have asked—Why so much surveillance of the
Panthers?—namely: Why so *little*? Why had the FBI failed to
apprehend the guilty not only in Betty's murder but in more than a
dozen others? Why were the Panthers able to operate for so long as
a criminal gang with a military arsenal, endangering the citizens of
major American cities? How could they commit so many crimes—
including extortion, arson and murder—without being brought to
the bar of justice?

The best review of Elaine's book and the best epitaph for her
Party are provided ironically by Elaine herself. In the wake of the

brutal and senseless whipping of Bobby Seale by a leader insane with drugs and political adulation, and a coterie too drugged with power themselves to resist, she reflects: "Faith was all there was. If I did not believe in the ultimate rightness of our goals and our party, then what we did, what Huey was doing, what he was, what I was, was horrible.

6

Treason of the Heart

I n 1965, I was twenty-six and living in London when *The Free
World Colossus*, a book I had written holding the United States
responsible for the Cold War, was published. At about that
time I received a phone call from a man with a thick Russian
accent who said he was with the Novosti Press Agency and
wanted to have lunch. I remember clearly that his first name was
Lev because I immediately associated it with Trotsky. Later on,
after the experience was over, I learned that Lev was the third man
in the Soviet embassy, a post usually reserved for officers of the
KGB.

Lev wore the badly-tailored black suits favored by Soviet officials and was a man of medium height with thin white hair and a
pasty Slavic complexion. In the course of our relationship, he
insisted always on calling me from a pay-phone, a precaution I
accepted as natural. This was not because I presumed from the outset that he was a spy, but because it was normal in the left to
assume that phones were tapped and that "sensitive" political matters should be discussed in person. The fact that Lev was a Soviet
official merely made the discretion seem particularly prudent.

Our meetings took place in London's more expensive restau-
rants, like Prunier's, where I first sampled Coquilles St. Jacques
and other elegant cuisines courtesy of the Soviet Union. My reaction to this treatment was a mixture of enjoyment—I could not

---

This is from an article based on my autobiography *Radical Son*, published
in *Heterodoxy*, January 1997.

myself afford such extravagances—and guilt. In my private thoughts I deplored the way the Soviet government was ready to squander wealth that properly belonged to Soviet workers on such luxuries, but it seemed rude to bring up such matters to my host, nor did I want to lose an opportunity to present my views to an influential Soviet official. My host routinely ordered a bottle of wine, which I did not hold well, so that by the middle of the meal I was always a little tipsy,

The topics of our discussions were wide-ranging and I did most of the talking. I took it as my mission to convert Lev to New Left ways of thinking. I advised him that it was important to publish Trotsky's writings in the Soviet Union and tried to persuade him that it was counter-productive to incarcerate dissidents in psychiatric institutions, the current Soviet practice. Repressive methods may have been necessary, I suggested, during the period of "primitive accumulation" when the Soviet Union was catching up with the industrial powers. But now that Russia was a superpower, the controls could be relaxed.

The focus of our discussions often shifted to the subject of Bertrand Russell, for whom I was working at that time, and his secretary, Ralph Schoenman. Lev wanted to know the answer to the question on everyone's mind. How influential was Schoenman in shaping the philosopher's political stands? Russell had made some public statements the Russians didn't like. Did they reflect his views or Ralph's? Later, I discussed these conversations with Ralph and he gave me some background to Lev's curiosity. The Johnson administration had recently begun bombing military targets in North Vietnam. At Ralph's prompting, Russell issued a public appeal to Moscow to supply MiG's to the North Vietnamese so they could shoot down the American planes. The Soviet consul general had summoned Ralph to a meeting. After explaining to him that sending Russian planes would mean war with the United States, the consul warned: "Mr. Schoenman, people who advocate World War III are either crazy or working for the CIA, and they get into trouble."

When Lev was not asking me questions about Russell and Schoenman, I lectured him on how the Soviet future could be reshaped. He didn't try to discourage me from the belief that I was making an impression. At the end of the second or third session he gave me a Parker fountain pen. It was still in the store box and wasn't wrapped like a present. I didn't know how to refuse it without insulting him. The next time we had lunch it was raining and I was wearing my trench coat. As we walked into the street at the end of the meal, he stuffed a thick white envelope into my left pocket.

I knew instinctively what it was, but was so frightened that I didn't dare remove it until I reached home. Without taking off my coat, I went into the bedroom and closed the door, laying the envelope out on the bed. Inside, there were 150 one-dollar bills. I was not so much surprised as dumbfounded. How could these people be so stupid in their own interest and so reckless with mine? *The Free World Colossus* was the first left-wing history of the Cold War that could not be tainted as the work of a Soviet apologist. It had taken me years to develop this perspective, which promised to be far more effective in persuading readers that America was responsible for the Cold War and far more valuable to the Soviets, if they wanted to look at it that way, than any information I might be able to obtain as an intelligence asset. Yet they thought nothing of putting my work in jeopardy by attempting to recruit me as an agent. The thought enraged me.

I returned the envelope at our next meeting and told him never to give me another. He was disappointed but not discouraged, especially since I agreed to go on with our lunches. But a few sessions later it became apparent that my rejection of the money had prompted a more drastic test. When we left the restaurant, he brought up my job as an instructor in a University of Maryland course at the American army base outside of London, and asked me if I would be willing to obtain information about NATO for him. We were standing in the middle of the street, but I screamed at him: "You're crazy. I'm not going to spy for you or anyone else.

Get the f—k away from me and don't ever contact me again." I walked away and never saw him again.

I was not the only radical courted by Lev. I had seen him with a Marxist economics tutor at the London School of Economics. I had discussed him in a veiled manner with the editor of the leftwing magazine *Views*, who had also been having lunches with him. Members of the *New Left Review* crowd knew him, as did activists I recognized from the Labour Party left. How many had failed to reject him as I did? How many had become suppliers of information to the KGB?

After my stint in London, I returned to the United States to join *Ramparts* magazine. Beginning in 1966, a series of sensational *Ramparts* stories drew a national spotlight to the magazine and expanded its circulation to 100,000 readers, making it the largest publication of the left. The stories featured the CIA and its global intrigues. The first had come to *Ramparts* courtesy of an obscure assistant professor of economics at Michigan State, named Stanley Sheinbaum, who had participated in a CIA-funded program to train police in South Vietnam. Sheinbaum's story provided a politically explosive link between the campus and the war. When a student came to *Ramparts* with information that the CIA was funneling secret funds to the National Student Association, a further connection was established. This scoop led to revelations about the Congress for Cultural Freedom and other liberal institutions that had been created to oppose the Communist offensive. In the hands of *Ramparts'* editors, a moral equivalence between Russia's police state and America's democracy was established. In the absence of similar stories about KGB operations among the organizations of the left or of links between the antiwar movement and the Communist forces in Vietnam, the *Ramparts* articles seemed to confirm the New Left view of the world.

One of the writers who worked on these stories was Sol Stern, whom I had met and gotten to know in Berkeley. In 1968 *Ramparts* sent Sol to Bratislava, along with Tom Hayden and an SDS delegation, to meet Madame Binh and other leaders of the

National Liberation Front. For the radicals attending, this was not just a fact-finding mission. The organizers allowed Sol to be present only after *Ramparts* agreed that he would not report on the "sensitive" political discussions taking place. Long afterwards, Sol told me what these were: "The SDS'ers held a seminar with the Communists on how to conduct their psychological warfare campaign against the United States." According to Sol, Hayden was particularly vocal in making suggestions on how to sabotage the American war effort. He also tried to get the group to endorse publicly the Communist line on the war, but Sol and the sociologist Christopher Jencks, who was also present, objected and Hayden's proposal was voted down.

Their dissent had consequences. Following the Bratislava meeting, members of the group were scheduled to go to North Vietnam. Hayden had already been there, publicly proclaiming that he had seen "rice-roots democracy" at work. As a consequence, he enjoyed the confidence of the Communist rulers and had become one of their gatekeepers, screening American radicals for his hosts. To punish Sol and Jencks, Hayden saw to it they were denied permission to go on with the others to Hanoi.

Hundreds, maybe even thousands of similar contacts and arrangements were made with the Communist enemy during the Sixties and after. Yet only a handful of New Leftists have ever written or talked about them. Few had the high-level contacts of Hayden, and only one, Carl Oglesby, was able to tell his story and remain a leftist in good standing. Others, like Phillip Abbott Luce and Larry Grathwohl, made their revelations as "renegades" and were attacked as "government agents," a stigma that warned others not to follow their example. Even after the collapse of Communism made its evils difficult to ignore, the cover-up by veterans of the New Left continued. Memoirs and historical monographs by New Left historians painted a virginal portrait of radical protesters, rewriting the history of the period on a scale that would have seemed impossible outside the Communist bloc. In his own memoir, Hayden includes pages of excerpts from his FBI file, interspersed with disingenuous presentations of his political career that keep his readers in the dark about many of the far-from-innocent activities in which he actualɪy engaged. The effect is to make the FBI's surveillance gratuitous and malign at the same time.

In the summer of 1972 Hayden paid a visit to the *Ramparts* offices. He told us he had been to Paris to meet with the National Liberation Front and representatives from Hanoi. He wanted us to publish an article he intended to write on the military situation. It was to be called "The Prospects of the Vietnamese Offensive" and was a detailed account of the battlefront in Vietnam and the political situation in America. In our office, he dictated all 13,000 words of the article into a tape-recorder in one sitting, while only referring to some notes he had brought with him. It was an impressive demonstration. The article concluded: "Vietnam, country of countless My Lais will be liberated. May we speed the time."

I knew that Hayden's article was Communist war propaganda. Peace negotiations had begun in Paris and the terms of any treaty would be critical to the war aims of both combatants. If the situation could be stabilized to preserve the regime in the South, the United States would prevail in the war. If conditions facilitated a Communist "liberation," the other side would win.

The Nixon administration wanted a truce signed before the November election. It had launched a dramatic gambit to pressure the Communists into a stabilizing peace. After more than two decades of quarantine, Nixon had recognized the Communist regime in China and, accompanied by his advisor Henry Kissinger, had made visits to Moscow and Peking. They hoped to persuade the Communist rulers to pressure Hanoi into a settlement on unfavorable terms. Hanoi responded with its own strategy, which was to launch an offensive in South Vietnam to alter the facts on the ground. The role of Hayden and other New Left radicals was to intensify the divisions in America, behind enemy lines.

I listened to Hayden's request to publish his propaganda piece with an anxious feeling. This was a "gut-check" present whenever Hayden asked for a political favor. One time he had summoned me to his Bateman Street house. When I got there, he asked me if I would hide a Black Panther in the shack behind my house. It occurred to me that the Panther, whose name was "Deacon" and who was later killed in a drug-related incident, might be wanted for an actual crime. But I ignored the thought for the same reason that everyone on the left ignored the crimes that leftists committed—the Panthers were a vanguard of the progressive future and were under attack. Equally important was my desire to impress Hayden with the fact that I was not just an intellectual but ready to put myself on the line when the need was there. Like other radicals I wanted to be regarded as an authentic revolutionary when the occasion presented itself.

The same consideration underlay my readiness to serve Hayden's purposes in placing his revolutionary propaganda before a large audience. Because I had acquired a reputation for being critical of the Communists, I even emphasized the gesture I was making. I told him I admired the way he was willing to offer his pen in the service of the Communists, because it would also serve the Vietnamese people. I did not really believe the Communists had the interests of the Vietnamese people at heart but I believed that the American "imperialists" had to be defeated. At the same time, I stressed to Hayden that my own task was one of remaining independent of any party line. Hayden eyed me with a cynical squint. I felt I had to warn him—since he was working directly with the Communists—that I was going to write an article in the same issue that would be critical of Hanoi's Communist allies in Moscow and Peking. By welcoming Nixon to their capitals, the Russians and Chinese were playing into his hands. Hayden refused to admit that there might be any conflict of interest between the Communist forces. Whether he actually believed this or was just playing the role he had assigned himself as a spokesman for Hanoi, I didn't know and never found out.

My piece, much shorter than Hayden's, was called "Nixon's Vietnam Strategy: How It Was Launched with the Aid of Brezhnev and Mao and How the Vietnamese Intend to Defeat It." The *Los*

Angeles Times ran a long article on its editorial page attacking what I wrote under the heading, "Bloodthirsty New Left Wants The War to Continue." One reader wrote a letter to the editor saying that an NBC reporter, also named David Horowitz, should be fired for expressing such views.

Neither my piece nor Hayden's was the most explosive feature of the August 1972 issue of *Ramparts*, however. That honor belonged to an unsigned article by a man who called himself Winslow Peck. It was titled "U.S. Electronic Espionage: A Memoir" and, as we soon discovered, publishing it would violate a section of the Espionage Act of 1918.

The article had literally come over the transom of our Berkeley office. It was passed on to me as *Ramparts'* expert on national-security subjects. At first I dismissed it as the work of a crank. The author claimed to know about top-secret military intelligence matters and included capitalized words like COMINT, ELINT, RADINT and SWAMP. I had no way of assessing those claims and was inclined to discard the manuscript without further thought. But before doing so I gave it to Bob Fitch, a writer we had hired after another staffer, Jan Austin, had left our staff to become a full-time member of the Red Family.

After reading the article, Fitch came back looking pale and frightened. It turned out that he was an ex-military man and had served as an intelligence operative in the 82nd Airborne Division during the Cuban Missile Crisis. As a result of his training, he recognized secret military codes in the text of the article—codes that he was under oath never to repeat. If we printed them, he said, we would all go to jail. Unfortunately for our country this turned out not to be the case. Once Fitch had authenticated the document, we arranged a meeting with Peck at a local Berkeley IHOP. We learned that Peck had been employed by a top-secret branch of intelligence called the National Security Agency, which encompassed 80 percent of U.S. intelligence but was unknown at the time. How unknown was indicated by an anecdote Peck told us. He was present at a briefing session with Vice President Hubert Humphrey in

1967 when Humphrey "asked a couple of pretty dumb questions that showed he didn't have the foggiest notion of what NSA was and what it did."

Peck's most sensational claim was that the NSA had cracked the Soviet intelligence code. That meant U.S. intelligence could read Soviet electronic communications at will:

As far as the Soviet Union is concerned, we know the whereabouts at any given time of all its aircraft, exclusive of small private planes, and its naval forces, including its missile-firing submarines. We know where their submarines are, what every one of their VIP's is doing and, generally their capabilities and the disposition of all their forces.

Peck himself was stationed at a base in Turkey and had listened to the last conversation between Soviet Premier Kosygin and a Soviet cosmonaut who had burned up in space. He also claimed to have intercepted and read the message to the front from Israeli headquarters in Tel Aviv recalling General Moshe Dayan during the 1967 war.

I was struck by what I thought were the momentous ramifications of Peck's disclosures. If we knew where every Soviet missile and tank was, there could be no surprise attacks or false "missile gaps" based on erroneous estimates, such as had underwritten Kennedy's arms-buildup in the Sixties. To print Peck's article would strike a blow against the war machine. It would promote peace on all sides—or so I deluded myself into thinking. In fact, as I realized after we had published Peck's story and the deed was done, what we had done was to expose the most carefully-guarded intelligence information of all: the knowledge that we had penetrated the Soviet code. Agents were killed to prevent the other side from knowing what their own side knew.

When I realized what we had done, I was beset with uncertainty and self-doubt. There was no one-time breaking of a code. The other side would always respond by creating a new one. By revealing to the Soviets that their security had been breached, we had merely alerted them that they needed to replace their code. Even if I had understood this, I might still have agreed to print his story anyway. My responsibility as a "revolutionary" was to hurt the United States. The overriding justification was one that weighed heavily on all the political decisions I made as a member of my radical generation. It was important that America should lose the Vietnam war. I did not believe that an NLF victory would mean "rice-roots" democracy, as Hayden had written. But I was convinced that America's loss would be Vietnam's gain. An American defeat would weaken oppression everywhere. Or so I believed.

When we told Fitch that we were going to run Peck's article, he panicked. We would all be tried for treason and go to jail, he whined. We brushed his fears aside, practically laughing in his face. Where was his revolutionary spine? Where was his commitment to the cause? When we refused to reconsider our decision, Fitch announced he was quitting the magazine. He was not about to go down in flames with us. We enjoyed seeing this rhetorical maximalist exposed as a coward, but his departure caused an internal lurch nonetheless. What if he was right? We had families. Were we ready to jeopardize their futures even for a grand gesture like this? We began to sense that we might be out of our depths.

Taking a step back, we decided to defer a final decision to publish the article until we could consult a lawyer. I thought of contacting the defense team for Daniel Ellsberg, the former Pentagon official who was then on trial in Los Angeles for leaking a classified report on American policy in Vietnam. We had just completed a *Ramparts* cover-feature on his case. I put in a call to Harvard law professor Charles Nesson, a member of the Ellsberg team. After I had outlined the situation, Nesson explained the law. Technically, he said, we would be violating the Espionage Act. But the act had been written in a peculiar way to apply to classified papers removed from government offices or material copied from government files. The government was able to indict Ellsberg because he had xeroxed actual papers. Therefore, Nesson explained, it was important for us not to acknowledge that any papers existed. If we took his advice, Nesson said, we might get away with publishing the article because to make its case in a court of law, the government would have to establish that we had indeed damaged national security. To do so it would be necessary to reveal more than the government might want the other side to know. In fact, the legal process would certainly force more information to light than the government would want anybody to have. On balance, there was a good chance that we would not be prosecuted.

I had just been given advice by a famous constitutional law professor on how to commit treason and get away with it.

We published the article and it became a journalistic coup, getting front-page coverage by *The New York Times*. But the *Times* story was disappointing because it did not even mention my notion that the NSA's technology made surprise attacks impossible. Instead, it focused on the more pertinent question of whether Peck's claim—that American agents had broken the Soviet code—was accurate. The *Times* story quoted experts to the effect that it was not. The *Times* account also revealed that the name of the man we knew as Winslow Peck was actually Perry Fellwock, a fact that could only have been learned from intelligence sources. After the *Times* story appeared, we held a press conference in the *Ramparts* offices which was attended by an impressive media cohort. We decided that one particular reporter was the CIA "plant" because he kept asking us whether we had any written documents. We held to the strategy that Nesson had devised and said there were none.

Thinking about these events, I have asked myself in retrospect whether there was any practical difference between my actions and those of radicals like Tom Hayden, who self-consciously served the Communist rulers in Vietnam. When Hayden and Jane Fonda went to North Vietnam and urged American troops to defect, it made me as uncomfortable as had Ralph Schoenman's broadcasts over Radio Hanoi during my days with Bertrand Russell. Remembering my parents' experience as members of the American Communist Party, when they were forced to become apologists for murder, I had long ago resolved that I would never commit myself to any regime or party that did not reflect my own political values. Yet war does not leave room for fine discriminations or intermediate stands. Looking back at what I actually did, my "critical independence" seems to me now a distinction without much of a practical difference. The same can be said for all those antiwar demonstrators who might have been critical of Communism but were willing to march behind slogans that called for the withdrawal of American troops, a policy that could only result in a Communist victory. They did not see Communism as a superior way of life the way Hayden did. But in regarding it as the lesser of two evils, they helped the enemy to win all the same.

As soon as the Communists did win, in April 1975, there were reports of a bloodbath in Indochina. The Khmer Rouge had swept across Cambodia leaving killing-fields in their wake. In Vietnam there were reports of a hundred thousand summary executions, a million and a half refugees and more than a million people imprisoned in "reeducation camps" and gulags in the South. These events produced a shock of recognition in some quarters of the left. Joan Baez took out a full-page ad in *The New York Times* to make an "Appeal to the Conscience of North Vietnam." She enlisted a number of former antiwar activists to sign the appeal. As soon as the statement appeared Baez was attacked by Tom Hayden and Jane Fonda as a tool of the CIA.[1] A counter-ad was organized by Cora Weiss, who had traveled with Fonda to Hanoi and collaborated with the regime in its torture of American POW's. The Weiss ad praised the Communists for their moderation in administering the peace.

---

[1] In politics, Baez never did anything else as worthy and remained a leftist. Years later, on one of the anniversaries of the fall of Saigon, I appeared with her on a television show discussing the events. She dismissed my views with hostility, saying, "I don't trust people with second thoughts." My response—which I did not get a chance to express on camera—was: "I don't trust people without them."

In 1973 Nixon and Kissinger had negotiated a peace treaty that was designed to keep the South Vietnamese regime in place and remove America's military presence. I knew that the outcome was not going to be the "liberation" we had promised. But with American forces out of the picture, I saw no compelling reason to remain politically in the fray. Hayden and others like him did. After the anti-draft movement had disintegrated in 1970, Hayden and Fonda organized an "Indochina Peace Campaign" to cut off remaining American support for the regimes in Cambodia and South Vietnam. For the next few years, the campaign worked tirelessly to ensure the victory of the North Vietnamese Communists and the Khmer Rouge. Accompanied by a camera team, Hayden and Fonda traveled to Hanoi and then to the NLF-controlled zones in South Vietnam to make a propaganda film. It was called *Introduction to the Enemy* and attempted to persuade viewers that the Communists were going to create a new "liberated" society in the South, where equality and social justice awaited its inhabitants if only America would cut off support for the Saigon regime.

Assisted by radical congressmen like Ron Dellums and Bella Abzug, Hayden set up a caucus in the Capitol building where he lectured congressional staffers on the need to end American aid. He directed his attention to Cambodia as well, lobbying for an accommodation with the Khmer Rouge guerrillas. When Nixon resigned over Watergate, it provided all the leverage Hayden and his activists needed. The Democrats won the midterm elections, bringing to Washington a new group of legislators who were determined to undermine the settlement that Nixon and Kissinger had achieved. The aid was cut, the Saigon regime fell, and the Khmer Rouge marched into the Cambodian capital. In the two years that followed, the victorious Communists killed more Indochinese than had been killed on both sides in all 13 years of the anti-Communist war.

It was the bloodbath that our opponents, the anti-Communist defenders of America's role in Southeast Asia, had predicted. But for the left there would be no looking back. Baez's appeal proved to be the farthest it was possible for them to go, which was not very far. The appeal did not begin to suggest that antiwar activists needed to reassess the role they had played in making these tragedies inevitable. Ironically, it was Hayden who eventually came closest to such self-recognition: "What continues to batter my sense of morality and judgment," he wrote in *Reunion*, "is that I could not even imagine that the worst stereotype of revolutionary madness was becoming a reality. Pol Pot and the Khmer Rouge became the Stalins and Hitlers of my lifetime, killing hundreds of thousands of people for being 'educated' or 'urban,' for attracting the paranoid attention of a secret police who saw conspiracies behind every failure of the grand plan to be achieved. Most Western estimates settle on 1.5 million killed." But having acknowledged those facts and his confusion over them, he could go no farther, and had no genuine second thoughts. The terrible result, which he had worked so hard to make possible, failed to prompt a reassessment of the people who had predicted the bloodbath if the Communists were to win and whose anti-Communist policies he had opposed: "None of this persuades me that Nixon and Kissinger were right."

Nixon and Kissinger were right, but the Democratic Party had been persuaded by its left wing to abandon the Vietnamese to their fate. This prompted other second thoughts about the way the left regarded America itself. As a student at Columbia, I had read Euripides' tragedy *The Trojan Women*, which was inspired by his countrymen's conquest of the small island of Melos. Euripides had intended for his play to arouse the moral sense of his fellow-Athenians about the war they had conducted and the suffering they had inflicted. When the Athenians saw Euripides's play, they wept for the people of Melos. In the eyes of my professor, Moses Hadas, this show of conscience was a tribute to Athenian civilization. How much greater, I thought, was the civilized response of America's democracy to the tragedy in Vietnam. I could not think of another historical instance where a nation had retreated from a field of battle it had dominated, because the conscience of its people had been touched. And yet, America had withdrawn for precisely that reason. The left believed that American policy was controlled by giant corporations, and that the war was being prosecuted for their imperial interests, which they would not relinquish. But the left had been proven wrong about this too. American democracy was not the "sham" we had said it was. When the American people turned against the war, there was no greater power to make it continue.

7

A Political Romance

hen I was a college literature student in the 1950s, my Shakespeare professor drew our attention to the way the poet turned to romance as he grew older, writing symbolic pastorals devoted to themes of redemption. According to my professor, this was a natural human progression, and he cited examples from other writers to prove his point. Youth is characterized by a hunger for information, he told us; age distills what it knows in parables, and returns to archetypal myths.

When Shakespeare wrote *The Tempest*, the most famous of his late romances and the very last of his plays, he was actually only forty-seven, more than a decade younger than I am now. Moreover, I have found my own experience to be exactly the opposite of what he predicted. Growing up in a progressive household, I found myself enveloped in the vapors of a romantic myth not unlike that of Shakespeare's pastorals or the fairy tales that had been read to me as a child. In the radical romance of our political lives, the world was said to have begun in innocence but to have fallen afterwards under an evil spell, afflicting the lives of all with great suffering and injustice. According to our myth, however, a happy ending beckoned. Through the efforts of progressives like us, the spell would one day be lifted and mankind freed from its trials. In this liberated future, social justice would be established, peace would reign and harmony prevail. Men and women would be utterly transformed.

This was printed as the epilogue to my 1999 book, *Hating Whitey and Other Progressive Causes.*

Being at the center of a heroic myth inspired passions that informed my youthful passage and guided me to the middle of my adult life. But then I was confronted by a reality so inescapable and harsh that it shattered the romance for good. A friend was brutally murdered by my political comrades, members of the very vanguard that had been appointed to redeem us all. Worse, since individuals may err, the deed was covered up by the vanguard itself, which hoped in so doing to preserve the faith.

If this personal tragedy had remained isolated perhaps the romance itself could have survived. But the murder of my friend was reflected and amplified in numerous others, most notably the slaughter of millions of poor peasants in Southeast Asia by the liberation fronts, the angels of progress whom my comrades and I had aided and defended. There was no happy ending. The injustice of the new orders was even greater than what had existed before. In retrospect it was apparent to me that most of the violence in my lifetime had been directed by utopians like myself against those who would not go along with their impossible dreams. "Idealism kills," the philosopher Nietzsche had warned before all this bloodshed began. But nobody listened.

As a result of my experience, I developed, in age, an aversion to romantic myths. What I experienced instead was a hunger for information—for the facts that would reveal to me the truth about the years I was a member of a heroic vanguard. The fall of the Communist empire and the opening of its secrets fed this passion. Preserved in the decoded Venona communications between Soviet agents in America and their contacts in the Kremlin is the record of the truths we had denied, and whose denial made our romance possible. The truths revealed that we were just what our enemies had always said we were. There were spies among us, and we were agents for a tainted cause. All of us had treason in our hearts in the name of a future that would never come.

In the battle of good and evil that formed the core of our romantic myth, we had enlisted—Old and New Left alike—on the wrong side of the historical conflict. We had set out as the proud harbingers of a progressive future. But what we had actually created were realities far worse than those we were seeking to escape. The enemies we scorned—patriots defending America—turned out to be the protectors of what was decent and pragmatically good, who had saved us from being consumed by our crimes.

It became clear to me that the world was not going to be changed into anything very different or better from what it had been. On this earth there would be no kingdom of freedom where swords would be turned into plowshares and lions would lie down with lambs. It should have been obvious when I began. Many things change, but people do not. Otherwise how could Shakespeare, or writers more ancient, capture in their creations a reality that we recognize, and that still moves us today?

These revelations of experience had a humbling effect. They took my attention away from the noble fantasies that had enveloped me and forced me to focus on my ordinary existence; to see how common it was; how un-heroic, ordinary and unredeemed. The revelations that shattered my faith allowed me, for the first time, to look at my mortality, at the fact that I was not going to be born again in a brave New World. That I was going to die like everyone else, and be forgotten.

And that is when I realized what our romance was about. It was not about a future that was socially just, or about a world redeemed. It was about averting our eyes from this ordinary fact. Our romance was a shield protecting us from the terror of our common human fate. And that was why we clung to our dream so fiercely, despite all the evidence that it had failed. That was why we continued to believe, despite everything we knew. For who would want to confront the terror of ordinary existence without some sustaining faith, unless forced to do so by circumstances beyond their control? Who would want to hear the voice of a future that was only calling them to oblivion?

And that is when I also realized that our progressive romance would go on. Some, like myself, might wake from its vapors under blows that caused great personal pain. But there would always be others, and in far greater number, who would not. A century of broken dreams and the slaughters they spawned would, in the end, teach nothing to those who had no reason to hear. Least of all would it cure them of their hunger for a romance that is really a desire not to know who we are.

8

Reflections on the Road Taken and Not

The other day I received an email from a stranger posing two questions that have been on my mind for some time, which made his message seemed uncannily personal. "I was curious," the writer said, "if you have ever looked at your political 'apostasy' and wondered whether, if circumstances had been different—if you had not been involved with the Panthers or if your friend had not been murdered by them—you would still be a Marxist today. Was your apostasy a result of an inexorable intellectual development, or were you forced into your second thoughts?"

In one form or another, that is a question just about everyone gets around to asking. If circumstances had been different, would my life have turned out differently? It is a question as old as philosophy—the puzzle of determinism and free will. Not everyone, of course, experiences such a dramatic turning-point in life as I did 25 years ago when the Black Panthers murdered Betty Van Patter. But we all can identify choices or decisions that changed our lives, moments when we suddenly set out on a new course. Each time those kinds of changes occur, they raise the question: Are they essential to our being, or only secondary to who and what we are?

In my case, I simply don't know whether the intensity of my ideological transformation would have been the same had it not

This article was published on October 25, 1999, http://archive. frontpagemag.com/Printable.aspx?ArtId=24339; http://www.salon.com/1999/10/25/reflections/

been provoked by an act of criminal brutality committed by my political allies and friends. But I am confident that the change would have come in any case. I have many friends and acquaintances who had similar "second thoughts" in which they found themselves rejecting the ideas and understandings that had motivated them when they were young; and I have no reason to suppose it would have been different for me. In fact, one of the first pieces I wrote about the incident that changed my political life was an article called "Why I Am No Longer a Leftist," which appeared in 1986 in *The Village Voice*. It drew explicit parallels between the crime the Panthers had committed and the much larger, more famous crimes that the broader left had committed— crimes that had caused people like me to reconsider our beliefs.

As a leftist I had developed habits of mind that caused me to look at "classes" rather than individuals, at social structures and general paradigms rather than at particular events or individual personalities that could be dismissed as incidental or unique. This way of looking at things led me to analyze events with an eye as to whether they were broadly characteristic or merely contingent, and to do so before I would consider allowing the lessons I drew from them to affect my outlook as a whole. I made such an analysis in the article I wrote for *The Village Voice*, as in my memoir, *Radical Son*.

The impact of these events in my case was dramatic. Nobody who knew me then and knows me now has failed to notice the differences in my life and attitudes. The trauma of this murder and the betrayal it represented had a profound effect on me, and made me a different person than I otherwise might have been. It was the pain that caused me to change. Every day, after Betty's murder, the pain spoke to me: "You cannot stay in this place. If you don't move, you will die." It is fear that normally keeps us in our personal grooves. But now I was caught between the fear of moving and the greater one of not moving. It was pain that inspired me to overcome inertia in order to escape what I felt was a spiritual death.

A second question raised in that email was unexpected, and even more perplexing than the first. "Do you ever feel that you are wasting your breath? Do you think that truth will ever matter? No matter what you prove or disprove, in the end the truth will remain in the shadows of what people want to hear and want to believe."

I agree with the observation more than I would like to. It is the human wish to be told lies that keeps us as primitive morally and socially as we are. But stoic realism is, after all, what being a conservative is about. It is about accepting the absolute limits that life places on human hope. One could define the viewpoint of the left as just the opposite. It is an obstinate, compulsive, destructive belief in the fantasy of change, in the hope of a human redemption.

I have watched my friends on the left, whose ideas created an empire of inhumanity, survive the catastrophe of their schemes and go on to unexpected triumphs by turning their backs on the ashes of their ideological defeats. Forced to witness the collapse of everything they had once dreamed of and worked to achieve, they have emerged unchastened and unchanged in pursuit of the same destructive illusions. And they have been rewarded for their misdeeds with a cultural cachet and unprecedented influence in the country most responsible for the worldwide defeat of their misguided schemes.

I cannot explain this dystopian paradox except by agreeing with my interlocutor that politics is indeed irrational; and that socialism is a wish that runs as deep as any religious faith. I do not know that the truth must necessarily remain in the shadows, as he writes. But I am persuaded that a lie grounded in human desire is too powerful for mere reason to kill.

9

Letter to the Past

Twenty-five years ago, on this date exactly, my friend Betty Van Patter disappeared from the Berkeley Square, a local tavern on University Avenue, and was never seen alive again. Six months earlier I had recruited Betty to keep the books of the Educational Opportunities Corporation, an entity I had created to run a school for the children of the Black Panther Party. By the time the police fished her battered body out of San Francisco Bay, I knew that she had been killed by the Panthers themselves.

At the time, the Panthers were still being defended by writers like Murray Kempton and Garry Wills in the pages of *The New York Times,* and by the governor of California, Jerry Brown. Indeed, the governor was a confidant of Elaine Brown, who had hired Betty and whom Huey Newton had appointed to stand in for him as the Panthers' leader when he fled to Cuba. At the time of Betty's death, Elaine was riding a wave of public approval. She was running for the Oakland City Council and had just secured a $250,000 grant from the Nixon Administration under a federal juvenile delinquency program. J. Anthony Kline, the *consigliere* to whom she had turned when the Party's enforcers got in trouble with the law, was about to be appointed to Governor Brown's cabinet (and is today a justice on the First Circuit Court of Appeals in San Francisco).

This article was published on Tuesday, December 14, 1999, http://archive.frontpagemag.com/Printable.aspx?ArtId=24348

In pursuit of answers to the mystery of Betty's death, I subsequently discovered that the Panthers had killed more than a dozen people in the course of conducting extortion, prostitution and drug rackets in the Oakland ghetto. While these criminal activities were taking place, they enjoyed the support of the American left, the Democratic Party, the Bay Area Trades Union Council, and even the Oakland business establishment. The head of the Clorox Corporation, Oakland's largest company, sat on the board of the Educational Opportunities Corporation I had created and whose books Betty had kept.

On a far smaller scale the Panther killings were an American version of the "Katyn massacre," the infamous murder of Polish officers carried out on Stalin's orders that the left had denied and concealed for decades, until the opening of the Soviet archives settled the dispute for good. The totalitarian nature of the Soviet state made it relatively simple to understand how the information that would settle the case could be kept hidden for years. It was much harder for me to understand why in democratic America the Panthers should be able to get away with these murders, and why the nation's press should turn such a blind eye to a group that law enforcement had made an object of its attentions.

Whatever the reasons, the fact remains that to this day not a single organization of the mainstream press has ever investigated the Panther murders, even though the story is one that touches the lives and political careers of the entire liberal establishment, including the First Lady and the Assistant Attorney General in charge of civil rights for the Clinton Administration. Both Hillary Clinton and Bill Lann Lee began their political careers as law students at Yale by organizing demonstrations in 1970 to shut down the University and stop the trial of Panther leaders who had tortured and then executed a black youth named Alex Rackley. This silence is even more puzzling since, despite a blackout by national media, the details of the story have managed to trickle out over the years. This has been the result of efforts by myself and my colleague Peter Collier, by radical journalists Kate Coleman and

Hugh Pearson and one or two others, including most particularly David Talbot and David Weir, the editor and managing editor of *Salon* magazine.

Because of our efforts, informed citizens are at least aware of these murders. On the other hand, unlike in the Soviet Union, where testimonies emerged as soon as the regime was toppled and the threat of retaliation gone, few additional witnesses have come forward to add to our knowledge about these American crimes. There are hundreds if not thousands of veterans of the Sixties who have some knowledge of the deeds but who have remained silent and complicit for 25 years. These include notable figures like Tom Hayden and journalists like the *Los Angeles Times* columnist Robert Scheer—both of whom promoted the Panthers as revolutionary heroes at the time, and who have failed to correct that impression ever since. But it also includes many lesser figures who worked day in and day out to facilitate the Panthers' rise to power and to cover up their crimes along the way. Evidently they have remained convinced that even though the crimes were committed, they somehow weren't. Or perhaps that if they were indeed committed, the crimes were and are no responsibility of theirs.

I am constantly asked by people who have read my autobiography *Radical Son*, or who have heard me talk about these events, how it is that my former comrades on the left can remain so stubbornly devoted to experiments that have failed, to doctrines that are false, to causes that are demonstrably wrong-headed and evil. Recently—on November 20, to be precise—an answer to these questions came from out of the blue, in a letter written by an old friend—Art Goldberg, a radical journalist who was deeply involved in the activities of the Panthers and their deceptions, and who remains a faithful keeper of the progressive flame today.

I had not heard from Art in fifteen years. We had grown up on the same block in Sunnyside, Long Island, a neighborhood of Queens that had been colonized by the Communist Party to which both our parents belonged. Because Art was a few years older than I, we weren't that close as children but became friends after college, when we found ourselves together in Berkeley as members of the nascent New Left. Art became a writer for the *Berkeley Barb* and other Movement papers and made himself particularly serviceable to the Black Panther Party. Toward the end of the Sixties Peter Collier and I were editing *Ramparts,* the most successful and well-heeled journalistic institution of the left. Because Art was an old friend of mine, we took him under our wing and gave him writing jobs that supplemented his income, while Peter devoted considerable time and effort to rewriting Art's pieces to meet the literary standards of a national magazine, which were somewhat more demanding than those of an underground paper like the *Berkeley Barb.*

So valuable was Art's propaganda to the Panthers that eventually Huey Newton assigned him to write the official biography of Charles Garry, the lawyer who defended Newton against charges that he had murdered a young policeman named John Frey. Newton had committed the murder, but in Art's account, as in all the writings of New Leftists at the time, Huey was presented as the innocent victim of a racist conspiracy by the state.

Art and another friend named Marty Kenner were the New Leftists closest to the Panthers of anyone I knew. Marty, a stockbroker who had organized the famous Leonard Bernstein party that Tom Wolfe satirized in *Radical Chic,* was working virtually full-time as Huey Newton's personal emissary and financial guru. In the Sixties I had kept my distance from the Party because I was frightened by their gun-toting style and hectoring posture. As the Seventies began, however, Newton announced that it was "time to put away the gun," and I became involved with the school-project I have already mentioned. At first I had intended just to raise the money for the school, but when Marty Kenner withdrew unexpectedly, telling me he was "burned out," I was left with the task of organizing the school myself. It was as a result of this responsibility that I recruited Betty Van Patter to keep its books.

I had not seen or heard from Art Goldberg or Marty Kenner for 15 years when I received Art's letter. On reflection it seems obvious what provoked the communication. I had just published a book called *Hating Whitey and Other Progressive Causes,* one of whose chapters was a memoir of Betty's death, called "Black Murder, Inc."[1] Obviously this chapter was what prompted him to contact me. In addition to Art's denial in the letter that he was political anymore, what I found most interesting was the fact that though I had written hundreds of pages on the details of Betty's murder, my sense of responsibility and guilt over what happened, and the devastating impact on myself and my family, Art seemed unaware of any of it.

> November 19, 1999
> Dear David,
> Every so often I hear about something you've written that pisses somebody off, but I don't much care because I have pretty much retired from politics. One thing I have been meaning to tell you for years, however, concerns the death of Betty Van Patter, the *Ramparts* bookkeeper. *In my mind, you are the person responsible for her death.* [Emphasis in original] Sending her in to audit the Panther's books at that particular time was tantamount to dressing her in a Ku Klux Klan white sheet and sending her up to 125th Street in Harlem or to West Oakland.
>
> I distinctly remember warning you to be careful about getting too involved with the Panthers because things were getting pretty crazy at the time you jumped in. I had pulled back, Marty Kenner had pulled back and so had Stew Albert. Had you asked Stew or myself, we would have urged you not to send Betty into the school under the circumstances in which you did.... The fact that you let Betty deal with them directly was incredibly naïve on your part, and shows you had no idea of what was going on with the Panthers at that time. If you had asked Stew, myself or Marty, we could have told you.... Kenner, after all, knew a lot about the Panther finances, as he was a major fundraiser. Nothing happened to him....

---

[1] See chapter 5, above.

The problem was that you were inexperienced and naïve and Betty Van Patter got killed because of it. That's why, whenever anyone brings up Betty's death, after you've written about it or alluded to it, I always say, "It was really Horowitz's fault. He set her up." As I said, it was like putting her in a white sheet and sending her up to Harlem.

Just wanted to let you know what I've been thinking.

Peace,

Art

Here is the answer I sent back:

December 12, 1999

Dear Art,

Unlike you I don't pretend to have "retired from politics," and unlike you I try not to lie to myself. Having become a conservative, I am prepared for how pathetic, vicious and disloyal some human beings can be, and how sublimely unaware of the disgusting image they present to others even as they preen their moral selves for their own approval. As a result, your letter does not really surprise me.

The fact that you should have spent ten seconds carrying around your insipid thoughts about Betty's death is laughable. Nonetheless, I thank you for revealing how ignorant you are about yourself and your friends, and how you are still wallowing in the evil that once engulfed us all.

Marty Kenner, my possible savior. If only I had thought of that! It was Marty, of course, who left the Panther school project in my hands—and without bothering to say why. The same Marty was so far from thinking the thugs he was among were bad guys that ten years later he attended the great Huey P. Newton's funeral as a fan, and then played the role of behind-the-scenes sponsor of Panther Field Marshal David Hilliard's self-glorifying book just before he became president of the Dr. Huey P. Newton Foundation, and resident tour guide of historic Panther sites. Stupid me! Why didn't I think of asking Marty for help?

"Nothing happened" to Marty, as you put it—nobody raped and tortured him and then bashed his head in (as I would phrase the same)—because his nose was so far up Huey's behind right to the end that he couldn't get his tongue loose to annoy them, even if it had occurred to him to do so.

Give this, at least, to Betty. She wasn't killed because she was white or stupid. She was killed because she had the integrity and the grit to talk back. She wasn't spineless, the way you and your friends are. She was killed because she wasn't a feckless servant of rapists and murderers like you and Marty were then and apparently still are now.

And Stew Albert!!! How could I have overlooked good old Stew when I was in need of advice? Stew Albert, the yippee genius who wrote a letter to *Ramparts* calling me a police agent because in an editorial I had condemned the Symbionese Liberation Army's assassination of a black father of three children, whose only crime was to have been a superintendent of schools.[2] According to Stew, my editorial gave a "green light" to law enforcement to carry out the richly deserved execution of Stew's beloved SLA fruitcakes! With stand up talent like this, Art, you should really go on Leno.

I see you are still crusading for social justice—going around telling anyone who has read my latest feeble attempt to right this historical record and show the world what we did, that "It was really Horowitz's fault. He set her up." Don't worry, my friend. I'm not going to return the favor and say you did it and I didn't. Of course, you did write all those rave notices and cover-ups, encouraging others to help feed the Panthers' criminal appetites (or has age affected your memory of this?). But I'm still not going to tell people it was your fault that I got involved with the Panthers or recruited Betty, or even that you kept your mouth shut all the time I was down in Oakland putting my life and hers in danger.

Of course, you've already prepared your alibi. You told me "things were getting pretty crazy at the time." What was I

---

[2]Marcus Foster. I have written about the SLA killings in "Pardoned Bombers," which is a chapter in my 2012 book, *Radicals: Portraits of a Destructive Passion*. Also see "Mercy for a Terrorist?" in *Progressives*, the second volume of this series.

supposed to make of that? "Crazy" could mean that the police were after them, that some of them were agents or that these pressures were creating internal conflicts I had to look out for. DID YOU TELL ME THAT HUEY NEWTON WAS A F—ING MURDERER AND MIGHT KILL ME?!!! Of course you didn't. In fact, everything you had written or said to me about Huey Newton told me exactly the opposite. And that is all that you've ever written to anyone or said to me about Huey and his progressive gang to this day.

But I still won't point my finger at you now, or blame you for what I did then. I won't do that because that's how I fell into this mess in the first place. By blaming others for what I did or did not do, blaming them for my own malaise. And that's what your self-serving politics is finally about, Art—yours and Marty's and Stew's. It's about putting responsibility where it doesn't belong. It's about blaming everyone but yourselves. It's about getting others to blame anybody besides themselves for who and what they are.

I'm glad you wrote this letter. It makes all the pain, and all the wounds inflicted on me by you and your comrades since then, seem worth it. Because it shows me what wretched human beings I was involved with when I was one of you, a member of the progressive vanguard and at war with the "enemies of the people."

Your letter shows me that in all these years you haven't changed a bit. But I have, and it's the only thing in this that I'm not sorry about.

The "Peace" benediction at the end of your letter was a really nice touch.

David

Think Twice Before You Bring the War Home

I am a former antiwar activist who helped organize the first campus demonstration against the war in Vietnam at the University of California, Berkeley in 1962. I appeal to all those young people, who participated in "antiwar" demonstrations on 150 college campuses this week, to think again and not join an antiwar effort against America's coming battle with international terrorism.

The hindsight of history has shown that our efforts in the 1960s to end the war in Vietnam had two practical effects. The first was to prolong the war itself. Every testimony by North Vietnamese generals in the postwar years has affirmed that they knew they could not defeat the United States on the battlefield, and that they counted on the division of our people at home to win the war for them. The Vietcong forces we were fighting in South Vietnam were destroyed in 1968. In other words, most of the war and most of the casualties in the war occurred because the dictatorship of North Vietnam counted on the hope that Americans would give up the battle rather than pay the price necessary to win it. This is what happened. The blood of hundreds of thousands of Vietnamese, and tens of thousands of Americans, is on the hands of the antiwar activists who prolonged the struggle and gave victory to the Communists.

This article was published on Thursday, September 27, 2001, http://archive.frontpagemag.com/Printable.aspx?ArtId=24224

The second effect of the war was to surrender South Vietnam to the forces of Communism. This resulted in the imposition of a monstrous police-state, the murder of hundreds of thousands of innocent South Vietnamese, the incarceration in "reeducation camps" of hundreds of thousands more, and a quarter-century of abject poverty imposed by crackpot Marxist economic plans, which continue to this day. This too is the responsibility of the so-called antiwar movement of the 1960s.

I say "so-called" because while many Americans were sincerely troubled by America's war effort, the organizers of this movement were Marxists and radicals who supported a Communist victory and an American defeat. Today the same people and their youthful followers are organizing the campus demonstrations to protest America's effort to defend its citizens against the forces of international terrorism and anti-American hatred which are responsible for the September attacks.

I know, better than most, the importance of protecting freedom of speech and the right of citizens to dissent. I also know, better than most, that there is a difference between honest dissent and malevolent hate, between criticism of national policy and sabotage of the nation's defenses. In the 1960s and 1970s, the tolerance of anti-American hatred was so high that the line between dissent and treason was eventually erased. Along with thousands of other New Leftists, I was one who crossed the line between dissent and treason. (I have written an account of these matters in my autobiography, *Radical Son*). I did so for what I thought were the noblest of reasons: to advance the cause of social justice and peace. I have lived to see how wrong I was and how much damage we did, especially to those whose cause we claimed to embrace, the peasants of Indochina who suffered grievously from our support of the Communist enemy. I came to see how precious are the freedoms and opportunities afforded by America to the poorest and most humble of its citizens, and how rare its virtues are in the world at large.

If I have one regret from my radical years, it is that this country was too tolerant toward the treason of its enemies within. If patriotic Americans had been more vigilant in the defense of their country, if they had called things by their right names, if they had confronted us with the seriousness of our attacks, they might have caught the attention of those of us who were well-meaning but utterly misguided. And they might have stopped us in our tracks.

This appeal is for those of you who are out there today attacking your country, full of your own self-righteousness, but who one day might also live to regret what you have done.

11

The End of Time

I have just published a new book, *The End of Time,* which is different from my other books. In the first place its subject is different, although I have written a memoir, *Radical Son,* and this is something of a memoir as well. In the second place its authorial voice is different. I have been engaged in the political wars for so long that people perceive me as someone perpetually in combat. Like most perceptions this is only partially correct. I actually have a soft side, and a reflective one. This is a book of lessons about life from one man's perspective.

Life. I didn't see it coming. That is a theme of this book. In fact none of us sees it coming when we start on our journeys. That is one of the paradoxes of our existence. We are all so different and unique. And yet in several crucial ways we are the same. And this is one of them: None of us sees life coming. Or as the Christian testament puts it: We see now through a glass darkly, not face to face.

My book is a kind of letter to the young, about what I have seen, about what to expect. And it is a consolation for the old, in the sense that it is about what all of us go through.

More than three hundred years ago a great scientist, a Catholic philosopher and poet of the soul named Blaise Pascal outlined our predicament. When he died at the youthful age of thirty-nine, Pascal left a collection of notes that he had stitched together with

This is a text of a talk I gave on the publication of *The End of Time,* a memoir and reflection. http://archive.frontpagemag.com/Printable.aspx?ArtId=8545

needle and thread and which were published after his death. Known as the *Pensées,* they have become a classic of Western thought. This is the fragment numbered 205:

> "When I consider the short duration of my life, swallowed up in the eternity before and after, ... engulfed in the infinite immensity of spaces of which I am ignorant and which know me not, I am frightened and astonished at being here rather than there. For there is no reason why here rather than there, why now rather than then. Who has put me here?"

For mortals like us there is no answer. In the words of St. John: "Believers and non-believers stand in the same darkness. Neither sees God."

Pascal was one of the greatest scientific minds that ever lived. He looked into the eye of the universe and could not find an answer. Without a Creator to make sense of it, he wrote, a human life is "intolerable."

What then are we to do? Pascal's answer to this question was his famous "Wager." Pascal was a physical scientist and also a mathematician who pioneered in the field of probability theory, devising formulas to calculate the odds of winning at games of chance.

Look on life, he said, as a game of chance. If you wager that there is a God who will make sense of all this, who will give meaning to our lives, who will provide us with a home in this infinite expanse of unexplored space, then there are two possibilities: If there is God, you win. If there is no God then you have lost nothing by wagering that He exists. Therefore wager that there is a God, and that life has meaning.

I am an agnostic. I do not know if there is a God or not. But I have lived my life as if what I do has meaning, and therefore I have, in a way, taken Pascal's advice.

As an agnostic I have also seen that there are ways of believing and of demanding meanings from life that are destructive and that are the source of great human suffering and grief.

Part of my book is about death and how death affects the lives we live. We live a great deal of our lives in denial of our end, as though we will go on forever. At least young people do. When you get to my age, you can see the horizon coming. Or rather, you can't avoid seeing the horizon coming.

This denial, and its impact on the purposes to which we devote ourselves, informs the title of my book, *The End of Time*. This title has two meanings. First, our time has an end; and second, knowledge of this fact should shape our ends.

In my book I refer to a story by Saul Bellow that provides an image for this denial. "When there is too much going on," Bellow writes, "more than you can bear, you may choose to assume that nothing in particular is happening, that your life is going round and round like a turntable."

Bellow doesn't say whether this is a turntable like the ones you find in playgrounds, or a turntable like those on which we used to play our music on vinyl records. Which are gone now like so much else.

Perhaps the denial Bellow is referring to is larger than the moment itself. Perhaps he is hinting that the music of your days can lull you into an illusion that the present will go on and on, and will never go anywhere else. Or perhaps, more simply, that your life is in motion when you think you are just standing still.

That is, until something happens. Until you get clobbered by events and wake up to the fact that the stillness is an illusion. That everything is changing about you, and that one day it will come to an end.

Bellow's own clobbering was the death of his mother from cancer when he was 17.

On the day this story takes place the young Bellow, who works for a local florist, is sent to deliver flowers to the funeral of a 15-year-old girl. Disoriented by the experience he goes to his uncle's office for comfort. But his uncle isn't in, and while the young man is in the building he encounters a sexual mystery-woman. The woman lures him to an apartment where she induces him to undress and then steals his money and clothes.

The humiliated youngster is forced to return home in a dress he has found in her closet. As he approaches his house, he fears his father's wrath. But then he remembers what's on his turntable. His mother is dying.

Ironically, remembering this produces in him immediate feelings of relief. He realizes that if his father is angry when he enters the door, it will mean his mother is still alive.

This is how Bellow describes the experience of his mother's death: "One day you are aware that what you took to be a turntable, smooth, flat and even, was in fact a whirlpool, a vortex."

The vortex of his mother's death sucked some part of Saul Bellow beneath the surface and it never came back. "My life was never the same after my mother died," Bellow said long after the event. In the story, he wrote: "I knew she was dying, and didn't allow myself to think about it—there's your turntable."

There are all kinds of turntables that draw us into life and lead us to think it will go on without end.

When I was in my fifties I fell in love with a younger woman, who came to me as an unexpected blessing in middle-age. Her name is April and this romance which blossomed into marriage became for me a new lease on life.

I bought a new house for us. It was perched like an eyrie on the palisades overlooking the Pacific. Because it cost more than my previous house I applied for a new insurance policy that would cover the mortgage for my wife in the event of my death.

I had to take a series of medical tests to qualify for the insurance. When they were completed the company told me my application was rejected because I had a PSA of 6.0. PSA is an acronym for prostate specific antigen. It is a number that can indicate the presence of a prostate cancer, so common in men that it is almost a feature of age.

I didn't believe the test result. I had just had a checkup a few months earlier and my PSA was only 4. How could it have gone up so fast? Moreover, friends of mine had PSA's of 9 and no cancer. I demanded another test which came back with a similar score.

I still was unconvinced. You could call this my turntable. I had as soon expected to get cancer in this life as to go on a voyage to the moon. I called my doctor and he ordered a biopsy for me. The biopsy showed that I did have a prostate cancer.

Obviously I hadn't paid much attention to things like cancer or to my body for that matter. Some of us are obsessed with our bodies and their care and feeding. Others live in their heads and consider time spent on their bodies as frivolous. It's funny how we all have these gravities of our being that determine who and what we are in such fundamental ways, yet hardly think about them or how we came to have them in the first place.

Some of us are optimists and expect good things to happen to us and are surprised when they don't. Others are pessimists who expect the worst and are pleasantly surprised when things turn out well. Obviously I was an optimist and a cockeyed one at that.

Three weeks later, I went into the hospital and had my prostate removed. I was lucky. I had a brilliant surgeon and with a little radiation afterward I was cancer-free.

Day in and day out, during my illness, my wife prayed for me. She prayed for my health and for my continued presence on this earth. Her brother Joe and his wife Marta, who attended a Catholic church, organized 30 Hispanic men, women and children, including my nieces, to pray for me too. There were others.

Every morning these relatives and strangers whispered my name in their intimate conversations with God, and implored him to spare me. I was touched and strengthened by their love and by their answered prayers. I had been saved and was grateful for that. I would be able to share life with April again, to be with my children and grandchildren, to rise in the morning and greet the sea.

Was God really behind this good fortune? Had he intervened to rescue an agnostic soul as a reward to the believers? Thankful as I was for their concern, I didn't like to think so. For if he had saved me to answer their prayers then I would also have to hold

Him responsible for the others, the ones whose prayers went unheard.

One of the patients who came regularly to the cancer ward at my appointed time was a young woman who seemed to be in her twenties. She came in a wheelchair accompanied by a sad woman who appeared to be her mother, and who had pushed her to the clinic from one of the recesses of the vast hospital complex we were part of.

She had barely begun life, but her eyes had already traveled to a distant space, displaying a vacancy that could have been equally the result of medications or resignation.

For her this life had become a waiting-room from which there was no exit. I could not help thinking, each time I saw her, of the many lives I had been privileged to live in my span, and of those she would not.

I was acutely conscious of the inhabitants of the cancer ward whose prospects were worse than mine. Along with those who loved them they had endured multiple operations, multiple setbacks, years of a crippled existence, and a fate on hold.

"Life is a hospital," the poet T.S. Eliot wrote. I could appreciate the metaphorical truth in the image, but it still felt like a violence to the reality that confronted me. Not all life's hospitals were equal and not all God's children were saved.

* * *

I had my biopsy four years ago in September 2001, two days before 9/11. Having spent the next four or five months in a battle for life, alongside others some of whom would make it and some who would not, ever conscious of the uncertainty of my fate, ever more conscious of the end of time, I was struck, reading about the 9/11 attackers, when I came across the phrase, "Love death."

It was a phrase that Mohammed Atta, the leader of the terrorists, had written in his instructions to his team. "Prepare for *jihad* and be lovers of death."

How can one love death? That is the enigma at the heart of human history, which is a narrative moved by war between tribes and nations. For how can men go to war unless they love death, or have a cause that they love more than life itself?

Lovers of *jihad* have such a cause. They believe they can redeem the world. This faith is what gives their lives meaning, puts order in the universe and restores justice to an unjust existence. By conquering the infidel world and instituting the law of the Koran they believe they can make the world holy and make it whole.

The world we live in—unjust, chaotic, suffused with suffering—is full of earthly redeemers. They are both secular and religious. They are people who cannot abide the life they have been given or who cannot wait to see if the end of their time on this earth will bring them a better time in the next. They are radicals who believe that without a divine intervention they can build a kingdom of heaven in this life, on this earth.

To realize their mission, both secular and religious radicals divide the world into two realms—the realm of those who are saved and the realm of those who are damned; believers and infidels, oppressors and oppressed. Radicals are permanently at war, their lives a perpetual *jihad.*

We all long for a judgment that will make the world right, for a God who will reward virtue and punish the wicked. Every God of Love is also a God of righteousness and death. And that is why the radical program of a redemption in this world is such a destructive force.

I once shared this radical faith. Life was intolerable to me without a redemptive hope. This quest for a world transformed brought tragedy to me as it has brought tragedy to the lives of so many others. The 20th century is a graveyard in which millions of corpses were sacrificed to the illusion of an earthly salvation.

Whether they are secular or religious radicals, those who believe we can become masters of our fate think they know more than Pascal.

But in their search for truth where do they imagine they have gone that he did not go before them? In the end, their confidence is only a mask for the inevitable defeat that is our common lot, an inverse mirror of their human need.

I understand Pascal's religion. I understand his anxious bewilderment at a life of no consequence. I understand his hope for a personal redemption and his search for an answer. But I no longer understand the faith of radicals who think they can change the world. I no longer share the belief that men by themselves, without a divine hand, can transform the world we live in and create paradise on earth.

Part of my book is a memoir, the story of how I met April, how she stood by me in my illness and nursed me through, and how I began a new chapter in life. I will not spoil the love story in this book by attempting to recount it here, but when April and I had been together for ten years, she said this: "When you die, I tell myself I'll be seeing you spiritually some day again. I don't know how I would live with the thought of you gone if I didn't believe that. I don't know how people who have no belief in God manage. It's a sad way to carry your heart through life."

But she knew I did just that. She said, "You need to respect God more. He's been good to you. When you came out of the operating room you were so handsome and your skin was magical, there was a glow on you. I knew that someone, maybe your grandma or your mom, was looking out for you." And then she said, "You have a mission. Most people are like me and don't. But you have a mission. God is protecting you."

It is a privilege to be loved. It can almost make you a believer, even if believing is not in you from the beginning. You give, and if you are lucky what you give comes back, and it comes back in ways you would never have imagined.

I could not so easily dismiss April's idea of a grace unseen. I knew I had taken risks that others prudently avoided, and had escaped unharmed. I had been felled by a cancer and was still around to talk about it. But what was the mission that might cause God to look out for me?

Why would the God of the Jews take a hand in the affairs of one of His children in any case? The Biblical point was that God gave us free will to determine our fates. Why would He intervene to change mine?

I had a mission once that tragedy altered and brought to an end. I had given up this idea of an earthly redemption. I had come to see the very dream as a vortex of destruction and had become an adversary of such illusions in others. That was the mission April meant.

But while I took pleasure in her romantic notion I could not flatter myself to think a providential eye was looking out for me. That was the very illusion I had escaped. The personal dream of every radical is to be at the center of creation and the renewal of the world. What I had learned in my life was that we were not at the center of anything but our own insignificance. There was nothing indispensable about us, about me, about anyone.

The wars of the social redeemers were as old as the Tower of Babel and would go on forever. With or without me. The dreamers would go on building towers to heaven, and just as inexorably they would come crashing to earth. Some would take to heart the lessons of the Fall, but others would fail to notice them or care.

Inspired by the dreamers who preceded them and innocent of their crimes, an unending cycle of generations would repeat what they had done. The suffering of the guilty and the innocent would continue without end, and nothing I could do or say would alter it.

The summons I had answered was more modest by far. I was a witness. I needed not to forget what I had learned through pain, and to pay my debt. I needed to warn whom I could and to protect whom I might, even if it was only one individual or two. If I had a mission to name, it was about wrestling with the most powerful and pernicious of all human follies, which is the desire to stifle truth in the name of hope.

Here is why you cannot change the world: Because we—all six billion of us—create it. We do so individually and relentlessly and in every generation. We shape the world as monarchs in our own homes and masters of others in the world beyond, when we cannot even master ourselves.

Every breeder of new generations is a stranger to his mate and a mystery to himself. Every offspring is a self-creator who learns through rebellion and surrender, through injury and error, and often not at all.

This is the root cause that makes us who and what we are—the good, the bad, the demented, the wise, the benevolent and the brute. We are creatures blind and ignorant, stumbling helplessly through a puff of time.

The future is a work of prejudice and malice inextricably bound with generosity and hope. Its fate is unalterably out of our control. Insofar as this work is manageable at all, it is carried out now and forever under the terrible anarchy of freedom that God has imposed on his children and will not take back.

Created by us each day at odds with each other, and created over and over, the world can never be made whole. It is irrevocably broken into billions of fragments, into microscopic bits of human unhappiness and earthly frustration. And no one can fix it.

Blaise Pascal was an agnostic of the intellect but a believer of the heart. He recognized that his condition was hopeless: only a divinity could heal his sickness and make him whole. Because science provided no answers to his questions, he trusted in the God of Abraham to provide what no mortal can. Pascal was a realist of faith. He drew a line between the sacred and the profane, and respected the gulf that separates this world from the next. He did not presume to achieve his own salvation in this world, or in anyone else's.

Not so the redeemers. They cannot live with themselves or the fault in creation, and therefore are at war with both. This makes them profoundly unhappy people. Because they are miserable in their own lives they cannot abide the happiness of others. To escape their suffering they seek Judgment, the rectification that will take them home.

If they do not believe in a God, they summon other men to act as gods. If they believe in God, they do not trust His justice but arrange their own. In either case, the consequence of their passion is the same catastrophe. This is because the devil they hate is in themselves and the sword of their vengeance is wielded by inhabitants of the very hell they wish to escape.

There is no redemption in this life. Generation after generation, we transmit our faults and pass on our sins. From parents to children, we create the world in our own image. And no power can stop us. Every life is an injustice. And no one can fix it. We are born and we die. If there is no God to rescue us, we are nothing.

In my time, I have found a solace and consolation in the written word. The universe I inhabit remains a mystery but I go on living and writing, nonetheless, as though there were a reason for both. Almost every day I create an order on the page, which reflects the order I see in the world. Whether it actually is an order doesn't matter as much as the fact that the quest moves me forward as though I were headed somewhere, and rescues me from the despair that would overwhelm me if I were not.

If I did not believe there was an order, I suppose I would not be able to pursue one at all. The pursuit is my comfort and the order my personal line of faith. They put oxygen into the air around me and allow me to breathe.

At the halfway mark of the last century, which to me does not seem so long ago, the gifted American writer William Faulkner won the Nobel Prize for Literature—an award, like every other human vanity, bestowed on the undeserving and the deserving alike.

Faulkner's most famous novel, *The Sound and the Fury*, is a title he took from Shakespeare's tragedy *Macbeth*. In pursuit of worldly gain, Macbeth betrays every human value and relationship that is meaningful to him. In the process he is stripped of all human companionship and respect, until he is only an empty and embittered shell.

Having emptied his own life of its spiritual supports, he turns against life itself. "It is a tale told by an idiot," he proclaims, "full of sound and fury, signifying nothing."

But when Faulkner mounted the podium in Oslo to receive his Nobel Prize, he struck a very different note. The year was 1950, the dawn of the nuclear era. Faulkner looked into the eye of its darkest prospect and declared, "I refuse to accept this. I believe that ... when the last ding-dong of doom has clanged and faded ... in the last dying red evening ... man will not merely endure; he will prevail."

Others criticized Faulkner's pronouncement as mere bravado. What basis could he have for such a claim? But this faith was not wisdom. It was the oxygen he needed to breathe.

April and I acquired a little Mexican dog with black and white markings, whose improbable name was Jacob and whose brain is smaller than my fist. When Jacob wags his tail for joy he does not hide his pleasure as we, burdened with consciousness, often do. Instead, his whole frame is swept into the movement as though life had no reality but this. Jacob is one of the myriad creatures on this earth, ridiculous and beautiful, whose origin is a mystery and who do not worry the significance of who or why or what they are.

In the morning when I step out of my shower this little self comes to me unbidden to lick the glistening drops from my feet. This is not a ritual of submission; it does not have any meaning for him at all. It is merely his pleasure. What is interesting is that I, a creature who lives by meanings, am also affected by this action. When he does not come, I feel the absence and miss him.

This is a microcosm of all the visits and vacancies that bring misery and happiness to our lives. We can embrace them or not. This choice, which we freely make, determines whether life will hollow us out and embitter us or provide us oxygen to breathe.

What is ahead of us? Like Pascal, we don't know. "Believers and non-believers stand in the same darkness. Neither sees God."

Therefore like Pascal we should wager on life. We should bear ourselves in this world as though we have seen God, be kind to each other, love wisely, and give to our children what we would have wished for ourselves.

12

Getting This
Conservative Wrong

In the introduction to *Rebels All!*, Kevin Mattson's unconventional look at conservatives, the historian acknow-ledges that conservative ideas need to be taken seriously. This is a refreshing departure from the wish of most liberals and all leftists that conservative ideas would disappear. It is also the reason I asked *Frontpage Magazine* editor Jamie Glazov to interview Mattson and promote his new book.[1] Readers of *Frontpage* know that I have conducted a five-year campaign to urge liberal-arts professors, most of whom are leftists, to assign conservative texts in their courses so that there might actually be two sides to the controversial issues they address. For my pains in conducting this effort to support an intellectual dialogue, I have been rewarded with the epithets "McCarthyite" and "chief organizer of the campus thought-police" by academic leftists who want to teach their political prejudices as though they were scientific facts.

Professor Mattson is unwilling to acknowledge his colleagues' role in this anti-intellectual assault. Instead he lays the blame for the lack of dialogue at the door of conservatives and their "shrill rhetoric." I suggest that he pay some attention to his colleagues' discourse when they pretend to deal with conservative ideas. He might also pay more attention to what conservatives actually do. This conservative magazine has invited numerous leftists like him

---

This was published as "How Liberals Get Conservatives Wrong," October 15, 2008, http://archive.frontpagemag.com/Printable.aspx?ArtId=32708
[1]October 13, 2008, http://archive.frontpagemag.com/readArticle.aspx?ARTID=32665

to come into its pages and promote their ideas and work; and we have treated them respectfully when they do. There has been no reciprocity from the other side.

Speaking just from personal experience, I have written ten books in the last decade, nine of which were dedicated to the analysis and refutation of leftwing practices and ideas. Only one of those nine books—*The Professors*—was reviewed or even discussed in the leftwing magazines for which Mattson writes—and then it was hardly to engage my ideas. "Ignore This Book" was actually the title of the review by Professor Cary Nelson that appeared in *Academe,* the official publication of the American Association of University Professors of which he is the head. Another leftwing "critic," Professor Michael Bérubé, has publicly explained that he only writes about my work to "ridicule" and "discredit" it.[2] In other words, to suppress rather than engage opposing ideas. As a conservative, I am certainly not alone in having my work treated this way by so-called intellectuals of the left.

As it happens, my name appears prominently in Kevin Mattson's new book, where I am described as an exemplar of "the postmodern conservative intellectual" and a leader of the contemporary conservative movement. His depiction of me and what I believe leaves much to be desired, and what follows is my response to his portrayal. As a courtesy, our editors informed Professor Mattson that I would be responding to his interview, once we had showcased his book, and he graciously accepted our offer.[3]

Let me begin by noting what is valuable in the portrait of modern conservatism to be found in *Rebels All!* Unlike most writers of the left, Kevin Mattson notices that there is a rebel element to contemporary American conservatism that distinguishes it from the status-quo Toryism of the past. Fifty-five years after William Buckley's protest against the liberal establishment at Yale, and 45

---

[2]September 12, 2007, http://archive.frontpagemag.com/readArticle.aspx?ARTID=28040
[3]Monday, October 13, 2008, http://archive.frontpagemag.com/readArticle.aspx?ARTID=32665

years after the Goldwater revolt against the Republican Party's political establishment, Professor Mattson has finally recognized these facts and attempted to make a thesis out of them. Unfortunately, in doing so, he regularly confuses style with substance, tactics with strategy, and generally fails to take conservative ideas seriously enough to understand them, or to make his book the interesting and rewarding read it could have been.

The profile Mattson has drawn of me, in particular, is a caricature, not a portrait. I do not subscribe to many of the views he attributes to me—post-modernism being the most obvious—and he seems entirely ignorant of the books I have written. This is no small fault in a historian. Disregarding all that I have thought and stood for, Mattson describes me as an "anti-intellectual," a "relativist" and an "extremist"—a characterization which reflects on all contemporary conservatives, of whom he regards me as an "exemplar." But contrary to Mattson, I am a defender of intellectual standards, an anti-relativist and a supporter of moderation in intellectual enterprises. Each of the labels Mattson ascribes to me, if correct, would render inexplicable my campaign for intellectual standards in the university and my efforts in the pages of this magazine to open a dialogue with dozens of intellectuals of the left. But they are not correct. The books I have written, if he would read them, are sustained civil arguments with leftist ideas and authors. They are hardly "anti-intellectual," let alone "extremist." If he had cared to look, Mattson could have found on my website archive tens of thousands of words I have written responding to leftist attacks, and tens of thousands more defending intellectual standards and the values and virtues of a liberal society, something he claims to cherish.

Because he has not read relevant texts I have written, Mattson picks up and repeats canards from the left that I have been forced time and again to answer and refute. Instead of taking on my arguments and trying to understand what I believe, Mattson writes sentences that describe me as "fighting the culture wars by writing numerous autobiographies about how he shed his sixties radicalism, arguing that slavery benefited African-Americans [and] sponsoring a Student Bill of Rights that would have state legislatures police classrooms for purported liberal content"—to all of which I can only say: "Not true." I wrote one autobiography, and I have never argued that slavery benefited African-Americans. If Mattson had only taken the time to read the little book I wrote about my reparations campaign, *Uncivil Wars*, he would know this.[4] Mattson's target of course is not just myself but all conservatives: "Horowitz's move from endorsing the Black Panther Party to saying that blacks should be grateful about slavery because it brought them to America—that trajectory serves conservative intellectuals well today."

Of course, I have never said that blacks should be grateful about slavery. What moron would? What I have said is that African-Americans should not turn their backs on America because of slavery, given the benefits that America has provided to blacks alive today who are more prosperous and free than the inhabitants of any African nation whose ancestors were not brought in chains to this country. This statement has been twisted by unscrupulous leftists into the false claim Mattson repeats.

Most importantly, since it is a focal point of Mattson's portrait, I have never sponsored any bill calling for state legislatures to police classrooms over liberal indoctrination or, for that matter, to monitor any kind of classroom content. On the contrary, I have stressed and supported the independence of academic institutions, and have never supported a legislative statute to enforce the Academic Bill of Rights. I specifically opposed legislation in Arizona that would have required professors to provide students with alternate texts if the ones they were assigned "offended" them. I opposed such legislation—as I explained in a published article available on my website—because this would take classroom authority away from the teacher. Even though I have a public

---

[4] See the fourth volume in this series, *Progressive Racism*, which contains my writing on slavery and reparations.

record of defending the independence of the university and opposing a measure that would have put students and professors on an equal footing, Mattson falsely describes me as a "populist" fomenting the overthrow of faculty authority.

Mattson also writes, "[Horowitz] does not sound conservative when he talks about defending right-wing students from left-wing bias." It's true, I wouldn't sound conservative if I had said that. But I didn't say that. I never attack leftwing "bias" because bias is another word for perspective and everybody has one. (I *have* attacked leftwing *ideas* because they are wrong-headed. But that is different from attempting to outlaw a political "bias.") The academic campaign I conducted is central to Mattson's analysis. One might think, therefore, that the one book Professor Mattson would have read is *The Professors*. One would be wrong. In the introduction to *The Professors* I wrote: "This book is not intended as a text about leftwing bias in the university and does not propose that a leftwing perspective on academic faculties is a problem in itself. Every individual, whether conservative or liberal, has a perspective and therefore a bias. Professors have every right to interpret the subjects they teach according to their points of view. That is the essence of academic freedom." What could be clearer? What could be more opposite to the view Mattson claims I hold?

Even if my words had not been so clear, my actions were. I defended Ward Churchill's right to hold reprehensible views and still be a professor. I defended the appointment of leftwing law professor Erwin Chemerinsky as dean of the new law school at UC Irvine when the appointment was withdrawn by the administration because prominent donors had complained about his political opinions. I have defended leftwing students against conservative professors. Yet Mattson ignores the clear public record of my words and deeds in order to misrepresent them and attack me.

Mattson associates me, for example, with advocates of Intelligent Design theory who want it included in the biology curriculum. I have publicly opposed this. He refers to me as an anti-foundationalist, post-modern relativist, which I am not. Mattson justifies this characterization with a single sentence from the Academic Bill of Rights (the sentence actually written by Stephen Balch): "Human knowledge is a never-ending pursuit of the truth [because] there is no humanly accessible truth that is not in principle open to challenge . . ." But what "post-modernist" would write that there is a "truth" that can be pursued in the first place? The statement in the Academic Bill of Rights is a carefully-worded, limited observation. It says that because no individual, faction, or party is in possession of absolute truth it is important to hear more than one side of a controversial issue. Who would object to this? Yet Mattson does.

Like many leftists, Mattson makes a federal case out of a little essay I wrote ten years ago called *The Art of Political War.*[5] An excerpt from the essay appears as the epigraph to his chapter on "Post-Modern Conservatism, the Politics of Outrage and Mindset of War." Mattson even exaggerates my role in the conservative movement in order to make my essay seem more influential than it was: "The 1960s had become a permanent fixture of Horowitz's identity, as it had for the country as a whole. Horowitz was the Sixties hipster marching in line with the 'Reagan Revolution,' and he determined the future of the conservative intellectual movement more than [Hilton] Kramer's or [Irving] Kristol's anguished, highbrow concern."

The fact is I wasn't a "hipster" in the 1960s. I was a Marxist who didn't smoke dope, didn't live in a commune, missed Woodstock, never went to a Grateful Dead concert or the Fillmore, didn't riot or throw stones at cops, and lived in a nuclear family. Moreover, my little pamphlet on *The Art of Political War* was not a working manual or political guide for intellectual conservatives or for the conservative movement. It was very specifically and explicitly a guide for conducting *electoral* campaigns before mass

---

[5]https://secure.donationreport.com/productlist.html?key=5DGIXY HTR-FJI

audiences where the contending parties are limited to 30-second TV sound-bites.

I have been attacked on this front before by leftists who want to turn *The Art of Political War* into a credo, which it is not. In fact, I devoted a whole chapter of my book *Indoctrination U* to refuting this claim when it was the focus of an attack by the Dean of the Faculty at Reed College. In responding to this attack I wrote: "The 'politics' to which *The Art of Political War* is addressed is *electoral* politics (or politics before masses), which would not include the controversies I normally engage in as a public intellectual or in the many other books I have written, or in the academic freedom campaign itself." What could be clearer? Unfortunately, Mattson hasn't read this book either, though it is entirely about the Academic Bill of Rights.

But he *has* read *The Art of Political War,* which makes the same point. Here is a passage that Mattson elides from the very excerpt he uses as the epigraph to his chapter: "You have only 30 seconds to make your point. Even if you had time to develop an argument, the audience you need to reach (the undecided and those in the middle who are not paying much attention) wouldn't get it.... Worse, while you've been making your argument the other side has already painted you as a mean-spirited, borderline racist controlled by religious zealots, securely in the pockets of the rich. Nobody who sees you this way is going to listen to you in any case. You're politically dead." This is quite obviously advice to Republicans running for election, not conservative intellectuals engaged in intellectual debates.

Mattson's book is an attempt to connect the conservatism of Buckley's generation with conservatism like mine. There are obvious connections between the two but Mattson is ultimately so uninterested in conservative ideas that the connections he makes are an impenetrable mosh. "Horowitz sees himself as a rebel today as much as he was in the 1960s. And he shares the same enemy conservatives chastised in the past—the 'liberal establishment.'"

No, I don't. The so-called "liberal establishment" today is a leftwing establishment. Unlike Buckley, I identify with 50s liberals like John F. Kennedy, whose politics in my view were identical to Ronald Reagan's. My political enemies today—Ward Churchill, bell hooks, Cornel West, Nicholas DeGenova, the editors of *The Nation*—have views of capitalism that are identical to those of the Cold War "progressives" who supported the Communist bloc and its cause. They have absolutely nothing in common with JFK or the liberal establishment at Yale in the 1950s whom William F. Buckley opposed. Mattson treats Buckley as the avatar of the conservative rebellion, a view I share. But I have never embraced a theocentric conservatism like that of Buckley, Russell Kirk and Whittaker Chambers, who anchored their conservatism in a religious faith. I do not. I am an agnostic. I have outlined my own conservative philosophy in *The Politics of Bad Faith*—a book Mattson also has not read. My conservatism is an effort to defend the principles of the American Founding. It is true that according to the Founders we derive inalienable rights from a creator. I agree that rights have to be derived from a source other than human will. If Mattson has another way to ground inalienable rights without invoking a Creator, I am all ears, but until then this agnostic will defer to the Founders.

Here is Mattson's vision of the conservative movement as expressed in his book and summed up in his *Frontpage* interview[6]:

> Postmodern conservatism takes from Buckley's model of the conservative the stance of the rebel.... From the Sixties, postmodern conservatism takes 'hipness' and the 'new sensibility.' And then it bundles these things together with an interest in the postmodern ideas of 'diversity' and 'anti-foundationalism.' Consider the use of the term 'diversity' in the original Academic Bill of Rights. The justification for ABOR also argued that 'there is no humanly accessible truth that is not in principle open to challenge.' The

argument is thus infused with postmodern theories about knowledge—knowledge as contingent, grounded in language games, never foundational, etc. But the conservative weds this postmodern outlook with a stance of war—the 'political war' that Horowitz outlines in one of his more popular books (popular among elected Republicans).

As I have just demonstrated this is a hodgepodge of misunderstood and misrepresented ideas which could have been corrected if Professor Mattson had done his homework, or picked up the phone and asked me what I meant.

13

What My Daughter Taught Me About Compassion

P resident Barack Obama has been in office nearly one year, making it two since my late daughter Sarah trudged through a freezing winter in Iowa to help him win the nomination. According to a Gallup poll conducted on the anniversary of the presidential vote, only 28 percent of Americans still believe that Mr. Obama will be "able to heal political divisions in the country." A year ago, 54 percent felt he would be able to do so.

When I read those figures I can't help thinking about Sarah. For the two of us reflected the country's political divisions in our own relationship—a case familiar to many American families. As a conservative and an active participant in political conflicts, I am acutely aware of how difficult it is, even with the best intentions, to change the tone in the midst of debate, and how many otherwise thoughtful people can be swept up in its passions.

Despite our political differences—the painful distances and predictable frustrations they created—Sarah and I ultimately came to the point where we were able to avoid the rancors of these public imbroglios. By the time she was overtaken by the medical complications deriving from a birth defect, which made efforts

---

This is a talk I gave on the publication of *A Cracking of the Heart.* December 29, 2009, http://online.wsj.com/article/SB10001424052748703 93940457456836197577086.html. Reading it today, I think it suggests a greater distance between us than actually was the case. We were never "estranged" in the sense in which that term is normally used, and there was only one seriously painful episode, which I have described in the book.

like her Iowa campaign extraordinarily difficult, we were quite close. Sarah and I were able to be respectful not only of the fact that we had such differences, but of the reasons we had them. After her death in March 2008, I decided to write a memoir of her remarkable life, and to include the story of our estrangement and reunion in the hope it might be helpful to others facing similar divisions. I called it *A Cracking of the Heart.*

My daughter was largely responsible for our reconciliation— although that term somewhat exaggerates the estrangement. She wanted to change the world, yet she knew this could only be accomplished one person at a time, and only by respecting the dignity of others. Despite her physical disabilities, Sarah traveled on buses and on foot across San Francisco, where she lived, to feed the homeless. Even though she was a vegetarian herself, she learned to prepare meat dishes for them because that was what they wanted. She stood vigil in bitter winters at San Quentin prison whenever there was an execution. But she did not think the criminals on behalf of whom she protested were innocent. Nor did she think they should be released. Sarah just felt that it was bad for the nation's soul to take a life.

Over the years, I came to realize that while some of my daughter's views were different from mine, the values they reflected, and more importantly the estimates of human character on which they were based, were not so different that I could not recognize them. A particular bone of contention between us had been over the Jewish concept of *tikkun olam*, which means "repair of the world" and is often wrongly conflated with the left's quest for "social justice." My life-experience had led me to conclude that the idea of changing the world was not only an impossible dream. It was the source of innumerable tragedies and of epic miseries that human beings had inflicted on each other through the failed utopias of Nazism and Communism. And so was the refusal to recognize it as such.

For more than a decade, Sarah and I argued across this gap with much disappointment until I came to realize that I was missing a crucial element that connected her view and mine. That realization was crystallized in an exchange we had over a book I had written called *The End of Time*. In the book, I had observed that while the prophets of all religions taught us to love each other as we love ourselves and to think that "there but for the grace of God go I," this advice was ultimately imprudent. Is it wise, I had asked, "to put our trust in strangers, or to love our enemies as ourselves? Would we advise our children to do so?"

Then came a passage to which Sarah took great exception: "I cannot embrace this radical faith. I feel no kinship with those who can cut short a human life without remorse; or with terrorists who target the innocent; or with adults who torment small children for the sexual thrill. I suspect no decent soul does either."

Sarah took those words as an attack on the very rationale of her life, and responded at first with anger. But she relented and then wrote me this: "My objection is that you're confusing compassion with gullibility. I do visit prisoners and I think it matters to make that human connection. That doesn't mean I'd necessarily trust them with my purse. I wouldn't let the State execute them in my name either. I don't think kinship with people who've crossed the line blurs my own morality. In fact, it gives it more clarity. If you see someone in the fullness of their humanity, you see how they are acting out their own confusion and suffering. This does not justify hurtful or evil acts. It doesn't even always inspire forgiveness. But if you see someone this way, you respond more in sadness than in anger. And that is simply a more excellent state of being."

A more excellent state of being. My daughter had not only understood the limits we face in trying to repair the world; she had taught me that compassion like hers could be informed by a sense of those limits as well. "Even if you've never had this experience," she continued, "respect the experience of those who have. I'm not talking about an idea either. This is a full-bodied understanding of another person. This practice has in fact transformed all my relationships, including ours by the way."

14

Something We Did

Just before Labor Day this year, a theater review in *The Washington Post* alerted me to the fact that someone had made me, or a fictional representation of me, into a principal character in his play. *Something You Did* purports to be a drama about the parole appeal of an actual person, Kathy Boudin, who forty years ago was a member of two violent organizations and was directly involved in the violent deaths of six human beings (although the play mentions only one). Despite the fact that I myself was never the member of any violent group and never so much as threw a rock in the Sixties, the playwright has cast my character as the bad guy, complicit in her crime, and an embodiment of the political forces that Boudin opposed at the time and that the playwright opposes now.

The day after the *Post* review appeared, I received a confirming email from my friend of nearly 60 years, Ron Radosh, who had just attended a performance and who sent me a scanned copy of a statement by the playwright explaining his play. In his note, the playwright identified me as the villain of his drama and said he had chosen me because I had written what he called the most "corrosive" attack on Kathy Boudin when she came up for parole; and also because I was "a former radical turned outspoken neo-conservative." It was, he said, his intention to have his play make a statement about the present. Finally, he described the play as asking

This was published on October 4, 2010; http://frontpagemag.com/
2010/david-horowitz/something-we-did-2/print/

and answering this question: "Whether the radical sins of the past can be forgiven even as the reactionary sins of the present multiply." With this loaded question, there could be no suspense as to the answer. Boudin is to be forgiven, because she has remained a radical and therefore her heart was and is in the right place. Never mind that she caused the deaths of three innocent people and left nine children fatherless. Whatever mistakes she committed, her intention was to save the Vietnamese and other oppressed people from conservatives like myself. Such was the thesis of the play.

A fiction based on reality can provide useful insights only if the structure of the facts remains intact. Unfortunately, this playwright so distorted the facts as to deprive his fiction of the ability to provide insights that are useful to an understanding of what happened. To begin, allow me to clear up his malicious claim that there is a moral parallel between Kathy Boudin's criminal acts and David Horowitz's "contribution" to the death of Betty van Patter at the hands of the Black Panthers. Kathy Boudin knowingly joined a radical group whose purpose was to conduct an actual war inside the United States. The Weather Underground set bombs, possibly murdered two police officers—there is a continuing cold-case investigation into this—and inadvertently blew up three of its own members when an anti-personnel device intended for others went off prematurely. When the Underground disintegrated and most of its leaders surfaced to return to civilian life, Kathy remained at war, joining a second violent group with identical goals. As a member of the "May 19 Communist Organization," she participated in an armed robbery in Nyack, New York to finance "the revolution." In the course of the robbery, three officers were murdered and nine children left fatherless.

There is no parallel between Kathy's criminal career and what I did as a New Left radical. I never broke a law or plotted to injure another human being. Although I raised money for a Black Panther school and attempted to help the Panthers develop a learning center, I never joined their organization or advocated that others should. The money I raised was to purchase and build a school. I became involved with the Panthers only after their leader, Huey Newton, had publicly proclaimed that it was "time to put away the gun." In those days *The New York Times* was comparing Newton to Mahatma Gandhi and Martin Luther—literally. When I recommended Betty van Patter to the Panthers as a bookkeeper, I accepted the left's view of the Panthers as victims of white racism and a noble force in the struggle for racial justice. I had no idea they were capable of cold-blooded murder.

After Betty was murdered, I realized I should have read the signs and known the dangers. I bore my responsibility for what had happened. Those recognitions are what the conservative part of my life has been about. I wrote an extensive memoir of those events in which I took full responsibility, in particular for not knowing what I should have known.[1] If Kathy Boudin had done the same—if she had attempted to re-examine the premises that led her to commit her crimes and had made a full accounting afterward—I would still have held her accountable but would not have judged her as harshly as I have.

A crucial fact about me that the play ignores is that I did not need to become a conservative to be critical of Kathy Boudin and the Weather Underground. Nor was I alone in this. In 1971, when still a radical, I wrote a widely-read article in *Ramparts* attacking the Weather Underground for its terrorist ideas and practices. My article focused on the explosion of the bomb that Boudin's Weather Underground cell was planning to detonate in a terrorist act. Three members of the cell were killed in that explosion, which destroyed the Greenwich Village townhouse they had turned into their bomb-factory. Boudin was in the townhouse at the time and survived. She then continued her chosen path of radical violence.

The townhouse episode includes crucial facts that the playwright suppresses in order to load his case for Boudin's redemption. In the play, the Boudin character, who is named Allison,

[1]*Radical Son: A Generational Odyssey*

claims that her terrorist acts were aimed at property, not people. She is thus presented as someone innocent of the purposes for which the bomb was to be used. In the play it is my character who persuades her to buy the nails that turn the bomb into an anti-personnel weapon. The black policeman who becomes the inadvertent victim of the bomb is killed by one of those nails. In the play Allison's innocence of the bomb's malicious purpose is central to the plot and to the playwright's twofold plan: to create sympathy and forgiveness for Allison/Kathy; and to indict my character, the neo-conservative, as the villain instead.

In fact, however, Kathy Boudin and her comrades were deliberately building an anti-personnel bomb filled with nails, intending to detonate it at a social dance at Fort Dix. The dance would be attended by 18-year-old draftees and their dates. The real Kathy Boudin was a calculating terrorist with no mercy for those she regarded as her political enemies, even if they were innocent draftees. My opposition to her parole, then and now, is because she committed heinous acts and has refused to face up to them—not because she opposed the Vietnam War.

The only article I ever wrote about her parole—which seems to have incensed the playwright—opens with this sen-tence: "The separate reality of radicals, which made them unable to comprehend their own deeds, was made vivid for me in a *New York Times* story I read later, about the parole appeal of ... Kathy Boudin."[2] The author of *Something You Did* never sought to interview me to find out what my real views were before defaming me in his play. He is a perfect example of radicals who inhabit a separate reality—who are unable to understand how others see them and therefore unable to understand themselves.

In *Something You Did* I am represented as a self-serving cynic and a representative specimen of the system I once opposed. My character, "Gene," cuts million-dollar deals on the basis of his fame as a radical turncoat and receives $50,000 speaking-fees to

---

[2]"Clinton's Pardoned Bombers" in *Left Illusions: An Intellectual Odyssey*

spread his noxious views. I wish. Perhaps the playwright was thinking of Cornel West or Michael Moore. If they do command such fees, it's because they have had no second thoughts and because their talk resonates with the prevailing views of the culturally-dominant left.

In addition to being materialistic and a narcissist, the character allegedly based on me is portrayed as an embittered racist and a xenophobic Jew. In constructing my character as that of a wealthy cynic the playwright chooses to confront a radical cliché rather than the person who in his eyes was Boudin's most corrosive critic. As far as my attitudes toward money and non-Jews and blacks, I am pretty much the same individual I was when I was on the left, though hopefully wiser. I am still a missionary driven by certain ideals, rather than the avaricious operator represented in the play. My conservative views are inspired by what I see as the destructive ambitions and practices of the left, and their negative impact on the very people—blacks, the poor, the Vietnamese— whom radicals have claimed to support. Any honest reader of my work would know that. A confrontation between a radical and a former radical who has had second thoughts about the practical results of his commitments would have provided a more interesting subject for this play than the progressive melodrama the playwright has settled on

But melodrama it is, and therefore the conservative must be exposed not only as an opponent of radical terrorists but as a racist; and since he is Jewish, a tribalist—in short, a "reactionary." In the play my character refers to the murder of two civil rights workers in Mississippi while deliberately omitting the third, James Chaney, because he was black. For this reactionary only Jews count. Those who have followed my career and writings will know, on the other hand, that I am more faithful to the civil-rights ideals of the Sixties, in which leftists claim to believe, than the author of this play. In my autobiography *Radical Son* the point I made about those issues, which the playwright grossly misrepresents, is that Jewish radicals like Kathy Boudin feel superior to the groups they are claiming to help, in this instance blacks, and so fail to understand them as individuals. The terrorist act that provides the basis for this play was committed by a group of violent black criminals whom Boudin mistook for black victims and comrades.

The climax of the play is Allison's parole-board appeal. She defends herself by claiming that whatever she did and whatever mistakes she made were in behalf of the Vietnamese and Cambodians, that the real criminals are the Americans who supported the anti-Communist cause. In other words, there is nothing she needs to regret about the political views that led her to commit her heinous acts, and anyway the acts her adversaries committed were worse. There are two problems with this attempted exculpation. The first is that Kathy Boudin and the anti-war left really didn't care that much about the Vietnamese and the Cambodians. When America left Indo-China in 1975 and the Cambodians and Vietnamese were being slaughtered by the Communists in one of the largest genocides of the 20th century, there were no protests by the American left of those atrocities—not by Kathy Boudin and not by her comrades-in-arms.

The second problem with Allison's appeal is that the factual premise on which it is based is a lie. Kathy Boudin was responsible for the death of a black policeman, Waverly Brown—actually the first black policeman ever hired by the Nyack police force. But the act that killed him was not and could not have been a protest against the Vietnam War. Officer Brown was killed by Kathy Boudin and her friends in 1981, eight years after American troops were withdrawn and six after the last American officials had left Vietnam, and at a time when the Communists were firmly in power.

This play is dishonest to its core. It misrepresents the reasons Kathy Boudin committed her crime; it misrepresents the crime itself; it whitewashes her culpability as a supporter of terrorist acts. Finally, on a personal note, it misrepresents who I am and why I opposed her parole.

15

Who I Am

L ast week an article appeared in the Jewish magazine *Tablet*, in which I am portrayed as politically "homeless" and depressed, while the institutional base from which I operate is described as long past its day. The article further alleges that I have come to a point in my life where I feel my efforts as a conservative have been "a waste." All of these allegations are demonstrably false. They are made by a writer who is a political leftist, tone-deaf and hostile to conservative ideas. As it happens, within the past year I published a book called *A Point in Time*, which is a summary of my views on life, of the battles I have waged, and which is also the strongest possible affirmation of the philosophy that underlies my conservative worldview. Far from being abandoned by other conservatives, I have received the strongest possible endorsements from conservative reviewers of this book, which Norman Podhoretz called "as moving as it is profound."

The David Horowitz Freedom Center is hardly past its peak. It is supported by 100,000 individual donors, which is more than three times the number of its supporters ten years ago. Conservatives who have spoken at the Center's events include four contenders for this year's Republican presidential nomination— Santorum, Gingrich, Bachmann and Cain—former president George Bush, his Secretary of Defense Donald Rumsfeld, his Attorney General John Ashcroft, Senator Marco Rubio and his colleagues

---

This article was published on May 9, 2012; http://frontpagemag.com/2012/david-horowitz/who-i-am/print/

John McCain, Jon Kyl, Jeff Sessions and Mitch McConnell, Speaker John Boehner, former Majority Leader, Tom DeLay, Rush Limbaugh, Sean Hannity, Glenn Beck, Ann Coulter and Victor Davis Hanson. A recent pamphlet I wrote called *Barack Obama's Rules for Revolution* has sold half-a-million copies, with another two million distributed. Notwithstanding *Tablet*'s description of the Center as a declining institution it has doubled its revenues in the last ten years and its influence in the conservative movement through its websites frontpagemag.com and discoverthenetworks.org is greater than ever.

I obviously made a mistake in agreeing to be interviewed by someone who misrepresented what I told him and ignored the evidence that contradicted his distortions. For being so unguarded, I owe an apology to my friends and supporters, several of whom expressed their dismay to me after reading the article. It is partly their concern that has prompted me to set the record straight. But in a perverse way I also appreciate the opportunity provided by the author of this tedious piece of writing because he has caused me to look at how integral to the conservative movement we at the David Horowitz Freedom Center are, and how deeply we are indebted to it as well.

When I received *Tablet*'s request for an interview, I was inclined to say yes because it came from a magazine with which I had a history, and which occasionally published first-rate conservative writers like Bret Stephens and Lee Smith. *Tablet* even published a defense of Nonie Darwish that I wrote when she was attacked by one of their writers. Then I was disarmed by the author himself who sent me an email about his intentions:

> I am a leftist, though not a dogmatic one, and I usually don't write directly about politics. For *The Nation*, I write mostly for the Books and Arts section, which isn't nearly as ideologically-driven as the magazine's editorial page.... So, we may not find much common ground politically, but that may make for a more stimulating piece. I'm less interested in debating Islamo-fascism than exploring your work's position at the intersection of autobi-

ography, politics, history, manners, and polemic. I think I can do
so fairly.

In the past, my work has been attacked by leftists who will
take a phrase from a fund-raising letter or a heated polemic and
then omit its context or distort its meaning to discredit my work.
The prospect of a leftist writer distinguishing the intellectual from
the polemical in my work appeared to be an opportunity to open a
conversation in a medium like *Tablet*, which is something I had
wanted to do.

When the article "David Horowitz Is Homeless" appeared, it
was obvious that none of its author's assurances was sincere. Here
is an example of his interest in literary styles rather than in scor-
ing political points: "If what was once labeled extremism is now
mainstream GOP boilerplate, then Horowitz deserves at least
some of the credit."

Not only was this a political attack, it was wildly inaccurate.
The Republican Party today finds itself defending policies that
were once the province of liberal Democrats like John F. Kennedy,
specifically capital-gains tax cuts, balanced books, strong defense
budgets, color-blind racial standards and aggressively anti-totalitarian foreign policies. Only an extremist of the left could so mis-
label a party that had just nominated a former Massachusetts
governor as its presidential candidate.

But the author wasn't done. He also wanted to pin Republican
"extremism" on me, the man whom conservatives had allegedly
abandoned: "In a widely distributed 2000 pamphlet called 'The Art
of Political War,' praised by Karl Rove and endorsed by 35 state
Republican party chairmen, Horowitz wrote: 'In political warfare
you do not fight just to prevail in an argument, but to destroy the
enemy's fighting ability. Republicans often seem to regard political
combats as they would a debate with the Oxford Political Union,
as though winning depended on rational arguments and carefully
articulated principles. But the audience of politics is not made up
of Oxford dons, and the rules are entirely different.... Politics is

war. Don't forget it.' If you can remember a time when conservative discourse sounded like an Oxford lecture hall, then you have a sense of how far Horowitz has helped to steer this ship off course." The missing context here is that the little pamphlet I wrote twelve years ago argued that it is *Democrats*—not Republicans—who have transformed the political arena into a combat zone, and who conduct politics as war by other means.

Of course the claim that I am responsible for changing the entire tenor of the Republicans' political strategy belies the thesis of the article, which is that I am "homeless." On the other hand I did remark to the author that Republicans haven't really heeded the advice I gave in *The Art of Political War.* Thirty-five state Republican Party chairmen did endorse the pamphlet, but none of them acted on its recommendations. Republicans have come a long way since I wrote it, thanks in the main to the emergence of the Tea Party. But they still have a long way to go. So yes, I am not happy with the state of the Republican Party on this score, but what conservative is? In the interview, I also said that the Republican presidential debates had made me ill, but what conservative was happy with the way the candidates tore into each other with ugly personal attacks, or insisted on arguing about contraceptives and theology while America's Nero fiddled and the country burned?

Here is the way *Tablet*'s article describes my alleged decline and fall on the right: "In his turn-of-the-21st-century heyday, shortly after publishing *Hating Whitey*, an assault on affirmative action and race-based quotas—or 'the anti-white racism of the left'—that preceded his campaign against reparations for slavery, Horowitz appeared on op-ed pages, talk radio, and television nearly every day. (He even wrote a bi-weekly *column*[1] for the liberal Salon.com.) But in 2012, his books are not just ignored by the *New York Times*, but by the *Weekly Standard* and *National Review*."

Again the facts are different. Even in my "heyday," I was never on television or talk radio nearly every day and, except for my

---

[1]http://www.salon.com/writer/david_horowitz/

Salon adventure, I never appeared regularly in any op-ed pages. *Salon's* editors dropped me when they decided to charge their readers for access, telling me that Salon's leftwing audience wouldn't pay for a publication that had a column by me in it. My book *Hating Whitey* did cost me my liberal New York publisher whose editor told me that the Free Press would never publish a book with the title I asked for: "Hating White People Is A Politically Correct Idea." It is true that *The New York Times* stopped reviewing my books when I became a conservative. But *Tablet's* claim that today my books are ignored by *The Weekly Standard* and *National Review* is just false. My last two books, published in 2011, received laudatory reviews in both magazines.

A half-truth lies behind the *Tablet* author's fabrication. I did tell him that a book I wrote with Ben Johnson, *Party of Defeat: How Democrats and Radicals Undermined America's War on Terror Before and After 9/11*, was not reviewed by the conservative press. This was especially troubling to me because its subject was important and because 18 sitting Republican senators and congressmen, including the ranking members of the armed services, intelligence and foreign affairs committees recommended the book in a blurb on its cover. In my view the conservative media may have avoided the book because the right is generally shy of holding Democrats' feet to the fire when it comes to issues of patriotism, even though the Democrats' disgraceful, not to say seditious behavior during the Iraq War certainly merited such scrutiny.

A more significant falsehood purveyed in "David Horowitz Is Homeless" is the insinuation that I look on the conservative half of my life as a "waste." This insidious suggestion goes to the heart of the author's failure to perform on his promise to "[explore] your work's position at the intersection of autobiography, politics, history, manners, and polemic." And to do so *fairly*.

The cause of that failure is once again the author's failure to respect conservative ideas: "One need not subscribe to the lurid pamphlets sold by his Freedom Center to get the sense that

Horowitz has sacrificed his intellectual capital to devote himself more fully to the movement," he writes. That is pure invention. The pamphlets I have written for the Center are indeed polemical, but they are only "lurid" to someone so far to the left that he cannot handle their insights. My essay, *Barack Obama's Rules for Revolution*, draws on a lifetime of experience with the left. Yes, it is a pamphlet and a polemic, but that is only the beginning of the story. Marx's most famous pamphlet, to take one obvious example, is an insidious and fallacious work, but it would never occur to the *Tablet* author—or to anyone—to suggest that Marx sacrificed his intellectual capital to write *The Communist Manifesto* just because it is a polemic.

There is another kind of intellectual work that I do, which has of late become a preferred vocation of mine, and which is the source of the author's final and most egregious claim that I consider my conservative work a waste. In two small volumes of which *A Point in Time* is one, I have attempted to summarize what I have learned about life in my seventy-three years on this earth. I have pursued this aspect of my work in between my political tasks. It is the failure to appreciate the disparate nature of the two efforts—one reflective, the other active—that has led the writer to his false conclusion. Here is the way the caricature concludes: "'I came out of the left through a lot of pain and a sense of enormous waste,' Horowitz said. 'I was an emotional powder keg. I had gotten to age 35—and I'm a very hard worker, and had written *a lot*—everything that I had done was a waste.' This is the part of the story when the apostate sees the light. Horowitz isn't sure he still does. 'Now that I'm older, I see that it's *all* a waste. I gotta live with that.'"

In fact, I still see the same light I saw when I turned my back on the political left and its malevolent agendas 30 years ago. The waste I experienced as an advocate for a bad cause was a bitter one. I had invested my life in a cause that was built on falsehoods and responsible for great evil. But the philosophical conclusions I have come to in my later years are quite different from those regrets. I am proud of what I have done for the conservative cause—for individual liberty and economic freedom, and for the defense of our country. My late-life conclusions are not those of an "apostate" and they are not about politics. They are about life itself. They are a recognition that, in the end, we are all going to disappear along with everything we have known. The entire world we inhabited will vanish. That is the existential truth which is our burden, and there is no way to escape it.

There are two principal ways that human beings deal with this truth, which is the theme of *A Point in Time*. Since, for most of us, a life that is empty of meaning is finally unlivable, we seek a redemption that will make our lives meaningful. One way to do this is to put our fate in the hands of a Creator, who will reveal its sense when our earthly journey is complete. Another is to invest our lives in a movement that promises to redeem this world by instituting social justice. The search for an earthly redemption is what the left is about, and it is the source of the greatest evils of our time. That is what I have learned in my life, and my radical detractors are incapable of understanding it.

16

Peter and Me

It is a real pleasure to be introducing my friend Peter Collier who has written a wonderful book about a remarkable conservative which he has titled, *Political Woman: The Big Little Life of Jeane Kirkpatrick*. Introducing Peter is also a challenge. It is not easy to present briefly someone who has been your closest friend, political ally and working partner for 40 years, let alone do him justice. So I concentrate on two gifts that Peter gave me which changed my life and career, and whose virtues are also evident in his book.

I first encountered Peter—that is the right word—when I was a teaching assistant in a Shakespeare course at the University of California, Berkeley. Peter still remembers the date—it was April 1961. I had just handed back a paper I had graded on *Richard III* when I saw out of the corner of my eye a student who was coming at me as though he was going to hit me. This was my introduction to Peter, who had missed a year of school—we are roughly the same age—and wound up as my student.

The paper had a big "C" on it, actually a C+, and he was not happy. As it happened, the plus reflected my own ambivalence about the grade I had given. It was a very well-written paper and C papers are never well written. But I was less interested in the writing than I was in the content, specifically the answer to the question I had posed when I gave out the assignment, and which I felt

---

This is the text of my introduction at a Wednesday Morning Club event on August 14, 2012 at the Four Seasons Hotel in Los Angeles.

his paper had failed to address. Nonetheless, there was still that literary style that no C student could produce.

To resolve my dilemma and defuse the situation, I suggested that he take his paper to the other teaching assistant for a second opinion and another grade. He took my offer and was given an A, which was a relief to both of us. He paid me back seven years later by mocking what I thought was the high point of my academic career, which was a dramatic lecture—Peter would say melodramatic—on *King Lear*. At the *Ramparts* offices where we were working, Peter would come around a corner and whine, "But I am bound upon a wheel of fire"—one of Lear's lines that I had favored in my lecture.

Peter was already an editor at *Ramparts* when I first arrived at its San Francisco offices in 1968. Improbably, we became office allies and then friends. Our relationship also picked up where we had left off. He became my critic and what I will call my chastener, the more so it seemed the closer we became. And close we did become, first as allies in a struggle to take control of *Ramparts* and then to run it and keep it alive.

We were a *yin* and *yang* couple. Peter had had a harsh childhood that made him skeptical about people, sometimes even cynical, and relentlessly realistic about the consequences one's actions might entail. Although we were both leftists, Peter's outlook was really conservative; he was what I would call an organic conservative. He had that core penchant for pessimism that conservatives do. He was always expecting things to turn out worse than they usually did, and pleasantly surprised when they didn't.

I was Peter's opposite, an optimist and a natural-born believer. I had grown up a sheltered child in a Marxist bubble, and was a dreamer of utopian dreams both personal and global. At the same time my vision was of the tunnel variety; Peter called it autistic. I rarely saw the ditches by the side of the road, while the horizons I contemplated were always bright.

The source of my optimism, which veered on the cockeyed, was my mother who protected and encouraged me. My father was the practical parent with his eye on the ditches. I didn't really appreciate him until I fell into one of those ditches, as it happened a very deep one. In the course of my troubles I consulted a therapist—in fact one whom Peter had recommended and about whom he would write an arresting portrait, published in a collection of "great American stories about therapy" titled *On the Couch.*

The therapist pointed out to me that my father had actually done me a favor by being so critical, by pointing out that life does have its pitfalls—in effect by being the one in the household with a conservative insight. The painful circumstances into which I had fallen, and which culminated in the murder of an innocent woman, now opened my eyes to the possibility that I might be wrong, tragically wrong, in the way I approached the world outside me and understood its actors. That was the conservative turning point in my life.

It also taught me to appreciate Peter, and what he has done for me over time. Peter has always been the harshest of my critics among those who were not motivated by politics to attack me. He was the critic therefore to whom I listened. Peter is my reality-check. And that is his first gift to me.

The second gift is reflected in that plus in the C+ I gave him when he was a student at Berkeley. Peter was always the writer in our partnership. When I first met him, I was a variation of the Jack Carson character in *Arsenic and Old Lace,* the cop who wants to be a playwright and says, "I got great ideas but I can't spell 'em."

Because of my interest in the ruling class, and a famous office-memo I wrote about the Rockefellers, Peter asked me to be his co-author on a biography of the Rockefeller family. I was a Marxist; I had no interest in biography and no idea of how to write one. But I said yes and the collaboration turned out to be a transforming one for me. It was in the course of writing this book and two subsequent biographies of American dynasties that Peter taught me what a narrative was, and what writing was about.

The Rockefeller book became a *New York Times* best-seller, but the lessons I had learned under Peter's sometimes harsh tutelage, and the self-righteous pig-headedness which was my radical birthright, led to a falling-out between us. We didn't speak for two years.

During this time I undertook an inventory of my failures both as an individual and as a missionary. The introspection enabled to me for the first time to listen to others, to appreciate that I might be wrong, and—more painful yet—culpable, which included my relationship with Peter. It was I who finally picked up the phone and called him. We met in a Berkeley coffee-shop and began catching up on what each of us had been doing during the two-year gap, sharing our war stories. And then, just as we were warming up to each other, Peter said from out of the blue: "We're mediocre." I wanted to hit him.

Depressed as I was at this juncture of my life, my delusions of grandeur had not entirely died. My optimism was in my DNA, which is why I needed a reality-checker—why I needed Peter. Peter was still and would always remain the *yin* in our couple, on the lookout for the downside before going forward.

He was and still is a beautiful writer. The biography he has written of Jeane Kirkpatrick is the kind of book, sensitive to character, elegant of style, appreciative of the trials of a human existence, that each of us would like to have written about ourselves.

PART II

Reflections on the Left

I

Goodbye to All That
(co-authored with Peter Collier)

When we tell our old radical friends that we voted for Ronald Reagan last November, the response is usually one of annoyed incredulity. After making sure that we are not putting them on, our old friends make nervous jokes about Jerry Falwell and Phyllis Schlafly, about gods that have failed, about aging yuppies ascending to consumer heaven in their BMWs. We remind them of an old adage: "Anyone under 40 who isn't a socialist has no heart; anyone over 40 who is a socialist has no brain."

Inevitably the talk becomes bitter. One old comrade, after a tirade in which she had denounced us as reactionaries and crypto-fascists, finally sputtered: "The worst thing is that you've turned your back on the Sixties!" That was exactly right. Casting our ballots for Ronald Reagan was indeed a way of finally saying goodbye to all that—to the self-aggrandizing romance with corrupt Third-Worldism; to the casual indulgence of Soviet totalitarianism; to the hypocritical and self-dramatizing anti-Americanism which is the New Left's bequest to mainstream politics.

The instruments of popular culture may perhaps be forgiven for continuing to portray the 1960s as a time of infectious idealism, but those of us who were active then have no excuse for abetting this banality. If in some ways it was the best of times, it was also the worst of times, an era of bloodthirsty fantasies as well as

---

*This article was published as "Lefties for Reagan" in a Sunday edition of *The Washington Post*, March 17, 1985.

spiritual ones. We ourselves experienced both aspects, starting as civil-rights and antiwar activists and ending as co-editors of the New Left magazine *Ramparts*. The magazine post allowed us to write about the rough beast slouching through America and also to urge it on through non-editorial activities we thought of as clandestine until we later read about them in the FBI and CIA files we both accumulated. Like other radicals in those days, we were against electoral politics, regarding voting as one of those charades used by the ruling class to legitimate its power. We were even more against Reagan, then governor of California, having been roughed up by his troopers during the People's Park demonstrations in Berkeley and tear-gassed by his National Guard helicopters during the University of California's Third World Liberation Front Strike. But neither elections nor elected officials seemed particularly important compared with the auguries of revolution the left saw everywhere by the end of the decade—in the way the nefarious Richard Nixon was widening the war in Indochina; in the unprovoked attacks by paramilitary police against the Black Panther Party; in the formation of the Weather Underground, a group willing to pick up the gun or the bomb. It was a time when the apocalypse struggling to be born seemed to need only the slightest assist from the radical midwife.

When we were in the voting-booth this past November—in different precincts but of the same mind—we both thought back to the day in 1969 when Tom Hayden came by the office and, after getting a Ramparts donation to buy gas masks and other combat issue for Black Panther "guerrillas," announced portentously: "Fascism is here, and we're all going to be in jail by the end of the year." We agreed wholeheartedly with this apocalyptic vision and in fact had just written in an editorial: "The system cannot be revitalized. It must be overthrown. As humanely as possible, but by any means necessary."

Every thought and perception in those days was filtered through the dark and distorting glass of the Vietnam War. The left was hooked on Vietnam. It was an addictive drug whose rush was a potent mix of melodrama, self-importance and moral rectitude. Vietnam was a universal solvent—the explanation for every evil we saw and the justification for every excess we committed. Trashing the windows of merchants on the main streets of America seemed warranted by the notion that these petty-bourgeois shopkeepers were cogs in the system of capitalist exploitation that was obliterating Vietnam. Fantasizing the death of local cops seemed warranted by the role they played as an occupying army in America's black ghettos, those mini-Vietnams we yearned to see explode in domestic wars of liberation. Vietnam caused us to acquire a new appreciation for foreign tyrants like Kim Il Sung of North Korea.[1] Vietnam also caused us to support the domestic extortionism and violence of groups like the Black Panthers, and to dismiss derisively Martin Luther King, Jr. as an "Uncle Tom." (The left has conveniently forgotten this fact now that it finds it expedient to invoke King's name and reputation to further its domestic politics.)

How naive was the New Left can be debated, but by the end of the 1960s we were not political novices. We knew that bad news from Southeast Asia—the reports of bogged-down campaigns and the weekly body-counts announced by Walter Cronkite—was good for the radical agenda. The more repressive our government in dealing with dissent at home, the more recruits for our cause and the sooner the appearance of the revolutionary Armageddon.

Our assumption that Vietnam would be the political and moral fulcrum by which we would tip this country toward revolution foresaw every possibility except one: that the United States would pull out. Never had we thought that the United States, the arch-imperial power, would of its own volition withdraw from Indochina. This

---

[1]Peter and I were not enthusiasts of Kim Il Sung (even if our *Ramparts* editor-in-chief Robert Scheer was). Nor did we share all of the New-Left attitudes summarized in this paragraph. In making our statements, we simply felt we should step up and own these kinds of excesses on behalf of the many in our generation, including ourselves, who had committed them.

development violated a primary article of our hand-me-down Marxism: that political action through normal channels could not alter the course of the war. The system we had wanted to overthrow worked tardily and only at great cost, but it worked.

When American troops finally came home, some of us took the occasion to begin a long and painful reexamination of our political assumptions and beliefs. Others did not. For the diehards, there was a post-Vietnam syndrome in its own way as debilitating as that suffered by people who had fought there—a sense of emptiness rather than exhilaration, a paradoxical desire to hold onto and breathe life back into the experience that had been their high for so many years.

As the post-Vietnam decade progressed, the diehards on the left ignored conclusions about the viability of democratic traditions that might have been drawn from America's exit from Vietnam and from the Watergate crisis that followed it—a time when the man whose ambitions they had feared most was removed from office by a constitutional process rather than by a coup. The only lessons of Vietnam that seemed to interest the left were those that emphasized the danger of American power abroad and the need to diminish it, a view that was injected into the Democratic Party with the triumph of the McGovern wing. The problem with this use of Vietnam as a moral text for American policy was that the pages following the fall of Saigon had been whited out.

No lesson, for instance, was seen in Hanoi's ruthless conquest of the South, the establishment of a police-state in Saigon and the political oblivion of the National Liberation Front, whose struggle we on the left had so passionately supported. It was not that credible information was lacking. Jean Lacouture wrote in 1976: "Never before have we had such proof of so many detained after a war. Not in Moscow in 1917. Not in Madrid in 1939, not in Paris and Rome in 1944, nor in Havana in 1959...." But this eminent French journalist, who had been regarded as something of an oracle when he was reporting America's derelictions during the war, was now dismissed as a "sellout."

In 1977, when some former antiwar activists signed an Appeal to the Conscience of Vietnam because of the more than 200,000 prisoners languishing in "reeducation centers" and a new round of self-immolations by Buddhist monks, they were chastised by activist David Dellinger, Institute for Policy Studies fellow Richard Barnet and other keepers of the flame in a *New York Times* advertisement that said in part: "The present government of Vietnam should be hailed for its moderation and for its extraordinary effort to achieve reconciliation among all of its people."

When tens of thousands of unreconciled "boat people" began to flee the repression of their Communist rulers, Joan Baez and others who spoke out in their behalf were attacked for breaking ranks with Hanoi.

Something might also have been learned from the fate of wretched Cambodia. But leftists seemed so addicted to finding an American cause at the root of every problem that they couldn't recognize indigenous evils. As the Khmer Rouge were about to take over, Noam Chomsky wrote that their advent heralded a Cambodian liberation, "a new era of economic development and social justice." The new era turned out to be the killing-fields that took the lives of two million Cambodians.

Finally, Vietnam emerged as an imperialist power, taking control of Laos, invading Cambodia and threatening Thailand. But in a recent editorial *The Nation* explains that the Vietnamese invaded Cambodia "to stop the killing and restore some semblance of civilized government to the devastated country." This bloody occupation, *The Nation* says, is actually a "rescue mission," and what has happened should not "obscure the responsibility of the United States for the disasters in Indochina," disasters that are being caused by our playing the "China card" and refusing to normalize relations with Vietnam. These acts on the part of the United States "make Vietnamese withdrawal from Cambodia unlikely;" only the White House can "remove the pressures on Vietnam from all sides [that] would bring peace to a ravaged land." Such reasoning recalls the wonderful line from the Costa-Gavras film *Z*: "Always blame the Americans. Even when you're wrong, you're right."

Another unacknowledged lesson from Indochina involves the way in which Vietnam has become a satellite of the Soviet Union: paying for foreign aid by sending labor-brigades to its benefactor. This development doesn't mesh well with the left's ongoing romantic vision of Hanoi. It also threatens the left's obstinate refusal to admit that during the mid-70s—a time when American democracy was trying to heal itself from the twin traumas of the war and Watergate—the U.S.S.R. was demonstrating that totalitarianism abhors a vacuum by moving into Africa, Central America, Southeast Asia and elsewhere. Instead of reevaluating the Soviets because of change in what we used to call "the objective conditions," the left rationalizes Soviet aggression as the spasms of a petrified bureaucracy whose policies are annoying mainly because they distract attention from U.S. malfeasance around the world.

If they were capable of looking intently at the Soviet Union, leftists and liberals alike would have to concur with Susan Sontag's contention—which many of them jeered at when she announced it—that communism is simply left-wing fascism.

One of the reasons the left has been so cautious in its reassessments of the Soviets is the fiction that the U.S.S.R. is on the side of history. This assumption is echoed in Fred Halliday's euphoric claim, in a recent issue of *New Left Review*, that Soviet support was crucial to 14 Third World revolutions during the era of "détente"—including such triumphs of human progress as Iran and South Yemen—and in Andrew Kopkind's fatuous observation that "the Soviet Union has almost always sided with the revolutionists, the liberationists, the insurgents." In Ethiopia? Propped up by 20,000 Cuban legionnaires, the Marxist government of Mengistu Haile Mariam has as its main accomplishment a "Red Campaign of Terror" (its official designation) that killed thousands of people. Where were those who cheer the Soviets' work in behalf of the socialist *Zeitgeist* when this episode took place? Or this past fall, when the Marxist liberator squandered more than $40 million on a party celebrating the tenth anniversary of his murderous rule while his people starved? Where were they to point out the moral when capitalist America rushed in 250 million metric tons of grain to help allay the Ethiopian starvation, while the Soviets were managing to contribute only ten million? Where are they now that Mengistu withholds emergency food supplies from the starving provinces of Eritrea and Tigre, because the people there are in rebellion against his tyranny?

Reagan is often upbraided for having described the Soviet Union as an evil empire. Those opposed to this term seem to be offended esthetically rather than politically. Just how wide of the mark is the president? Oppressing an array of nationalities whose populations far outnumber its own, Russia is the last of the old European empires, keeping in subjugation not only formerly independent states such as Estonia, Latvia and Lithuania—Hitler's gift to Stalin—but also the nations of Eastern Europe. Every country "liberated" into the Soviet bloc has been transformed into a national prison, where the borders are guarded to keep the inmates in rather than the foreigners out.

The war in Afghanistan is much more a metaphor for the Soviets' view of the world than Vietnam ever was for America's. Of the approximately 16 million people living in Afghanistan at the time of the Soviet invasion, an estimated one million have already been killed and wounded. There are now about four million refugees, a figure that does not include "internal" refugees—the hundreds of thousands of villagers forced to leave their scorched earth for the Soviet-controlled big cities, the only places where food is available. Or the thousands of Afghan children who been taken to the Soviet Union to be "educated" and who will eventually be returned to their native land as spies and quislings.

Soviet strategy is based on a brutal rejoinder to Mao's poetic notion—which we old New Leftists used to enjoy citing—about guerrillas as fish swimming in a sea of popular support. The Soviet solution is to boil the sea and drain it, leaving the fish exposed and gasping on barren land. The Russian presence is characterized by systematic destruction of crops and medical facilities, indiscriminate terror against the civilian population, carpet-bombings and the deadly "yellow rain" that even the leftist Peoples' Tribunal in Paris—successor to the Bertrand Russell War Crimes Tribunal—has said is being used in Afghanistan.

During each December anniversary of the Soviet invasion, when liberal politicians rediscover the *mujahedin* guerrillas in the hills after eleven months of moral amnesia, there are blithe references to Afghanistan as "Russia's Vietnam." Those who invoke the analogy seem to think that simply by doing so they have doomed the Russian stormtroopers to defeat. But this analogy is based on a misunderstanding of what Vietnam was and what Afghanistan is. Unlike America's high-tech television war, Afghanistan is one of those old-fashioned encounters that take place in the dark. The Soviets make no attempt to win hearts and minds; the My Lais that are daily occurrences there cause no shock because they do not appear on Moscow TV; there are no scenes of the peasant children whose hands and faces have been destroyed by antipersonnel bombs in the shapes of toy trucks and butterflies that the Soviets have strewn over the Afghan countryside; there are no images of body-bags being offloaded from Soviet transports. Because there is no media coverage, there can be no growing revulsion on the home front, no protests on Soviet campuses and in Soviet streets, no clamor to bring the boys home.

Afghanistan is not the Soviets' Vietnam for another reason. Not only are the Soviet people kept from seeing the atrocities their government has committed; the rest of the world is blacked out too. At the height of the Vietnam War there was a noncombatant army of foreign journalists present to witness its conduct. In Afghanistan they are forbidden, as are the Red Cross and all other international relief agencies that were integral to what happened in Vietnam. Without those witnesses, Afghanistan is a matter of "out of sight, out of mind." In Vietnam we waged a war against ourselves and lost. The Soviets will not let that happen to them. The truth of the Vietnam analogy is not that guerrillas must inevitably bog down and defeat a superior force of invaders, but that a war against indigenous forces by a superpower can be won if it is waged against a backdrop of international ignorance and apathy. The proper analogy for Afghanistan is not Vietnam at all but rather 1930s Spain—not in the nature of the war, but in the symbolic value it has for our time, or should have, in terms of democracy's will to resist aggression. Aid to the mujahedin should not be a dirty little secret of the CIA but a matter of public policy and national honor.

Perhaps the leading feature of the left today is the moral selectivity that French social critic Jean-François Revel has identified as "the syndrome of the cross-eyed left." Leftists can describe Vietnam's conquest and colonization of Cambodia as a "rescue mission," while reviling Ronald Reagan for applying the same term to the Grenada operation, although better than 90 percent of the island's population told independent pollsters they were grateful for the arrival of U.S. troops. Forgetting for a moment that Afghanistan is "Russia's Vietnam," leftists call Grenada "America's Afghanistan," although people in Afghanistan—as one member of the resistance there told us—would literally die for the elections held in Grenada.

The left's memory can be as selective as its morality. When it comes to past commitments that have failed, the leftist mentality is utterly unable to produce a coherent balance-sheet, let alone a profit-and-loss statement. The attitude toward Soviet penetration of the Americas is a good example. Current enthusiasm for the Sandinista regime in Nicaragua should recall to those of us old enough to remember a previous enthusiasm for Cuba 25 years ago. Many of us began our New Leftism with the Fair Play for Cuba demonstrations. We raised our voices and chanted, "Cuba Si! Yanqui No!" We embraced Fidel Castro not only because of the flamboyant personal style of the *barbudos* of his 26th of July Movement but also because Castro assured the world that his revolution belonged to neither Communists nor capitalists, that it was neither red nor black but Cuban olive-green.

We attributed Castro's expanding links with Moscow to the U.S.-sponsored invasion of the Bay of Pigs, and then to the "secret war" waged against Cuba by U.S. intelligence and paramilitary organizations. But while Castro's apologists in the United States may find it expedient to maintain these fictions, Carlos Franqui and other old Fidelistas now in exile have made it clear that Castro embraced the Soviets even before the U.S. hostility became decisive, and that he steered his country into the Soviet bloc with considerable enthusiasm. Before the Bay of Pigs he put a Soviet general in charge of Cuban forces. Before the Bay of Pigs he destroyed Cuba's democratic trade-union movement, although its elected leadership was drawn from his own 26th of July Movement. He did so because he knew that the Stalinists of Cuba's Communist Party would be dependable cheerleaders and efficient policemen of his emerging dictatorship.

A symbolic event along the way that many of us missed was Castro's imprisonment of his old comrade Huber Matos, liberator of Matanzas province and one of the four key military leaders of the revolution. Matos's crime: criticizing the growing influence of Cuban Communists, thereby jeopardizing Castro's plans to use them as his palace-guard. Matos's sentence: 20 years in a four-by-eleven-foot concrete box. Given such a precedent, how can we fail to support Edén Pastora for taking up arms against early signs of similar totalitarianism in Nicaragua?

What has come of Cuba's revolution to break the chains of American imperialism? Soviets administer the still one-crop Cuban economy; Soviets train the Cuban army; and Soviet subsidies, fully one-quarter of Cuba's gross national product, prevent the Cuban treasury from going broke. Before the revolution there were more than 35 independent newspapers and radio stations in Havana. Now, there is only the official voice of *Granma*, the Cuban *Pravda*, and a handful of other outlets spouting the same party line. Today Cuba is a more abject and deformed colony of the Soviet empire than it ever was of America. The arch-rebel of our youth, Fidel Castro, has become a party hack who cheerfully endorsed the rape of Czechoslovakia in 1968 and endorses the ongoing plunder of Afghanistan today—an aging pimp who sells his young men to the Russians for use in their military adventures in return for $10 billion a year.

In leftist circles, of course, such arguments are anathema, and no historical precedent, however daunting, can prevent outbreaks of radical chic. That perennial delinquent Abbie Hoffman will lead his Potemkin-village tours of Managua. The Hollywood stars will dish up Nicaraguan president Daniel Ortega as an exotic *hors d'oeuvre* on the Beverly Hills cocktail circuit. In the self-righteous moral glow accompanying such gatherings, it will be forgotten that, through the offices of the U.S. government, more economic and military aid was provided the Sandinistas in the first 18 months following their takeover than was given to Somoza in the previous 20 years, and that this aid was cut off primarily because of clear signs that political pluralism in Nicaragua was being terminated.

Adherents of today's version of radical chic may never take seriously the words of Sandinista directorate member Bayardo Arce when he says that elections are a "hindrance" to the goal of "a dictatorship of the proletariat" and necessary only "as an expedient to deprive our enemies of an argument." They will ignore former Sandinista hero and now *contra* leader Edén Pastora who sees the junta as traitors who have sold out the revolutionary dream: "Now that we are occupied by foreign forces from Cuba and Russia, now that we are governed by a dictatorial government of nine men, now more than ever the [anti-]Sandinista struggle is justified." They will ignore opposition leader Arturo Cruz, an early supporter of the Sandinista revolution and previously critical of the contras, when the worsening situation makes him change his mind and ask the Reagan administration to support the *contras* in a statement that should have the same weight as Andrei Sakharov's plea to the West to match the Soviet arms buildup.

American leftists propose solutions for the people of Central America that they wouldn't dare propose for themselves. These armchair revolutionaries project their self-hatred and their contempt for the privileges of democracy—which allow them to live well and to think badly—onto people who would be only too grateful for the luxuries they disdain. Dismissing "bourgeois" rights as a decadent frill that the peoples of the Third World can't afford, leftists spread-eagle the Central Americans between dictators of the right and dictators of the left. The latter, of course, are their chosen instruments for bringing social justice and economic well-being, although no leftist revolution has yet provided impressive returns in either area,, and most have made the lives of their people considerably more wretched than they were before.

Voting is symbolic behavior, a way of evaluating what one's country has been as well as what it might become. We do not accept Reagan's policies chapter-and-verse—especially in domestic policy, which we haven't discussed here—but we agree with his vision of the world as a place increasingly inhospitable to democracy and increasingly dangerous for America.

One of the few saving-graces of age is a deeper perspective on the passions of youth. Looking back on the left's revolutionary enthusiasms of the last 25 years, we have painfully learned what should have been obvious all along: we live in an imperfect world that is bettered only with great difficulty and easily made worse—much worse. This is a conservative assessment, but on the basis of half a lifetime's experience it seems about right.

2

My Vietnam Lessons

When I see today's protesters in the flush of youthful idealism with their signs proclaiming "No Vietnams in Central America," a feeling of ineffable sadness overtakes me. For 20 years ago I was one of them. In 1962, as a graduate student at Berkeley, I wrote the first book of New Left protest, *Student,* and helped to organize perhaps the first anti-war demonstration opposing what we denounced as U.S. intervention in Vietnam. In the mid-Sixties I went to England and helped to organize the Vietnam Solidarity Campaign, which supported what we called the Vietnamese struggle for independence from the United States, as well as the International War Crimes Tribunal, which brought American war atrocities under intense and damning scrutiny but ignored atrocities committed by Communist forces in Vietnam. While in England I also wrote *The Free World Colossus,* a New Left history of the Cold War, which was used as a radical text in colleges and in the growing movement against the Vietnam War. At the end of the Sixties I returned to America as an editor of *Ramparts,* the most widely read New Left magazine. Our most famous cover appeared during Richard Nixon's campaign in 1972 for a second term. It featured a photograph of the My Lai massacre with a sign superimposed and planted among the corpses, saying "Re-Elect the President."

This was a speech to a congressional seminar on the tenth anniversary of the fall of Saigon, April 10, 1985.

Let me make this perfectly clear. Those of us who inspired and then led the antiwar movement did not want just to stop the killing, as so many veterans of those domestic battles now claim. We wanted the Communists to win. It is true that some of us may have said we only wanted the United States to get out of Vietnam, but we understood that this meant the Communists would win. "Bring the troops home" was our slogan; the fall of Saigon was the result.

There was a political force in American life that did want a peace, which would not also mean a Communist victory—a peace that would deny Hanoi its conquest and preserve the integrity of South Vietnam. That force was led by our archenemy, President Richard Nixon, whose campaign slogans were "Peace with Honor" in Vietnam and "Law and Order" at home. But we did not want "honor" because that meant preserving the government of South Vietnam; and we did not respect "law and order" because respecting the democratic process would have meant that the majority in America, who supported President Nixon and South Vietnam, would have prevailed.

Like today's young radicals, we Sixties activists had a double standard when it came to making moral and political judgments. We judged other countries and political movements—meaning socialist countries and revolutionary movements—by the futures we imagined they could have if only the United States and its allies would get out of their way. We judged America, on the other hand, by its actual performance, which we held up to a standard of high and even impossible ideals. Of course, if we had been able to look at the facts we would have seen that America was more tolerant, more democratic, and more open to change than the countries and movements to whom we gave our support. But we were unable to do that. We were, in the then-fashionable term, "alienated" from what was near to us, unable to judge it objectively.

Some of this alienation—a perennial and essential ingredient of all political leftism—could be attributed to youth itself, the feeling that we could understand the world better and accomplish more than our elders could. But there was another dimension to our disaffection, an ideology that committed us to "truths" behind the common-sense surface of things. Like most of the left's leaders, I was a Marxist and a socialist. I believed in the "dialectic" of history and therefore, even though I knew that the societies calling themselves Marxist were ruled by ruthless dictatorships, I believed they would soon evolve into socialist democracies. I attributed their negative features to under-development and to the capitalist pasts from which they had emerged. I believed that Marxist economic planning was the most rational solution to their underdevelopment and would soon bring them unparalleled prosperity—an idea refuted as dramatically by the experience of the last 70 years as the ancillary notion that private property is the source of all tyranny and that socialist states would soon become free. (They might become free, but only by giving up their socialist delusions.) The same Marxist analysis told me that America, however amenable to reform in the past, was set on a course that would make it increasingly rigid, repressive, and ultimately fascist. The United States was the leviathan of a global imperialist system under attack at home and abroad. Its ruling class could not afford to retreat from this challenge; it could only grow more reactionary and repressive.

Those expectations, wrong in every respect, were not an idiosyncratic theory of mine but the core of the New Left's view of the world generally and of its opposition to America's Vietnam War in particular. The New Left believed that in Vietnam America's corporate liberal empire had reached a point of no return. As a result, electoral politics and any effort to reform them were futile and counterproductive. The only way to alter America's imperial course was to take to the streets—first to organize resistance to the war and then to liberate ourselves from the corporate capitalist system. That was why we were in the streets in the first place, and why we did not take a hard stand against the bomb-throwers in our midst.

What took place that changed my views and gave me second thoughts? As our opposition to the war grew more violent and our prophecies of impending fascism more intense, I took note of how we were actually being treated by the system we condemned. By the decade's end we had deliberately crossed the line of legitimate dissent and abused every First Amendment privilege and right reserved to us as Americans. While American boys were dying overseas, we spat on the flag, broke the law, denigrated and disrupted the institutions of government and education, gave comfort and aid, even revealing classified secrets, to the enemy. Some of us, like Tom Hayden and Jane Fonda, provided a protective propaganda shield for Hanoi's Communist regime while it tortured American war-prisoners; others engaged in violent sabotage against the war effort. All the time I thought to myself: If we did this in any other country, the very least of our punishments would be long prison terms and the pariah status of traitors. In any of the socialist countries we supported—from Cuba to North Vietnam—we would spend most of our lives in jail and, more probably, be shot.

What actually happened to us in repressive, capitalist America? Here and there our wrists were slapped—some of us went to trial, some spent months in jail—but basically the country tolerated us. And listened to us. We began as a peripheral minority, but as the war dragged on without an end in sight, people joined us: first in thousands and then in tens of thousands, swelling our ranks until finally we reached the conscience of the nation. America itself became troubled about its presence in Vietnam, about the justice and morality of the war it had gone there to fight. And because the nation became so troubled, it lost its will to continue the war and withdrew.

Out the window for me went all those pre-conceptions we had had about the rigidity of American politics, about the controlled capitalist media, which, in fact, provided the data that fueled our attacks on the war, and about the ruling-class stranglehold on American foreign policy. That policy had shown itself in its most critical dimension responsive to the will of ordinary people and to their sense of justice and morality. As something of a historian, I believe I am correct in my judgment that America's withdrawal from the battlefront in Vietnam because of domestic opposition is unique in human history. I know no other case on record of a major power retreating from a war in response to the moral opposition of its own citizenry.

If America's response to this test of fire gave me an entirely new understanding of American institutions and of the culture of democracy that informed and supported them, the aftermath of the U.S. retreat gave me a new appreciation of the Communist adversary. America not only withdrew its forces from Vietnam, as we on the left had said it could never do, but from Laos and Cambodia and, ultimately, from its role as guardian of the international status-quo. But far from increasing the freedom and wellbeing of Third World nations, as we on the left had predicted, America's withdrawal resulted in an international power-vacuum that was quickly filled by the armies of Russia, Cuba, and the mass-murderers of the Khmer Rouge, not to mention the non-Communist but no less bloodthirsty fanatics of revolutionary Islam. All this bloodshed and misery was the direct result of America's post-Vietnam withdrawal, the end of *Pax Americana*, which we had ardently desired and helped to bring about.

In Vietnam itself, the war's aftermath showed beyond any doubt that the struggle there was not ultimately to achieve or prevent self-determination but—as various presidents had said and we denied—a Communist conquest of the South. Today the National Liberation Front of South Vietnam, whose cause we supported, no longer exists. Its leaders are dead, in detention camps, under house arrest, in exile, powerless. America left Vietnam ten years ago; but today Hanoi's army is the fourth-largest in the world, while Vietnam has emerged as a Soviet satellite and imperialist aggressor in its own right, subverting the independence of Laos, invading and colonizing Cambodia.

Those events confronted me with a supreme irony: the nation I had believed to be governed by corporate interests, a fountainhead of world reaction, was halted in mid-course by its conscience-stricken and morally aroused populace; the forces I had identified with progress, once freed from the grip of U.S. "imperialism," revealed themselves to be oppressive, unspeakably ruthless and predatory. I was left with this question: What true friend of the South Vietnamese, or the Cambodians, or the Ethiopians, or the Afghans, would not wish that *Pax Americana* were still in force?

There was yet another Vietnam lesson for me when I pondered the question put by Jeane Kirkpatrick to the still-active veterans of the New Left: "How can it be that persons so deeply committed to the liberation of South Vietnam and Cambodia from Generals Thieu and Lon Nol were so little affected by the enslavement that followed their liberation? Why was there so little anguish among the American accomplices who helped Pol Pot to power?" Indeed, why have those passionate advocates of Third World liberation not raised their voices in protest over the rape of Afghanistan or the Cuban-abetted slaughter in Ethiopia?

Not only has the left failed to make a cause of those Marxist atrocities; it has failed to consider the implications of what we now know about Hanoi's role in South Vietnam's so-called "civil war." For North Vietnam's victors have boldly acknowledged that early in the war they had intruded even more regular troops into the South than was claimed by the Lyndon Johnson's White Paper that had been used to justify America's original commitment of military forces—a White Paper that we leftists had scorned as a fiction based on anti-Communist paranoia and deception. But today's left is too busy denigrating Ronald Reagan's White Papers on Soviet and Cuban intervention in Central America to consider the implications of the past.

My experience has convinced me that historical ignorance and moral blindness are endemic to the American left, necessary conditions of its existence. The left does not value the bounty it actually has in this country. In the effort to achieve a historically bankrupt fantasy called "socialism," it undermines the very privileges and rights it is the first to claim. The lesson I learned from Vietnam was not a lesson in theory but a lesson in practice.

Observing this nation go through its worst historical hour from a vantage point on the other side of the barricade, I came to understand that democratic values are easily lost and, as history attests, only rarely achieved; that America is a precious gift, a unique presence in the world of nations. Because it is the strongest of the few democratic societies that mankind has managed to create, it is also a fortress that stands between the free nations of the world and the dark, totalitarian forces that threaten to engulf them.

My values have not changed, but my sense of what supports and makes them possible has. I no longer can join "antiwar" movements that seek to disarm the Western democracies in the face of the danger that confronts them. I support the current efforts of America's leadership to rebuild our dangerously weakened military defenses; and I endorse the conservative argument that America needs to be vigilant, strong, and clear of purpose in its life-and-death struggle with its global totalitarian enemies. As an ex-radical, I would only add that in this struggle Americans need to respect and encourage their own generosity—their tolerance for internal dissent and their willingness to come to the aid of people who are fighting for their freedom.

3

Semper *Fidel*

Twenty-five years ago, as one of the founders of the New Left, I was an organizer of the first political demonstrations on this Berkeley campus—and indeed on any campus—to protest our government's anti-Communist policies in Cuba and Vietnam. Tonight, I come before you as a man I used to tell myself I would never be: a supporter of President Reagan, a committed opponent of Communist rule in Nicaragua. I make no apologies for my present position. It was what I believed to be the humanity of the Marxist idea that made me what I was then; it is the inhumanity of what I have seen to be the Marxist reality that has made me what I am now. If my former comrades who support the Sandinista cause were to pause for a moment and then plunge their busy political minds into the human legacies of their activist pasts, they would instantly drown in an ocean of blood.

The real issue before us is not whether it is morally right for the United States to arm the anti-Sandinista *contras,* or whether there are unpleasant men among them. The issue before us and before all people who cherish freedom is how to oppose a Soviet imperialism so vicious and so vast as to dwarf any previously known. An "ocean of blood" is no metaphor. As we speak here tonight, this empire—whose axis runs through Havana and now Managua—is killing hundreds of thousands of Ethiopians to

---

This was a speech given at a debate on Nicaragua at the University of California at Berkeley, April 4, 1986 and published in *Commentary,* June 1986.

consolidate a dictatorship whose policies against its black citizens make the South African government look civilized and humane.

There is another issue at stake here, especially important to me: the credibility and commitment of the American left, whose attitudes to American power have gained a far-reaching influence since the end of the Vietnam War. In his speech on Nicaragua, President Reagan rightly invoked the precedent of the Truman Doctrine, the first attempt to oppose Soviet expansion through revolutionary surrogates in Greece. The first protest of my radical life was against the Truman Doctrine in a May Day march in 1948. I was with the left defending revolutions in Russia and China, in Eastern Europe and Cuba, in Cambodia and Vietnam—just as the left defends the Sandinistas now. And I remember clearly the arguments with which we made our case in forums like this, and what the other side said, too—the presidents who came and went, and the anti-Communists on the right, the William Buckleys and the Ronald Reagans. And, in every case, without exception, time has proven the left *wrong*—tragically and destructively wrong—wrong in its views of the revolutionaries' intentions and wrong about the facts of their revolutionary rule. And just as consistently, the anti-Communists have been proven right.

Just as the left now dismisses the president's warnings about Soviet expansion—calling them anti-Communist paranoia, a threat to peace, a mask for American imperialism—so we attacked President Truman as a warmonger and aggressor then. Russia's control of Eastern Europe, we said, was only a defensive buffer, a temporary response to American power; first because Russia had no nuclear weapons, and then because it lacked the missiles to deliver them. Today the Soviet Union is a nuclear superpower, missiles and all, but it has not given up an inch of the empire it gained during the Second World War—not Eastern Europe; not the Baltic states that Hitler delivered to Stalin, whose nationhood Stalin erased and which are now all but forgotten; not even the Kurile islands that were once part of Japan.

Not only have the Soviets failed to relinquish their conquests in all these years—years of dramatic, total decolonization in the West—but their growing strength and the wounds of Vietnam, a scab liberals and leftists continue to pick, have encouraged them to reach for more. South Vietnam, Cambodia, Laos, Ethiopia, Yemen, Mozambique, and Angola are among the nations that have recently fallen into the Soviet orbit. To expand their territorial core—which their apologists still call a "defensive perimeter"— Moscow has already slaughtered a million peasants in Afghanistan, an atrocity warmly endorsed by the Sandinista government. Its Minister of Defense, Humberto Ortega, describes the army of the conquerors, whose scorched-earth policy has driven half the population of Afghanistan from its homes, as the "pillar of peace" in the world today. To any self-respecting socialist, praise for such barbarism would be an inconceivable outrage, as it was to the former Sandinista, now *contra*, Edén Pastora. But praise for the barbarians is sincere tribute coming from the Sandinista rulers, who see themselves as an integral part of the Soviet empire.

"The struggle of man against power is the struggle of memory against forgetting." So wrote the Czech writer Milan Kundera, whose name and work no longer exist in his homeland. In all the Americas, Fidel Castro was the only head of state to cheer the Russian tanks as they rolled over the brave people of Prague. Cheering right along with Fidel were Carlos Fonseca, Tomás Borge, Humberto Ortega and the other creators of the present Nicaraguan regime. One way to assess what has happened in Nicaragua is to realize that wherever Soviet tanks crush freedom in the future, there will now be two governments in the Americas supporting them all the way—Cuba, where Castro sells his young men as Soviet legionnaires for billions of dollars a year, and Nicaragua, whose time to provide Soviet conscripts for empire will come, if and when the American left manages to cut the *contras* adrift.

Memory against power: about its own crimes and for its own criminals the left has no memory at all, which is the only reason it can wag its finger at President Reagan and the anti-Communist Right. In the eyes of the left in which I grew up, as well as in those of the Sandinista founders, Stalin's Russia was a socialist paradise, the model of mankind's liberated future: Literacy to the uneducated, power to the weak, justice to the forgotten. We praised Russia then, just as the left praises the Sandinistas now. And just as they ignore warnings like Violeta Chamorro's—"With all my heart, I tell you it is worse here now than it was in the times of the Somoza dictatorship"—so we dismissed as anti-Soviet lies the testimonies about Stalinist repression.

In the society we hailed as a new human dawn, tens of millions of people were confined in slave-labor camps, in conditions rivaling Auschwitz and Buchenwald. Between 30 and 40 million people were killed, in peacetime, in the daily routine of socialist rule. While leftists applauded the Soviet Union's progressive policies and guarded its frontiers, Soviet Marxists killed more peasants, more workers, and even more Communists than all the capitalist governments together since the beginning of time. And for the entire duration of this nightmare, the William Buckleys and Ronald Reagans and other anti-Communists went on telling the world exactly what was happening. And all that time the pro-Soviet left and its fellow travelers went on denouncing them as reactionaries and liars, using the same contemptuous terms with which the left attacks the president today.

In fact, the left would *still* be denying the Soviet atrocities if the perpetrators themselves had not finally acknowledged their crimes. In 1956, in a secret speech to the party elite, Khrushchev made the crimes a Communist fact; but it was only the CIA that actually made the crimes public, allowing radicals to come to terms with what they had done. Khrushchev and his cohorts could not have cared less about the misplaced faiths and misspent lives of their naive supporters on the left. The Soviet rulers were concerned about themselves. Stalin's mania had spread the slaughter into their own ranks. His henchmen wanted to make totalitarianism safe for its rulers—Stalinism without Stalin. In place of a dictator whose paranoia could not be controlled, they instituted a dictatorship by directorate, which not coincidentally is the form of rule in Nicaragua today. In the future, Soviet repression would work one way only: from the privileged top of society to the powerless bottom.

The year 1956, which is the year Soviet tanks flattened the freedom-fighters of Budapest, tells us who the Sandinistas really are. In that year, the Khrushchev Report made the facts about the Stalin era unavoidable, even for the faithful, and the left all over the world was forced to redefine itself in relation to the truth. China's Communist leader, Mao, decided he liked Stalin's way better. As a result of Mao's sinister folly, 25 million people died in the "great leaps" and "cultural revolutions" he then launched. But in Europe and America a new anti-Stalinist left was born. This "New Left," of which I was one of the founders, was repelled by the evils it was now forced to see, and embarrassed by the tarnish the totalitarians had brought to the socialist cause. It turned its back on the Soviet model of Stalin and his heirs.

In Nicaragua, however, the Sandinista vanguard was neither embarrassed nor repelled. The following year, 1957, Carlos Fonseca, the revered founding father of the Sandinista Front, visited Russia and its new and improved totalitarian state. To Fonseca, as to Borge and his other comrades, the Soviet monstrosity was their revolutionary dream come true. In his pamphlet *A Nicaraguan in Moscow,* Fonseca proclaimed Soviet Communism his model for Latin America's revolutionary future. A second step in this vision of a Communist America is now being realized in Nicaragua. The *comandante* directorate, the army and the secret police are already mirrors of the Soviet state, not only structurally but in their personnel, which is trained and often manned by agents of the Soviet axis.

Yet the most important figure in this transformation is not a Nicaraguan at all but Cuba's first Communist, Fidel Castro. From 1959, when Carlos Fonseca and Tomas Borge arrived in Havana, and for 20 years after, the Sandinista leaders became disciples of

Fidel and with his blessings went on to Moscow, where Stalin's henchman completed their revolutionary course. Humberto Ortega, Daniel's less visible but more important brother, is Fidel's personal protégé. Humberto is the author of the *tercerista* strategy, which allied their minuscule sect to a coalition of democrats contending for power. Fidel is not only the image in which the Sandinista leadership has created itself and the author of its victorious strategy; he is the architect of its politburo, the *comandante* directorate. The directorate was personally created by Fidel in Havana on the eve of the final struggle, sealed with a pledge of military aid against the Somoza regime. Without Castro's intervention, Arturo Cruz and the other anti-Somoza, pro-democratic *contras* would be the government of Nicaragua today. It was Fidel who showed the Sandinistas how to steal the revolution after its victory and how to secure their theft by manipulating their most important allies: the American left and its liberal sympathizers.

Twenty-five years ago, when the Sandinistas began their apprenticeship, Fidel was our revolutionary hero. Like today's campus radicals, some of us became "coffee-pickers" and passengers on the revolutionary tour. We wrote glowingly about literacy campaigns, health clinics, and other wonders of the new world a-coming. When Fidel spoke, his words were revolutionary music to our ears. "Freedom with bread. Bread without terror." "A revolution neither red nor black but Cuban olive-green." And so in Managua today: "Not Communism but Nicaraguan *Sandinismo*" is the formula his imitators proclaim.

So persuasive were Fidel's political poems that radicals all over the world fell under his spell. Jean-Paul Sartre wrote one of the first and most influential books admiring the new leader: "If this man asked me for the moon," the philosopher wrote, "I would give it to him. Because he would have a need for it."

When I listen to today's enthusiasts for the Sandinista redeemers with their scorn for the contra rebels, the fate of a *fidelista* hero comes to my mind: one of the liberators of Cuba, whose role in the revolution was the equal of Che Guevara's. For in the year that Jean-Paul Sartre came to Havana and fell in love with the humanitarian Fidel, Huber Matos embarked on a long, windowless night of the soul.

Huber Matos's fate came to pass with Fidel's second revolution. All the fine gestures and words with which Fidel had seduced us and won our support—the open Marxism, the socialist humanism, the independent path—were calculated lies. For even as he proclaimed his color to be olive-green, he was planning to make his revolution Moscow-red. So cynical was Fidel's strategy that at the time it was difficult for many to comprehend. One by one Fidel removed his own comrades from the revolutionary regime and replaced them with Cuban Communists. At the time, the Communists were a party in disgrace. They had opposed the revolution; they had even served in the cabinet of the tyrant Batista while the revolution was taking place. But this was all incidental to Fidel. Fidel knew how to use people. And Fidel was planning a *new* revolution that he could trust the Communists to support. He had decided to turn Cuba into a Soviet state. Moreover, Fidel also knew that he could no longer trust his *fidelista* comrades, because they had made a revolution they thought was going to be Cuban olive-green.

Although Fidel was a party of one and the Sandinistas are a party of nine, and though Fidel removed socialists and they removed democrats, the pattern of betrayal has been the same: to gain power, the Sandinistas concealed their true intention (a Soviet state) behind a revolutionary lie (a pluralist democracy). To consolidate power they fashioned a second lie—democracy, but only within the revolution—and those who believed in the first lie were removed. At the end of the process there will be no democracy in Nicaragua at all, which is exactly what Fonseca and the Sandinistas had intended when they began. When the Sandinistas removed their anti-Somoza allies, they did not need Nicaraguan Communists because they had Fidel and thousands of agents and technicians from the Soviet bloc.

When Huber Matos saw Fidel's strategy unfolding in Cuba, he got on the telephone with other Fidelistas to discuss what they should do. That was a mistake. In the first year of Cuba's liberation, the phones of revolutionary legends like Huber Matos were already tapped by Fidel's secret police. Huber Matos was arrested.

In the bad old days of Batista oppression, Fidel had been arrested himself. His crime was not words on a telephone but leading an attack on a military barracks to overthrow the Batista regime. Twelve people were killed. For his offense, Fidel spent a total of 18 months in the tyrant's jail writing a book. Huber Matos was not so lucky. Fidel was no Batista, and the revolution was no two-bit dictatorship, like the one it replaced. For his phone call, Huber Matos was tried in such secrecy that not even members of the government were privy to the proceeding. Afterward he was consigned to solitary confinement in a windowless cell, where he remained for the next 20 years. And even as Fidel had buried alive his former friend and comrade, he went on singing songs of revolutionary humanism and social justice.

In another context, Milan Kundera explains the meaning of this revolutionary parable of Huber Matos and Fidel. Recalling the French Communist Paul Eluard, who wrote poems praising brotherhood while his friend was murdered by Eluard's comrades in Communist Prague, Kundera remarked: "The hangman killed while the poet sang." He explained the words thus. "People like to say: Revolution is beautiful, it is only the terror arising from it which is evil. But this is not true. The evil is already present in the beautiful, hell is already contained in the dream of paradise. . . . To condemn gulags is easy, but to reject the totalitarian poetry which leads to the gulag by way of paradise is as difficult as ever." Words to bear in mind today as we consider Nicaragua and its revolution of poets.

To believe in the revolutionary dream is the tragedy of its supporters; to exploit the dream is the talent of its dictators. Revolutionary cynicism, the source of this talent, is Fidel's most important teaching imparted to his Sandinista disciples. That is the faculty which allows the *comandantes* to emulate Fidel himself: to be poets and hangmen at the same time; to promise democracy and organize repression; to attack imperialism and join an empire; to talk peace and plan war; to champion justice and to deliver Nicaragua to a fraternity of inhumane, repressive, militarized, economically crippled states.

"We used to have one main prison, now we have many," laments a former Fidelista for the socialist paradise that Nicaragua has gained. "We used to have a few barracks; now we have many. We used to have many plantations; now we have only one, and it belongs to Fidel. Who enjoys the fruits of the revolution? The houses of the rich, the luxuries of the rich? The *comandante* and his court."[1]

Nicaragua is in the grip of utterly cynical and utterly ruthless men whose purpose is to crush its society from top to bottom, to institute totalitarian rule, and to use Nicaragua as a base to spread Communist terror and regimes throughout the hemisphere. The Sandinista anthem that proclaims the Yankee to be the "enemy of mankind" expresses precisely the revolutionaries' sentiment and goal. That goal is not to create new societies—the sordid record of Communist states would dissuade any reformer from choosing the Communist path—but to destroy societies that already exist. For Nicaragua, a *contra* victory would mean the restoration of the democratic leadership from whom the Sandinistas stole the revolution—the government that Nicaragua would have had if Cuba had not intervened in the first place. For the Americas, it would mean a halt to the Communist march that threatens its freedoms and its peace. Support for the *contras* is a first line of defense. If *the contras* fail, it will hasten the time when Americans will have to defend themselves.

A final word to my former comrades and successors on the left. It is no accident that the greatest atrocities of the 20th century have been committed by Marxist radicals; and it is no accident that they have been committed by radicals in power against their own people. Hatred of self, and by extension one's country, is the

---

[1] Carlos Franqui, *Family Portrait With Fidel*, 1984

root of the radical cause. As American radicals, the most egregious sin you commit is to betray the privileges and freedoms which ordinary people from all over the world have come to this country to create—privileges and freedoms that ordinary people all over the world would feel blessed to have for themselves. But the worst of it is this: you betray all of the tangible good that you can see around you for a socialist pie-in-the-sky that has meant horrible deaths and miserable lives for the hundreds of millions who have fallen under its sway.

4

A Decade Overrated and Unmourned

(co-authored with Peter Collier)

From its earliest battle-cry—"You can't trust anyone over 30"—until the end of its brief strut on the stage of national attention, the Sixties generation saw itself as a scouting party for a new world. It was the master of ceremonies presenting a "cultural revolution" that would better the lot of inmates in the prison of linear thought. It was the social horticulturist whose "greening of America" would allow the long-stalled post-industrialist age finally to break through the crust of the Puritan past. It was the avenging angel that would destroy the evil empire of "Amerikkka" and free the captive peoples of color around the world. The Sixties generation had created a new age, the Age of Aquarius, whose kingdom was surely at hand.

It is little wonder that people who lived through the Sixties, or who felt the nostalgia for it that such films as *The Big Chill* conveyed, regard this decade as the last good time. The images that remain are of youth—kids arriving in buses from all over America to converge on Haight-Ashbury, kids sharing their dope and bodies with newcomers who dropped into their communes, kids with pictures of the outlaw-heroes Bonnie and Clyde on their walls. It was a time of eternal youth; even the adults acted like kids.

Has any other generation ever been so successful in promoting its claims of Utopia? Looking at the era two decades later, we only see the images that reflected in the glass of Sixties' narcissism. We

---

A version of this article originally appeared in *Playboy*, January 1989.

are assured that it was a time of great idealism, populated by individuals who wanted nothing more than to give peace a chance; a time when dewy-eyed young people in the throes of moral passion sought to remake the world. Were they driven to extreme remedies? It was because the world was governed by cruel power. Did they burn out quickly? It was because a dark world greedily consumed their glorious light.

The reality was less exalted. If not quite the low, dishonest decade of the Thirties, the Sixties was nonetheless a time when what began as American mischief matured into real destructiveness. It was a time when a gang of ghetto thugs like the Black Panthers could be anointed as political visionaries; when Merry Pranksters of all stripes went into business as social evangelists spreading a chemical gospel. It was the most self-dramatizing of decades, a time when the only indispensable props were a soapbox, a megaphone, and a suppository.

If God had died in the Fifties, the victim in the Sixties was the "System," that collection of inherited values and assumptions which provide guidelines for the individual and the nation. As one center of authority after another was discredited under our assault, we convinced ourselves that we murdered to create. But what we proposed to put in the place of destroyed authority—a new social order, a new system of human relationships—turned out to be dangerous Utopias infected with banal dreams and totalitarian passions.

New decades rarely start on time. The election of John Kennedy, however, was such a calculated attempt to break with the past—substituting youth for Eisenhower's age, and Kennedy's "vigah" for the old president's evident exhaustion with the ambiguities of the post-war world—that 1960 seemed like a watershed. Kennedy did lend the office an existential *brio*, but his thousand days were spent playing out the themes of the Fifties. What we think of as the Sixties—that historical interlude that would have such a distinctive style and tone—really began the day the assassin came to Dallas. The "lone, crazed gunman," a specter that would haunt the era, had been loosed. JFK became a melancholy ghost rattling his chains for the rest of the decade—a symbol first of its betrayed promise and then of its corrupted innocence.

Even during his three years in office, Kennedy had been a bystander at the most crucial event of the beginning of the decade. This was the civil-rights movement, which opened America to its black outcasts. The summary moment of the civil rights movement came three months before Kennedy's death, when Martin Luther King, Jr. stood in front of the Lincoln Memorial and delivered his "I Have a Dream" speech. It seemed at the time that the speech might have set the tone for the Sixties. What was surprising about King's movement, however, was not how quickly it arrived—for it was preeminently a movement of the Fifties—but how quickly it passed.

By 1965, when the high Sixties were in gear, King was on the defensive, under attack by a new radical generation. With Stokely Carmichael as their representative figure, black militants rejected nonviolence and social integration, calling instead for "black power." They used threats of violence to exclude traditional civil-rights leaders like Roy Wilkins and Whitney Young from their protest and put pressure on King himself. The torching of the urban ghettos, beginning with Watts in 1965, provided the light by which the black-power movement wrote a violent and chaotic epilogue to King's history of decency and courage.

King continued to speak, before diminishing audiences, about peaceful and creative change, about building a movement of love and hope. The black activists opposed to him rode his coattails at the same time they were privately deriding him as "Uncle Martin" and "de Lawd." In a gesture characteristic of the nihilism that was coming to be the most typical feature of Sixties politics, they made it clear that they wanted no part of King's American dream. They were not interested in being integrated into a "System" they had decided was irredeemably racist; in fact, they wanted only to bring the "System" to its knees. King talked about brotherhood; Carmichael preached the doctrine that blacks were a "colony" and called for "national liberation" from America itself.

The guerrilla army of this liberation was to be the Black Panthers. While King had enriched the national dialogue on race and civil rights, the Panthers completed the debasement of political language and process with totalitarian slogans like "Off the pigs," "Power grows out of the barrel of a gun," and "If you're not part of the solution, you're part of the problem." As investigations later revealed, they were using the Santa Cruz Mountains as a killing-field to solve their internal power struggles while at the same time using rhetoric to titillate whites momentarily enamored of "revolutionary violence."

Except for the Panthers' murders of several of their own and their gun battles with local police, black militancy was primarily talk. But even talk had consequences. A daunting example of the impact that the loose talk and heavy rhetoric of the Sixties had on policy can be seen in the way the black family—a time-bomb ticking ominously, and exploding with daily detonations—got pushed off the political agenda.

While Carmichael, Huey Newton and others were launching a revolutionary front against the system, the Johnson administration was contemplating a commitment to use the power of the federal government to end the economic and social inequalities that still plagued American blacks. A presidential task force under Daniel Patrick Moynihan was given a mandate to identify the obstacles preventing blacks from seizing opportunities that had been grasped by other minority groups in the previous 50 years of American history. At about the same time as the passage of the Voting Rights Act of 1965, Moynihan published findings that emphasized the central importance of family in shaping an individual life and noted with alarm that 21 percent of black families were headed by single women. "[The] one unmistakable lesson in American history," he warned, is that a country that allows "a large number of young men to grow up in broken families, dominated by women, never acquiring any stable relationship to male authority, never acquiring any set of rational expectations about the future—that community asks for and gets chaos. Crime, violence, unrest, disorder—most particularly the furious, unrestrained lashing out at the whole social struc-ture—that is not only to be expected; it is very near to inevitable."

Moynihan proposed that the government confront this prob-lem as a priority; but his conclusions were bitterly attacked by black radicals and white liberals, who joined in an alliance of anger and self-flagellation and quickly closed the window of opportunity Moynihan had opened. They condemned his report as racist not only in its conclusions but also in its conception; e.g., it had failed to stress the evils of the "capitalistic system." This rejectionist coalition did not want a program for social change so much as a confession of guilt. For them the only "non-racist" gesture the president could make would be acceptance of their demand for $400 million in "reparations" for 400 years of slavery. The White House retreated before this onslaught and took the black family off the agenda. As Moynihan said later, "From being buoyantly open to ideas and enterprises, [Johnson] became near contemptuous of civil-rights leaders who he now believed cared only for symbols." In his next State of the Union address, the president devoted only 45 words of his speech to the problems confronting blacks.

It is an archetypal Sixties case history—the rejection of real solutions in favor of demands that are made with the knowledge they cannot be met. The consequences of this syndrome have become, with time, painfully clear. While in 1950 some 30 percent of Americans had been poor according to official definitions, the normal workings of the system had reduced the figure to 13 per-cent by 1968 when Great Society programs were just beginning. Over the next 12 years, federal spending on poverty would quadru-ple but without the intended effect. In 1980, 13 percent of Ameri-cans were still classified as poor, the same figure as 12 years and more than $100 billion earlier. What had changed was the nature of poverty itself. It had become increasingly youthful, black, femi-nized and entrenched. Unwed black teen mothers had become the norm rather than the exception in the black community.

It is a problem that the present-day apologists for the Sixties blame on the "System." By 1970, however, black families which were intact and living outside the South, both adults having a high-school education, had attained income equality with their white counterparts. These were blacks who had remained committed to the opportunity-system Martin Luther King had embraced. These are the blacks who today have entered the professional and managerial class in huge numbers, an increase of 63 percent during the Eighties alone; a decade when, for the first time in U.S. history, the black middle-class outnumbered the black poor.

But radical leaders who had pushed King aside continued to condemn the system and advised blacks to buy out of it so vehemently that a commitment to self-betterment almost had to be made against the grain of black life. In 1950, when America did have a racist system but did not have a self-anointed priesthood denouncing its evils, 9.5 percent of black teenagers, as opposed to 8.7 percent of white teens, were unemployed. In 1980, after a decade-and-a-half of Sixties rhetoric, some 38 percent of black teens were unemployed. Obviously the bad-mouthing of America was not the only cause for this disastrous turn of events, but it was an instance of contributory negligence on the part of radicals. A part of the black community has made advances since 1960. But those accomplishments are in spite of Sixties figures like Stokely Carmichael, who opted for a privileged exile in totalitarian Guinea after a frightening run-in with the Panthers; or like Huey Newton, who was charged with one felony after another before his sordid death on an Oakland street-corner in 1989. The success of the black middle-class is a reward for following Martin Luther King's advice to commit to the American dream; while others were trapped in the self-pitying victimhood so adroitly exploited by radical demagogues.

Black radicals who reviled King during his lifetime as an Uncle Tom now kneel with cynical reverence at his shrine, although they still reject his vision. Blacks still face poverty and unemployment; but chief among their disabilities are Sixties leftovers, like the opportunistic Jesse Jackson, who have revived the anti-Americanism and infatuation with Third-World totalitarianism exhibited by

King's radical opponents 20 years ago. How would King have regarded Jackson's remarks about "Hymies" or his praise for a black fascist like Louis Farrakhan? Probably in much the same way he regarded white demagogues in the Sixties who talked about "niggers" and praised white fascists in robes.

Another reason for the degradation of the civil-rights movement was the willingness of its radical leaders to buy into the notion—part of the vulgar Marxism in vogue during the Sixties—that blacks were victims not only of discrimination and prejudice but of the American empire, of America itself. Like other destructive ideas that fastened themselves like an exotic jungle fungus on our national self-conception, this notion came directly by way of Vietnam.

If the struggle for civil rights was the central movement of the Sixties, the war in Vietnam was the central fact. The war informed the life of an entire generation. It was such a pervasive experience that even non-combatants felt as though they had been waist-deep in rice paddies and occasionally experienced a sudden stab of fear at the staccato rhythms of helicopter blades. The war continued to be fought well into the Eighties in literature and film as well as in foreign policy. Should the United States have gone into Vietnam? Could we have won?

To argue these questions is to become mired in the battles long after the war has been lost. It is also to lose sight of the most important fact about Vietnam: It was a cultural occasion as much as an historical event. The destructive anti-Americanism that eventually came to characterize the era had been off-limits, intellectually and morally, at the beginning of the decade; the Vietnam War was the justification the movement needed to cross the line.

The first antiwar protests—by those who had been part of the civil-rights movement as it developed under King—were caused by what people saw as the inhumanity of the war. But this moral dimension was soon replaced in the antiwar movement by an irrational hatred of America and all it stood for. The war corrupted everything—the people who protested against it as well as those

who fought. The movement soon determined that what it perceived as the lies of the U.S. government must be fought by lies of
its own. These lies were sentimental—Ho Chi Minh, a life-long
Comintern agent, was simply a misunderstood nationalist, the
George Washington of his country. Or the lies were strategic—
North Vietnamese regular troops were not fighting in the South
alongside the NLF. Truth was the first casualty, in the war at home
as much as in Vietnam.

After it was over and movement "activists," as the media generously called them, were looking for a way to make their revolt
seem like a patriotic act, they created the myth that they had
detoured into hard-line positions because this was the only way to
stop the war. In fact, like Voltaire's God, Vietnam would have had
to be invented if it hadn't existed, because it justified the anti-
Americanism that was part of the movement from its very beginnings. Tom Hayden let that particular cat out of the bag later on,
when speaking about the founding charter of Students for a Democratic Society, the 1962 Port Huron Statement: "We were
opposed . . . to doctrines imposed from the past. In that sense we
were not Marxist. . . . But we were conscious of what we were driv-
ing at, which was a revolutionary change in the American structure. We were never reformers who became disillusioned and,
therefore, more radical." In other words, the war in Vietnam was a
gift of chance that allowed radical leaders to convince others of the
need for a social apocalypse and of the necessity for their destructive strategies.

As the war escalated, the treason of the heart committed by the
many became treason in fact for a few. In 1969 SDS splintered into
factions, the chief of which was the Weathermen. That year its
leadership went to Havana to form the Venceremos Brigade. While
they were there, they held discussions with the Vietnamese and
Cubans that led them to return home with plans for a wave of terrorism cut short only because their high command blew itself up
in a Manhattan townhouse.

Like other wounds suffered by Sixties radicals, this one was self-inflicted. Despite their incessant complaints of police brutality, Sixties radicals lived for the most part in a no-fault system, demanding their constitutional rights at the same time they were abusing and denouncing the Constitution. They knew they had the option, which many ultimately used, of diving back into the system when they tired of being extrinsic. For this reason, New Leftism, although discredited in politics, continues to thrive in the "academic work" of former radicals who returned for post-graduate degrees to the universities they had earlier tried to destroy. It was an example of the cynicism that marked the Sixties—an underlying awareness that America was exactly the sort of flexible and forgiving society the leftists condemned it for failing to be.

The radicals' assault in the Sixties was never directed against conservatives. The target was liberalism itself. It had been liberalism that had guided America to power in the postwar world. It was liberalism that had gotten the United States into Vietnam. Centrist liberalism was the balance wheel giving synchronicity to the entire political system. But now radicals assaulted the center; if it could not hold, America would fall. Liberals were bashed not only over foreign affairs but also for the domestic program installed by the New Deal. Radicals in the university began a systematic revisionism that challenged the whole achievement of the American liberal tradition—from the origins of the Constitution to the origins of the Cold War.

The decisive moment in the assault against liberalism was the destruction of the last Democratic Party presidential candidate in this tradition, Hubert Humphrey. The instrument was the riot that a handful of radical leaders organized for the 1968 Democratic Party convention in Chicago. Tom Hayden and the other leaders knew that Chicago's Mayor Richard Daley, in the wake of the riots after Martin Luther King's assassination, had called for the shooting of "looters" on sight. They knew that "the whole world was watching." They knew that a confrontation on the streets of

Chicago would inevitably lead to violence and explode in political shocks felt across the globe.

The Chicago demonstrations became the Tet Offensive of the antiwar movement: the military defeat on the battlefield that won a political victory in Washington. In the wake of the riots, Humphrey was defeated, and four years later the New Left vision possessed the Democratic Party—the "cold war" liberals' ability to fight the takeover having been destroyed by the Chicago debacle. The left's candidate lost, but its vision prevailed. George McGovern's candidacy became for the left what Barry Goldwater's eight years earlier had been for the right—a way of entering and eventually possessing a party. A sign of the times was the way Tom Hayden, who had destroyed the Democrats' chances in Chicago in 1968, resurfaced as a party regular in California in the mid-Seventies.

Vietnam was a powerful narcotic. One of the self-revealing comments of the anti-war movement came when the Communists first agreed to negotiate. "We fight, fight, fight, and then they sell us out!" was the despairing response of Harlem Maoist Bill Epton. The movement was addicted to the sense of being invincibly correct and utterly moral that the war had given it. And so a feeling of emptiness came over the Sixties generation when the withdrawal from Vietnam began.

By the time the last U.S. personnel had ingloriously left, Sixties radicals were already searching for new connections, in Africa and Central America, that would restore the "high" they had lost. They turned their backs on Vietnam. Their moral outrage did not come into play when Hanoi conquered the South. The only "lessons" of Vietnam that interested them were those that confirmed American guilt. The left wasn't interested in the curriculum involving Communist genocide in Cambodia or the imperialism of Moscow and Hanoi. Their moral amnesia allowed them to ignore the fact that more Indochinese were killed in the first two years of the Communist peace than had been killed on all sides in a decade of the anti-Communist war.

At the same time they ignored these realities, the Sixties radicals were making sure that the war, or at least their version of it, would linger in the nation's consciousness. Just as the Sixties had been dominated by the fact of Vietnam, so the postwar era was dominated by the Vietnam metaphor. Until the Sixties, the dominant political image had been provided by Munich, which encapsulated the lessons of the Thirties as a warning to democracies to arm themselves against aggressors who talked about peace. But the Munich metaphor was repeatedly assaulted in the Sixties by those who claimed that it had lured us into the Southeast Asian war. In the Seventies, "Munich" was replaced by "Vietnam," an experience with the opposite moral—that anti-communism led to "quagmire" and a vigilant democracy to "abuses of power;" and that totalitarian Third-World movements were actually manifestations of harmless nationalism.

The Vietnam metaphor dominated the politics of the Eighties as the Vietnam War had the politics of the Sixties. It *made* policy. Whenever America even considered acting in its self-defense, opponents of such action merely invoked the specter of Vietnam. They talked about the "holocaust" in Indochina, with full awareness of the symbolic resonance in comparing America to Nazi Germany. "Another Vietnam" was a curse on action. Less an argument than an incantation, it became an irresistible pressure for passivity, isolationism and appeasement.

The battle-cry "No Vietnams in Central America" showed the Vietnam metaphor in action. The slogan smothered all distinctions of time and place that separated these conflicts and defined their meanings. Playing on fears of another quagmire that would again bleed this country, the slogan became a persuasion to do nothing about the expansionism of Marxist-Leninist regimes or about dominoes that might fall in our own hemisphere. For nostalgic radicals, "No Vietnams in Central America" has also been an unfulfilled wish. The Sixties is still seen as the last good time by these people, who are like the Japanese soldiers wandering in a cerebral jungle—unwilling to admit that the war is over. They really want another Vietnam, another cultural upheaval; another defeat for the United States; another drama of moral self-inflation; another orgy of guilt and recrimination; a reprise, in short, of the Sixties.

In the Vietnam metaphor, we have the tunnel at the end of the light.

During the Sixties, we also became a culture of splinter-groups, of people who identified ourselves according to ethnicity, gender, special interests—a galaxy of minorities, united only by a sensibility that now regarded society at large with suspicion. The political philosopher Michael Walzer unconsciously expressed this sensibility when he confessed, in a recent article in *The New Republic*, "It is still true that only when I go to Washington to demonstrate do I feel at home there." Within the culture the Sixties created, its minorities exist in a perpetual adversarial relationship to America, inspired by assumptions about its malign intent, which they "learned" as a result of the symbiosis between the black revolution and the war in Vietnam. This factionalization and division, this readiness to believe the worst about our home-ground, is the enduring legacy of the Sixties.

"Liberation" was the radical watchword. Where did it lead us? No cause followed so swiftly or so instructively along the path cleared by its radical vanguard as the one in behalf of American women. Even before feminism was able to proclaim itself as an independent cause of the era, a contrite American power-structure had included women in the compact it made with the civil-rights movement led by Martin Luther King. In 1963, the first federal statute requiring "equal pay for equal work" sailed through Congress, and the Civil Rights Act of 1964 specifically extended its protection to women, banning discrimination on the basis of "race, color, religion, sex, or national origin."

But like its black counterpart, the women's movement had already been seized by the radical passion. Its manifesto, Betty Friedan's *The Feminine Mystique*, went beyond a plea for equality in the system to an indictment of the system itself: "Our culture does not permit women to accept or gratify their basic need to grow and fulfill their potentialities as human beings."

There was an important truth in the claim that America's women had been denied their place in its dream, a truth that the victories of the next decade would confirm, permanently expanding their horizons and opportunities as dramatically as the civil-rights revolution had done for America's blacks. But the exaggerations in the indictment were equally important and consequential. The culture that Friedan had indicted because it did not permit women to grow had provided Friedan herself with an Ivy League education and an opportunity not only to have three children but a writing career subsidized by her working husband. The family that she claimed was a "concentration camp" for American women had supported her in the years of her labor. Far from denying her recognition, her "masculine" profession had rewarded her with the hyperbolic acclaim of reviewers who hailed her work as "the most important book of the 20th century."

But in 1966, when Friedan and her associates founded the National Organization of Women, the radical enthusiasms of the time blinded them to positive American realities like this and committed them instead to a rhetoric that was rejectionist. To the feminists of NOW, women were an "oppressed majority," the victims of a "sexism" that paralleled racism and was imposed by the "patriarchal" character of the American system. Women's liberation could not be achieved by extending the "rights" of such an oppressive system to American women, but only by a "cultural revolution" that would "restructure" American society. Such a revolution must abolish the "gender roles" that the system had imposed, along with the legal and moral restraints that denied women control over their bodies and delivered them to "the tyranny of their reproductive biology."

In the name of liberation, the radicals crusaded against laws that recognized differences between men and women, providing special protections for women in the workplace, the family, and society at large. To radicals, the family was nothing more than a target of opportunity. Gloria Steinem denounced marriage as a form of prostitution, while 50,000 feminists marked the anniversary of women's suffrage with a march on Fifth Avenue and expressive slogans like "Don't Cook Dinner—Starve a Rat Today." Radical feminists linked all the Sixties revolutions. "We want to destroy the three pillars of class and caste society—the family, private property, and the state."

Eventually, the sorcerer's apprentices of the feminist movement would draw back in horror from what they had unloosed. Referring to the excessive "Second Wave" of the movement she had begun, Friedan decried the way that the feminine mystique had been superseded "by a feminist mystique which denied that core of women's person hood that is fulfilled through love, nurture, home." Feminists like Andrea Dworkin began to warn that "sexual liberation only made life harder for women."

The toll of this sexual confusion on the emotional life and psyche of a generation is difficult to assess. But consequences of the revolutionary feminism that outlasted the Sixties are measurable. Between 1960 and 1980, the percentage of illegitimate births more than doubled. "Only a minority of American children may now expect to reach age 18 having lived continuously with their natural parents," New York Senator Daniel Moynihan noted in January 1987. "Sixty percent of children now being born may expect at one time or another to live in a single-parent family and nine in ten of such families are headed by females." Of the nation's 33.7 million poor in 1984, 35 percent lived in female-headed households. Without the sharp increase in the number of such families, U.S. poverty would have dropped significantly between 1960 and 1984.

Friedan and other feminists may now be chastened by the unforeseen consequences of their attack on the American family. But the nation whose institutions they assaulted is finding its equilibrium less easy to recover. As previous revolutions have shown, it is far more difficult to restore protective traditions that have been destroyed than it was to destroy them in the first place.

This grim historical lesson is underscored by another of the Sixties' cultural liberations, one of the unintended consequences of which is a venereal epidemic that now threatens a death-toll many times greater than that of the war in Vietnam. Basking in the reflected glow of the Sixties, gays cast off the chains of a moral tradition they denounced as oppressive and established their own "liberated zones" where they pursued an ideal of free sex for more than a decade. Their bathhouses became institutional symbols and political organizing-halls as well as the sexual gymnasiums of the gay movement. In time they also came to resemble petri dishes, culturing the dangerous diseases that began to afflict the gay community.

Public-health officials in San Francisco, Los Angeles and New York watched with alarm as a succession of serious venereal epidemics—rectal gonorrhea, Hepatitis B, CMV—swept through these communities—epidemics so extensive that they cost taxpayers in excess of $1 million a day to provide treatment. In the past, action would have been taken; this time there was no action. The liberated gay culture was "doing its thing." Public-health officials were intimidated from speaking out, lest they trespass against a "minority lifestyle;" proven public-health measures were rejected as an infringement on "civil rights."[1]

Even after AIDS appeared at the beginning of the Eighties, the situation did not change. In San Francisco, gay activists and their liberal allies in the city's political machine prevented action to close the bathhouses. This coalition obscured life-and-death matters with fusty Sixties rhetoric about "pink triangles" and "final solutions." The political and public-health establishments caved in to this rhetoric and withheld warnings during crucial years when the virus first spread—warnings that would have educated the gay public about the sexual transmission of AIDS—a fact that was, at first, obdurately denied by leading gay activists. They also denied the snowballing evidence that the epidemic was caused by reckless promiscuity and anal intercourse. Even today, the phrase

---

[1]Authors' interview with Don Francis of the Centers for Disease Control in Atlanta

"promiscuous anal intercourse" is still censored out of the "educa-tion" literature that government agencies provide as the corner-stone of official anti-AIDS programs, because they are politically unacceptable to gay activists.

The attitudes struck and the policies adopted in San Francisco set the standard for the rest of the country. Gay leaders and the public-health officials they so easily cowed refused to pursue strategies that might have slowed or isolated the epidemic, for fear they would infringe on a liberated lifestyle. Instead, with true Six-ties gall, they indicted the government as "homophobic" for not providing more money for AIDS research. America was to blame. Ronald Reagan had somehow caused AIDS by failing to mention it often enough. It was the sort of logic that might have been retrieved from a Sixties time-capsule.

It is now too late for many of the public-health measures that are a community's first line of defense against a virulent epidemic. The AIDS virus is in place. It has now infected three-quarters of San Francisco's gay men and more than one million people nation-wide. Other proven public-health procedures like mandatory test-ing and contact-tracing have been blocked by gay and liberal activists in the name of "civil rights." That it is in name only is clear from the tactic of "outing" practiced by radical gay groups themselves. The purpose of "outing" is to expose prominent gays still in the closet; a gay tabloid called *Outweek* provides the means. There has been no protest in the gay political community over this calculated invasion of privacy, despite the fact that pro-tection of "confidentiality" is alleged as the primary reason for opposition to testing.

Meanwhile, the rhetorical excess continues. At the first national gay civil-rights "March on Washington," a reprise of King's moment in history, which was attended by 200,000 activists in December 1987, a prominent slogan proclaimed: "Rea-gan No, Sodomy Yes." It was as if anal sex had not been firmly established as one of the two principal modes of AIDS transmis-sion, along with the sharing of needles. In a feature essay in *The*

Village Voice, writer Richard Goldstein described AIDS imbecilely as the metaphor of the present generation in the way that Vietnam had been for the previous one. He declared: "The sharing of needles must be understood in the same context as anal sex—as an ecstatic act that enhances social solidarity."

The same lesson about liberation can be learned from social epidemics as from venereal ones. The unprecedented increase in violent crimes that has infected America over the past two decades is an example. The Sixties defined itself by its efforts to delegitimize the police as an "army of occupation," while also celebrating crime as a form of existential rebellion and the outlaw as a perceptive social critic. There was a numbing barrage against what was derided as "law and order" seen in slogans like "off the pigs," in the insistence that "all minority prisoners are political prisoners," and in the romanticizing of murderers like George Jackson who deserved to be locked deeper in the prison system rather than becoming international symbols of American "injustice."

The Sixties raised incalculably what we now regard as an acceptable level of violence and menace in our workaday existence—the crime equivalent of Muzak murmuring in the background of our lives. Once again, however, the most prominent victims were the intended beneficiaries of this liberation: the black communities of the inner cities, who watch helplessly as crime tears their lives apart. But the social theorists and Sixties nostalgia-artists are as uncaring of those people as they were for the millions they delivered into the hands of the Communists in Vietnam.

And finally there is the Eighties' drug epidemic, a delayed gift from the Sixties and its ideology of consciousness-expansion. For people like Ken Kesey and Timothy Leary, drugs were the weapons of a folk revolution, a democratization of the sublime, America in Wonderland. For political radicals, drugs were a shortcut to potentially revolutionary alienation and repudiation of the social mainstream. In 1969, during the People's Park uprising in Berkeley, Tom Hayden and other radicals drew up the "Berkeley Liberation Program" that promised, among other things, to "protect and expand our drug culture" and to recognize "the right of people to use those drugs which are known from experience to be harmful." Before the movement's successes, drugs had been quarantined in the social underground; now they had become part of an individual's bill-of-rights. This moral imbecility stood out even in the Sixties theater of the absurd. Yet the political ethos behind it survives to this day. Thus *The Nation*, a leftist publication, condemned Reagan's anti-drug policies as "an ideological mobilization like the war against Communism ... with its redolence of racism, its anti-Third World and anti-Sixties overtones."

The nihilism that was part of the Sixties' advertisement for itself makes it tempting to blame the decade for everything that has gone wrong since then. But to leave such an impression would be uncharitable and untrue. In some ways, it was the best of times. There was an expansion of consciousness, of social space, of tolerance, of experience itself. It was exciting to be alive, to find oneself swimming in the rush of history's stream-of-consciousness. But while the beauty of the Sixties was that it was a decade of youth, its defect was an inability to grow up. It was constitutionally unable to see the other side of the ledger—condemned to ignore the fact that, as in physics, there are equal and opposite reactions in society—social costs for social acts.

In the end, the words of Lennon decipher the truth of the era in a way that the works of the other Lenin, who enjoyed a brief but depressing vogue among radicals of the day, did not:

> *You say you want a revolution?*
> *Well you know,*
> *We all want to change the world.*
> *You say you got a real solution?*
> *Well you know,*
> *We'd all love to see the plan.*

But when all the posturing and self-dramatization was over, there was no plan, no idea about how to replace what had been destroyed.

Schizophrenic to its core, the era was never clear whether its primary identity was that of creator or destroyer. Its ambivalence was suggested by the two groups that dominated its popular music—perhaps the only real artistic achievement of the time. Was the inner voice of the Sixties that of the Beatles, innocent minstrels on a "magical mystery tour?" Or that of the Rolling Stones, the vandals presiding at its "beggars' banquet?"

For a while, these groups reigned jointly over popular culture, expressing the audacious delusion of the Sixties that it was beyond consequences, beyond good and evil, able to have it all. It was possible to assault the cops by word and deed but also be safe on the streets; to reject authority and yet live coherently; to be an outlaw culture and yet a humane and harmoniously ordered one.

Listening to the Beatles and the Stones, Sixties rebels registered these ideas with growing grandiosity, believing they had gone from counterculture to counter-nation once they planted the flag of discovery at Woodstock. A place consecrated by love, holy to the Sixties in the way the Paris commune was to Marxists, Woodstock institutionalized the right to live outside the rules. Unlike the doomed inhabitants of "Amerika," the citizens of this new nation could have joyous copulation and access to illegal drugs. If the drugs caused bad trips or the sex carried disease, the caring immigrants of Woodstock would be there to care for their own.

But the Woodstock Nation was an illusion as ungrounded in reality as the hallucinations induced by the LSD that was its national chemical. A few months after its founding, the decade began to draw toward its apocalyptic close. As a portent of things to come, the Beatles were breaking up. The title-song of the album *Let It Be* might be taken as a recognition of the destructiveness of the Sixties crusade against established order. The Rolling Stones answered this act of contrition with the title-song of their album *Let It Bleed.* Then came Altamont, the *Kristallnacht* of the Woodstock Nation. At Altamont, the gentle folk of Woodstock met the Hell's Angels—not only criminals but suppliers of the drugs that were destroying the new nation from within. While the Stones were singing *Sympathy for the Devil,* a black man lunged near the stage with a knife in his hand and was beaten to death in front of everyone by the Angels. Devils and Angels: it all came together and all came apart.

Appalled at what had happened, Mick Jagger dropped the song from his repertory. He saw that the Sixties were over. It was time to go back to the dressing-room, time to stop posturing as the "satanic majesties" of an era, time to grow up and simply become part of the rock scene again.

The rest of us had to do the same thing: learn to live with adulthood. And so the Sixties faded into gauzy memory—the good old days when we were all so bad, a time of limitless possibilities and wild dreams made all the brighter by the somber and complex world that succeeded it. The paradoxical reason for the Sixties' growing appeal is this: it created the tawdry world that we now measure and find wanting by comparison to it.

There is truth in the nostalgia. It is the memory of the era that is false. The Pandora's box the Sixties opened then is still unclosed; the malign influences the Sixties released then still plague us today.

5

Keepers of the Flame
(co-authored with Peter Collier)

The Church of Radicalism administers a harsh communion and has no patience with apostates. We knew this before and discovered it again when we published *Destructive Generation*. The book is not a plea for grace but an attempt to understand the varieties of religious experience that characterized the movement in its heyday and among its hard core; to understand what went wrong with the Sixties left, what responsibility people like ourselves bear, and how the faith of leftism has been kept going in our own time despite an unrelieved record of disaster.

In writing *Destructive Generation,* of course, we expected to be excommunicated from the Church of the Left yet again. But this time, in addition to being shown the exit sign at the gates of Eden, we found ourselves stigmatized as something even worse than anti-left. We were anti-Sixties. In writing about the decade, we had stumbled into the nostalgia factory where the touch-up artists of radical history work with airbrushes to erase unpleasant memories and smooth out rough moments. We had seen the smithy where the myths of this golden age are forged; myths intended to restore the power of the radical dream and to make sure that our present political culture doesn't learn from its history so that it will be condemned to repeat it.

Of these myths about the Sixties, the first and most pernicious is the doctrine of original innocence. This holds that the left is

---

This article appeared in *The New Republic* on June 26, 1989, in response to radical critics of *Destructive Generation*.

purer of heart and therefore better—more compassionate, more idealistic, more peace-loving, more humane—than all other political movements. To remake this innocence, defenders of Sixties radicalism must now propose that groups such as the Black Panther Party and the Weatherman terrorists—groups of which we had enough first-hand knowledge to write about them plausibly in *Destructive Generation*—were nothing more than a lunatic fringe that had only minuscule support 20 years ago and have no legitimate standing as historical metaphors today. There might have been excesses back then—justifications of "revolutionary violence," a fashion for zany neo-Marxist creeds. But those involved in such things were part of what university administrators once called "a small but vociferous minority"—a minority that gets smaller with each passing year as yesterday's radicals pop out of their cocoons and take wing as today's progressives.

"It wasn't us, babe," these fluttering revisionists say today. "We were not violent. You might have been, but not us. We were not proponents of revolution or even radical change. Of course, somebody did it. Since you admit in your book that these things took place, you are guilty." Such is the fate of those who use the second-person plural as part of the grammar of collective responsibility.

For us, there is an irony in being called the last New Left extremists. Having actually drawn back from the Sixties left during its heaviest weather, we thought that when *Destructive Generation* appeared we might be criticized by remnants of the hardcore as being inauthentic. "Where were you when we were getting ready for the armed revolution?" we imagined them asking. But we obviously misjudged the strength of the historical rewrite now under way. Instead of clenching the fist, our old comrades have pointed the finger. "You guys were part of the lunatic fringe then, and you're part of it now," they have told us. "You've just exchanged one radicalism for another, while the rest of us have been integrating ourselves back into society and getting on with our lives." Or, as *New Republic* editor Hendrik Hertzberg complained to us in a recent conversation, "You were apologists for communism then and you are apologists for anti-communism now." As though these postures were morally equivalent.

Tom Hayden, Bobby Seale and all the other quick-change artists of the left have a right to get on with their lives. But they have no right to deface the truth of the Sixties to ease their mid-life transits. In Hayden's autobiography *Reunion*, one looks in vain for any serious admission of complicity in the North Vietnamese rape of South Vietnam. Or for any illumination of the year or so he spent perpetually out of breath from trying to inflate the revolutionary legend of the Black Panthers as "America's Viet Cong." Or for any mention of his experiences in the hills of northern California doing target-practice under the tutelage of the Minister of Defense of the "Red Family" in giddy anticipation of the fascism he thought Richard Nixon might install, thus giving a little goose to the revolution that had then entered a period of dry labor. Hayden was no worse than many at the time. But he is no better now because he has decided to subtract these facts from his own life and from the history of the movement in the interests of getting on with it. This lack of second thoughts is the telltale heart of the American left.

Why no reckoning? Because reckonings are conservative. They counsel against the heedless rush to redeem the ambiguous and mottled realities of the human condition. They prove that life is made better only incrementally and with great difficulty, but it is made worse—much worse—very easily. Reckonings examine the toxic waste that revolutionary enthusiasms leave in their wake. Reckonings open the mass graves to examine the shards of bone that are all that is left of the New Men and Women created by utopias past.

Because they want to continue their crusades, our old comrades not only don't want second thoughts of their own. They don't want us to have them either. They not only want to protect their sense of moral superiority as a special generation formed by a crucial decade. They also want to keep that decade inviolate, so that some future radical generation can use it as a model when it decides to pull the sword from the stone.

A second myth of Sixties nostalgia artists is that "we" were actually more sinned against than sinning. In fact, "we" never really "knew sin" at all (to use Todd Gitlin's phrase in *The Sixties*) until the end of the decade, when the unending war had blunted our moral affect and driven us into a state of temporary insanity. In the battle between memory and forgetting, this is an example not only of amnesia but of auto-lobotomy. The New Left bit the apple the first time the first journalist thrust the first microphone into its face and told it that it was a "prophetic minority." It knew sin early in the Sixties in the founding sessions of Students for a Democratic Society, when Hayden and others proposed a moral equivalence between the United States and the USSR; in the middle of the decade when it claimed that Ho Chi Minh was the George Washington of his country; and at the end of the decade when it transmuted the slogan "Bring the troops home" into "Bring the war home."

To serve memory means admitting that we radicals generically (not just we two) did not love this country enough. We did not do all we could to stop the war without hating our heritage root-and-branch. If we did not carry North Vietnamese flags ourselves, we did not face down those who did. If we did not spell Amerika with a "k" ourselves, we failed to repudiate those who did. There was enough sin to go around in the Sixties, sins of omission as well as commission, sins of the heart as well as the hand.

The fault-lines around the Sixties and the left go deep in our culture. Exactly how deep we realized when *Village Voice* leftist Paul Berman, who had attacked us in print on several previous occasions as "renegades"—a term of the Thirties that has outlived the Stalinist neo-logicians who created it—was given our book by *The New Republic* for an unusually lengthy review. Because our position on issues such as the spread of totalitarianism in Central America were closer to the magazine's than those of Berman, who has vacillated between being a cheerleader for the Sandinistas and a fence-sitter in the struggle over Nicaragua's future, this assignment had the feel of a political hit.

A 1986 Berman article in *Mother Jones,* magazine of the long radical exile, opens with a scene in which the author is in Managua chumming it up with Omar Cabezas, the number-two cop in Tomás Borge's Ministry of the Interior. It seems that he had just read Cabezas's autobiography *Fire from the Mountain* and was "astonished"—not by the fact that Cabezas had falsified the history of the revolution, but rather by the intoxicating discovery that "backwater Nicaragua was the world center of the New Left." Proceeding from this *aperçu,* Berman wrote: "Elsewhere, the dream of Che led to stupid posturings. [But] in León [where Cabezas had launched his Sandinista career] the dream of Che was the road to the Ministry of the Interior. Fantasy elsewhere was realism in Nicaragua."

Here is the authentic voice of the Sixties left thrown as if by ventriloquism into the present. Twenty years ago we saw the Fidelistas as archetypal New Leftists, the ones who had done it while we pampered Americans were only fantasizing about it. Cuba having proved unpalatable, it is now the Sandinistas who have the authenticity that America's radicals never achieved. There is no acknowledgment that in Cuba Che's New-Left dream led directly to Fidel's *gulag.* Here it might be different, Berman muses, while sitting in the headquarters of the Sandinista police state batting his eyes at another dreamer of Che's dream.

Berman typifies those intellectuals of the left who—for all their birdwalking and backtracking—always wind up on the wrong side. Determined to locate the good part of the New Left in this newest workers' paradise, he dons his Mexican wedding-shirt and *huaraches* and wanders through Managua in pinched-face concentration searching for evidence that socialism cares about people. We saw him there in the fall of 1987; we were amused by his mumbled apologies for the *bêtise* of staying two nights in the Intercontinental Hotel and by the quick dash he made every morning to breathe the heady fumes of the *barrio.*

It is not surprising that the whole literary repertory of leftism is on display in his attack on our book—the shameless mendacity, the tabulation of history, the brain-dwarfing moral smugness, and above all the insuperable intellectual mediocrity. Berman is not only ignorant about basic realities of the decade we write about, he is also tone-deaf to the era's complexity. This is shown by what he writes about the Black Panthers. Collier and Horowitz alone, he fatuously suggests, got an illicit thrill from those heavy dudes. Only *we* were intrigued by their Promethean willingness to pick up the gun; only *we* suspended our disbelief when they said they had put the gun down in favor of serving the people.

The Panthers were, in fact, an icon for the great mass of worshipers in the Church of Leftism, a larger and more joyous congregation then than now. The posters of Huey P. Newton sitting on his Zulu throne adorned the walls of hip lawyers as well as college students. Leonard Bernstein didn't invite just anyone into his living room even in those balmy days. Berman has the gall to ignore it all. Ain't nobody here but us moderates, he says; we didn't believe in no Black Panthers back then.

The irony is that it was only after the early Seventies, when the so-called violent Panther faction of Eldridge Cleaver's followers had been expelled from the party, that people like us, who had remained aloof from the Panthers during their maximalist phase, did get involved. As we point out in *Destructive Generation*, we did so because Huey Newton claimed not only to have put down the gun but to have embraced exactly the sort of community-organizing and development passionately believed in by that tiny group of social democrats among whom Berman counts himself. Like Berman and his ilk today, we wanted back then to continue to believe in the left. We were searching for a soulful socialism in the Oakland ghetto just as he now searches for it in the *barrio* of Managua. Of course we were wrong 15 years ago, just as he is today. The "sane" wing of the Black Panther Party turned out to be filled with insane killers.

But if we were wrong, we were not, as Berman claims, alone in our self-delusion. At about the time we became involved in the Panthers' "survival" programs, Bobby Seale came surprisingly close to being elected mayor of Oakland. In the spring of 1973, *The Nation* ran a long article explaining the change for the better that had taken place in the party. Rutgers political scientist Ross Baker assured readers that it was safe to support the Panthers once again because they had "outgrown their rhetoric."

A few months after the two of us had become involved with the Panthers, the much-adulated liberal journalist Murray Kempton wrote a front-page review of Newton's *Revolutionary Suicide* in *The New York Times Book Review* that concludes with this peroration: "We must hear him out because we suspect that he comes not as avenger but as healer. Here is the only visible American who has managed to arrive at the Platonic conception of himself." In a final flourish, Kempton noted that Huey had run a joint seminar at Yale with Erik Erikson, using the reference to compare the Panther leader favorably to Luther and Gandhi. That was in May 1973. A few weeks later, Kempton's book on the "Panther 21," *The Briar Patch,* was published. And it was favorably reviewed by another *soi-disant* social democrat, Garry Wills, who served up another front-page *Times* review containing such gems about the Panthers—the Eldridge Cleaver Panthers, no less—as these: "Never, it would seem, have people threatened more and been guilty of less.... And in the end there is a sense of the almost incredible ability of men to find dignity in resisting the viciousness of other men—like lifting a 500-pound weight with one hand while stooped under a 1,000-pound weight kept on one's back."

The image is as awkward as many of Berman's own, but the message is clear: these noble Panthers were victims. Thus Kempton and Wills said in the liberal *New York Times* what even we, at this stage, would have thought a bit much. So our sin is not in being the only ones who enthused over the Black Panthers in 1973, but being the only ones who care to remember today the nasty things that took place back then when Huey Newton was still a fetish for liberals and social democrats as well as for scraggly West Coast radicals.

The story we tell of the Panther *Götterdamerung,* moreover, would remain trapped in the memory-hole of the left if not for our book *Destructive Generation.* We alone have pointed out what Berman now claims is obvious: that the Panthers, for all their success in blandishing liberals and social democrats, had never been anything more than a violent street-gang. Protective of the faith, Berman bristles when we apply this term to the hardcore left as a whole. Lest we forget, however, Bonnie and Clyde ("We rob banks") were as much cult-heroes in the Sixties as Huey and Eldridge were. More prototypically, Stalin had a gang that also robbed banks. SDS wound up, after elemental mitosis, as a gang of terrorists called Weatherman. The Sandinistas are a gang in power; the FMLN is a gang in El Salvador that's out of power so far; Castro is the last great revolutionary gangster in the Soviet world.

The metaphor may not be perfect but it is apt, because the gang, like the left, is ruled by power, not law; the gang aims only to perpetuate itself; the gang uses rackets and scams to accumulate its wealth—shaking down the Oakland ghetto or shaking down the *campesinos.* The gang thrives on feudalism and backwardness; and as that darkness is lifted, as we see today in the Soviet bloc, the gang's hold is threatened. Of course, criminal gangs are often candid about themselves in a way that the gangs of the left never are. Criminal gangs never say they are serving the people, or midwifing the birth of a socialist utopia.

Looking for love in all the wrong places, Berman is one of those socialist butterflies for whom the bloody and bankrupt history of socialism has no conclusive meaning. That is why he continues to travel to Managua and bring back reports that careen between agonizing reappraisal and reaffirmation of belief.

At home Berman postures as an independent, if sympathetic, critic of the revolution. In Managua, however, the desire to be a communicant in the Church of Socialism gets the better of him. He goes to see Cabezas and reports back that the Sandinistas are the only New Leftists who actually made it happen. The image of someone who postures as a leftist of conscience sitting in the headquarters of the secret police has a cognitive dissonance right out of the Sixties.

6

Carl Bernstein's Communist Problem & Mine

M ore than a decade ago, when I was in my late 30s, I was visited by an elderly woman named Ann Colloms, the mother of my best childhood friend. Like my own parents and indeed all the adults I knew in the years I was growing up, Ann had been a member of the Communist Party. She had come to discuss an incident that occurred when she was in the Party and that still troubled her nearly 20 years later. Although I still considered myself part of the left at that time, I had already developed some publicly-expressed doubts about the radical heritage we all shared. It was for this reason that Ann now sought me out: to confess her complicity in a crime committed when she was a Communist long ago.

Ann and my parents belonged to a colony of Jewish Communists who, in the early Forties, had settled in a ten-block neighborhood of working-class Catholics in Sunnyside, Queens. The members of this colony lived two lives. Outwardly they were middle-class: scrupulous in their respect for the *mores* of the community and unfailing in their obedience to its civil laws. They always identified themselves publicly as "progressives," espousing views that were liberal and democratic. They thought of themselves, and were perceived by others, as "socially conscious" and "idealistic;"
This article appeared in the July 1989 issue of *Commentary*.

they were active in trade unions and civil-rights groups and in the progressive wing of the Democratic Party.

This article appeared in the July 1989 issue of *Commentary*.

The picture is consistent with that myth now struggling to be born in our literary culture that such people were "small-c" communists whose belief in democratic values outweighed their commitment to big "C" Communism. But this is a myth with malevolent implications. In fact the members of this colony, like Ann and my parents, also inhabited another, secret world as soldiers in the Third International founded by Lenin. In their eyes, a sixth of humanity had entered an entirely new stage of history in Soviet Russia in 1917—a triumphant humanity that would be extended all over the world by the actions of the vanguard they had joined. The world of liberal and progressive politics may have been the world in which outsiders saw them; but their secret membership in this revolutionary army was the world that really mattered to Ann, to my parents and to all their political friends. It was the world that gave significance and meaning to what otherwise were modest and rather ordinary lives.

In their own minds, Ann and my parents were secret agents. When they joined the Communist Party, they had even been given secret names for the time when their true objective would require them to abandon the facade of their liberal politics and go underground to take the lead in the revolutionary struggle. (My mother's secret name was "Anne Powers," which always struck me as terribly WASP-y.) All their legitimate political activities were merely preparations or fronts for the real tasks of their political commitment, which they could discuss only with other secret agents like themselves. Their activities in the democratic organizations they entered and controlled and in the liberal campaigns they promoted were all part of their secret service. Their real purpose in pursuing them was not to advance liberal or democratic values but to serve the interests of the Soviet state—because in their minds the Soviet Union was the place where the future had already begun. For those in the Party, the revolutionary role was not the *kitsch* fantasy it seems in retrospect but something that was very real and ultimately sinister. The story that Ann told me was proof enough.

No more than five feet tall in her stocking feet, Ann had been a high-school teacher of foreign languages. Her only flirtation with a reality beyond the prudent bounds of her middle-class existence was, in fact, her membership in the Communist Party. But even her Party life—despite its little Bolshevik rituals and conspiratorial overtones—was organized around activities that were quite unextraordinary: raising funds for the volunteers of loyalist Spain, marching for civil rights, and playing the part of a loyal cadre in the New York City Teacher's Union, which the Party controlled. But on one occasion Ann was chosen for a task that was not like the others—one that would burden her with guilt for the rest of her life.

In 1940 the Party selected Ann, then a new mother, for a special mission. The nature of the mission required that its purpose not be revealed, even to her, and that its details be concealed even from her Party comrades. In any other area of Ann's life, the suggestions of illegality and the dangers inherent in such a proposal would have provoked intolerable anxieties and suspicions in a person of her middle-class temperament and sheltered experience. But it was the Party that had made the request. And because it was the Party, the same elements had an opposite effect. The fear that was present only emphasized the importance of the cause that beckoned. The prospect of danger only heightened the honor of receiving a call from the vanguard Party. She understood instinctively that it was the very insignificance of her life up to that moment—its unobtrusiveness—that made her suitable for the task she was being called perform. It was the Party that spoke but it was History that called, and she answered.

Ann left her infant son with her husband in New York and took a plane to Mexico. There she delivered a sealed envelope to a contact the Party had designated. After making the delivery, she flew back to New York and resumed the life she had lived before. It was as simple as that. Yet it was not simple at all. As Ann soon discovered, she had become a small but decisive link in the chain by which Joseph Stalin reached out from Moscow to Cayocoán, Mexico, to put an ice-pick in Leon Trotsky's head.

One of the most disturbing elements in Ann's story lay in the fact that she had waited so long to tell it, and then only to me. It had been 20 years after Khrushchev's report exposing to the Party faithful the crimes that Stalin had committed. It was at that time that she and my parents had left the Communist Party. Twenty years later she had come to me to tell her story and relieve her guilt. But neither she nor my parents had ever thought to tell me this or similar stories to warn me of the minefields I might encounter when, as a young man, I started on my own career in the left. They had never told their stories publicly, nor would they approve of my doing so now. The attitude of Ann and my parents toward historical truth was a telling one. Like thousands of others, they had left the Party but could not leave the faith.

Al Bernstein, the father of Watergate journalist Carl Bernstein, had been a member of the Communist Party and a secret agent in the same way that Ann and my parents were secret agents. Like them, Al Bernstein is one of those progressives who left the Party but could never leave its political faith. When Carl Bernstein approached his father about a book he intended to write on "the witch-hunts leading up to the McCarthy era," Al Bernstein stonewalled him, refusing to be interviewed even by his own son. He did not approve his son's proposed quest for the truth about his Communist past. He did not want his son to discover the truth about his experience in the Communist Party or about the Party's role in American life. He did not want him to write about it. Even to ask the questions his son was asking indicated an incorrect political attitude. "I think your focus on the Party is cockeyed. You're up the wrong tree. The right tree is what people did.... I worry about your premise. The *right* premise, the premise of a lot of recent books about the period, is that people were persecuted because of what they did, not because of their affiliation. Because once you admit affiliation you get into all that Stalinist crap." (emphasis in the original)

Not to accept the "right" premise was more than politically incorrect; it was dangerous. "The premise people eventually accepted after the McCarthy period was that the victims weren't Communists. If you're going to write a book that says McCarthy was right, that a lot of us were Communists, you're going to write a dangerous book.... You're going to prove McCarthy right, because all he was saying was that the system was loaded with Communists. And he was right."

In Al Bernstein's view, even though McCarthy was right about the presence of Communists posing as liberals in the political woodwork, and even though virtually all of McCarthy's targets were Communists, the fact that they were Communists who lied about being Communists had nothing to do with their being singled out: "Was I 'oppressed' because I was a Communist? ... No. It was incidental. I was 'oppressed' because of what I did, because I was affiliated with a left-wing union."

We should not be misled by this fatuous catechism. The sacrament that the father rams down the son's throat is brutal as well as tasteless. In point of fact, Al Bernstein was a Communist. He was not merely "affiliated with" the United Public Workers of America; he was a leader of the union. The United Public Workers of America was not merely a "left-wing union" but a union under Communist Party control. And the fact that it was a union under Communist control—despite Al Bernstein's protestations—made it entirely different than other unions that were not Communist-controlled.

The difference was manifested most dramatically in the Cold War year 1948, which began with the Communist coup in Czechoslovakia. Coming ten years after Munich, the event sent shock waves through the capitals of the West. In an effort to halt the march of Soviet power, the Truman administration announced it was launching the Marshall Plan—an economic-aid program to revive the war-shattered economies of Western Europe and to shore up its democracies against their own Communist threats. While most American unions supported the Marshall Plan as an economic boon for their members and a necessary defense measure for the West, Al Bernstein's union did not. Along with all the other Communist-controlled unions in America, Al Bernstein's United Public Workers attacked the Marshall Plan as a Cold War plot and launched an all-out campaign against it. On the political front, Al Bernstein and his comrades bolted the Democratic Party and organized the Progressive Party candidacy of Henry Wallace in the hope of unseating Truman and ending his anti-Communist program. Their actions were in fact a Soviet-orchestrated plot to sabotage the defense of Europe against Soviet aggression.

Most unions were not agents of the Soviet Union as Al Bernstein's was. In response to their sedition, Al Bernstein's union and other Communist-controlled unions were purged from the CIO. They were purged not by McCarthy or by Harry Truman and his Loyalty Board but by patriotic unionists like Philip Murray and Walter Reuther, who as liberal socialists would not go along with the Communist betrayal of their country and their union members in the service of the Soviet Union. Phillip Murray, who is cited in Carl Bernstein's *Loyalties* for his principled opposition to the Loyalty Boards, also told the CIO convention in 1948 that he opposed the Communists "because they have subverted every decent movement into which they have infiltrated themselves in the course of their unholy career."

At 70-plus years of age, more than three decades after Senator McCarthy's death, Al Bernstein is still actively practicing his old Stalinist deceits, still taking the Fifth Amendment towards any inquiry, however innocent, into his commitments and beliefs, still hiding his Communist agendas behind a liberal façade—and not only to the world at large but to his own pathetically inquisitive son. To be called a witch-hunter by your father for trying, however ineffectually, to sort out the Oedipal tangle must be a daunting experience.

Carl, whose memoir is utterly innocent of the vast literature on American Communism—which refutes virtually every page of this little book he took eleven years to write—measures the dimensions of his filial love in a passage that occurs a little less than halfway through the text: "Many years later, ... [I] realized that it is my father for whom I write, whose judgment I most respect, whose approval I still seek." *Loyalties* is little more than a unilateral withdrawal from the Oedipal struggle.

In the end, it is the sheer desperation of this filial hunger that overwhelms the text Carl Bernstein intended to write and that explains the deficiencies of the preposterous book he has had the bad judgment to publish. (Even the title—originally *Disloyal*—has been changed to fit the fashions of the paternal party line.) He resists his father's "correct premise," manfully at the outset. But by the final chapters of *Loyalties* he has capitulated and even joined up. Al Bernstein's Communist Party loyalties didn't matter, not to him and not to those who pursued him—or so Carl avows. Al Bernstein and all the other agents of the Communist cause were targeted solely for their activities on behalf of trade unionism and civil rights; the internal security program of the Truman administration "really was a war against liberals."

This is not a book about the Communist Party and its discontents but a lecture on the need to keep the tattered faith at whatever cost to one's integrity. As Al Bernstein, shrewder and intellectually stronger than his wayward son, impatiently observes, "the right premise"—the Communist Party's premise— is "the premise of a lot of recent books about the period." Thus the standard academic work on the subject of American universities in the loyalty-oath era—*No Ivory Tower* by Princeton professor Eleanor Schrecker—is written from this neo-Stalinist perspective, as are most other recent studies written by academic leftists about the early Cold War security conflicts.

Even more striking support for Al Bernstein's perspective is offered by the notices of *Loyalties* in the prestigious book-reviews of the Sunday *New York Times*, *The Washington Post* and *Los Angeles Times*. In each, Carl had his literary knuckles rapped by leftist reviewers who chided him for not justifying his parents' Communist politics *enough*. Thus, Paul Robeson's neo-Stalinist biographer Professor Martin Duberman complained in *The Washington Post Book World*: "In his dedication, Carl Bernstein asserts that he is proud of the choices his parents made. But he never provides enough argued detail about what went into those choices to allow most Americans to join him—as surely they should—in his approbation." Indeed.

What are the tenets of the neo-Stalinist faith that has so unexpectedly resurfaced in American letters? Basically there are two: first, that Communists were peace-loving, do-gooding, civil-rights activists and American patriots; second, that they were the innocent victims of a fascist America. Carl has it down pat: "*'It was a reign of terror.'* I have never heard my father talk like that, have never known him to reach for a cliché. But this was no cliché." (emphasis in original). Correct: it was not a cliché; it is a lie.

No, Carl, we in America didn't have a reign of terror, not the way that phrase is understood to apply to the Stalinist world out of which our families both came and where it means blood in the gutters. In America, my mother elected to take an early disability retirement from the New York school-system rather than answer questions about her membership in the Party. But with the help of Party friends and liberal sympathizers she immediately went on to other, better careers, as secretary to the head of the National Lawyers Guild and research librarian for Planned Parenthood. Your father became a small-time entrepreneur and you got a job, through his personal connections, as a reporter at *The Washington Star.* When later you were at the *Post* and about to help topple a sitting president during the Watergate scandal, you went to managing editor Ben Bradlee to reveal the terrible secret about your parents' Communist past, and what did he do? Remove you from the case? No; in horrific, anti-Communist, paranoid America, the home of McCarthy's reign of terror, the editor of *The Washington Post* told you to get on with the story. And what did you learn from that? Exactly nothing.

That is my ultimate complaint about *Loyalties* and its pseudo-account of the anti-Communist era. As in all the recent rewrites of this history, whose premise is to keep the faith, the reality of the postwar domestic conflict between Communists and anti-Communists goes unreported. In a fleeting episode of *Loyalties*, Carl's friend and former boss Ben Bradlee recalls over dinner that he had always thought of progressives like Carl's parents, whom he did not personally know, as "awful people." Even in the jagged structure of this book, the observation is jarring. But even more unnerving is the fact that the famous investigative reporter of Watergate does not pursue the remark to inquire what memories might lie behind it. The same lack of inquisitiveness is seen in his feeble efforts to understand the nature of his parents' true commitments. He describes his mother, then in her 70s, as a woman who is "very forgiving." But when she refers to a political adversary of 30 years ago as a "vicious bastard," her son simply ignores the emotional signal, missing anything that it might tell us about the polarized psyches and virulent hatreds of progressives like his parents.

Elsewhere he describes how his grandfather would take him to a Jewish bookstore to buy the Yiddish-language Communist newspaper *Freiheit*. "Until the day he died in 1967 he had no use for the [non-Communist] *Forward*—or the [non-Communist] *Socialists*. 'Fareters,' traitors of the cause, he called them, and he didn't much like having any of them into his house. . . ." This life-long hatred toward non-Communist leftists, coupled with casual vitriolic abuse, was a staple of the personalities of Bernstein's parents and of the other "victims" of the postwar "purge." In attempting to explain to Carl, at another point in the text, why Al Bernstein joined the party, family friend and fellow-Communist Bob Treuhaft observed: "There was a feeling that unless you joined and were with us you were the enemy." Carl lets this one slip by, too.

These progressive activists had many enemies. John L. Lewis, head of the CIO's United Mine Workers, had once been a party ally; but when he refused to go along with the Communist-supported no-strike pledge after the German invasion of Russia, the party attacked him as a "pro-Nazi" who was committing "treason." The Communists also routinely denounced civil rights leader A. Philip Randolph, the organizer of the war-time March on Washington, as "a fascist helping defeatism," because Randolph had refused to shelve the struggle for civil rights—as the party demanded—in favor of joining the effort to help save the USSR from defeat. So much for the fantasy that Communist Party members were at bottom only unionists and civil-rights activists, or that progressives love peace.

Not only were progressives not libertarians; they were also, despite their pious wails later on, notorious masters of the political blacklist in all the organizations they managed to control. It was partly for these reasons that when the loyalty boards and congressional committees finally did come to town, there were a lot of people—a lot of liberal people—waiting to settle scores with the Communists. To them, Communists were not the civil-libertarian idealists of Carl Bernstein's book but political conspirators who had infiltrated, manipulated and taken over their own liberal organizations to subvert them for hidden agendas; had slandered, libeled, and blacklisted people who opposed the party line; and had then lied to the public, pretending they were not Marxists or Soviet loyalists when questions about their political affiliations were asked.

The Communists lied to everyone then, and the new keepers of their faith are still lying today. "If you're going to write a book that says McCarthy was right, that a lot of us were Communists, you're going to write a dangerous book," Al Bernstein had warned. Look for a moment at this logic: To admit that they were Communists is to lend credence to the claims of Joe McCarthy. Why is this dangerous at so late a date? Is not McCarthy himself the most irretrievable political corpse of the McCarthy era? It is dangerous for progressives to admit the truth not because it will bring *persecution* but because it will remove the final veil and show progressive life to be simple service to the totalitarian cause.

It is not a fear of smearing "innocents" that haunts the political left when it looks at its disgraceful past. It is something more like the fear that haunted the conscience of deconstructionist scholar

Paul De Man: embarrassment over a terrible guilt. "'Look,'
[Al Bernstein] snapped, 'you've read Lillian Hellman's book. She
skirts these questions [about Communist Party membership]
very neatly. She's too sharp to leave herself open to that kind of
embarrassment.'"

As always, Al Bernstein's old Stalinist politics reveal a judgment sharper than that of his born-again son. Embarrassment is
the problem, not a sham reign of terror. It is the shame of being
exposed as a loyal supporter of a mass-murderer like Stalin for all
those years. The struggle now is not over the fact, but what it actually meant to be a Communist then and an apologist for Communists now. Civil rights, trade unionism, human brotherhood and
peace: That's what we were—they now stubbornly claim as their
fallback position—that was our cause. Communism? Marxism?
Socialism? Those were incidental—irrelevant to who we were and
what we did.

Loyalties reveals the secret of how the progressive left aims to
be born again—by erasing the embarrassment of its disreputable
past; by hiding the shame of having supported Stalin and Mao and
Fidel and Ho and all the terrible purges, murders, and other despicable means that finally served no beneficial ends. The ultimate
embarrassment is of having been so stubbornly and perversely on
the wrong side of history; of having embraced "solutions" that
were politically, economically and morally bankrupt in the great
struggles of our time. As Joseph Stalin was the first socialist leader
to understand, the airbrushing of history is the only sure means to
preserve the honor of the left. In this, as no doubt in other parts of
his undiscovered life, Al Bernstein follows right along the Stalinist
path. And his son walks in lockstep behind him, picking up his
mess.

7

Political Cross-Dresser: Michael Lind Perpetrates a Hoax

L ast winter, while working on my autobiography, I received a phone-call from my friend Ronald Radosh telling me about an article Michael Lind had written for the socialist magazine *Dissent*. The article was called "The Death of Intellectual Conservatism" and was Lind's explanation of the political transformation that had led him to abandon his career as a journalist ostensibly on the political right. The article was announced with great fanfare on his part and accepted by the left, Lind's new home, as a *God That Failed* in reverse. Prior to the appearance of Lind's article, and despite the fact that we were presumably both members of a relatively small community of conservative intellectuals, I had only been vaguely conscious of his existence. Although I was an inveterate reader of conservative magazines and books, and familiar with most if not all of the intellectual lights of the movement, I knew Lind only as a name on the masthead of Irving Kristol's foreign-policy magazine, *The National Interest*, and as the author of one or two articles whose subjects and arguments had not left a lasting impression.

Despite Lind's obscurity, there were reasons for the interest that news of his apostasy now aroused in me. To begin with, there was the appearance of a parallel career, as someone who seemed to be stepping onto a path that both Radosh and I had previously trod, albeit in the opposite direction. The path had begun in 1952, when

Published May 15, 1998 on www.frontpagemag.com; http://archive.front-pagemag.com/Printable.aspx?ArtId=24322

Radosh and I had gotten to know each other at a meeting of his chapter of the Labor Youth League, a Communist Party front in lower Manhattan, where I had come to recruit writers for the *Daily Worker*'s "youth page," which had been launched improbably at my suggestion since I was only 13 at the time. (My parents were friends with Joe North, one of the paper's editors.) The youth page lasted for only one issue but Ron and I became lifelong friends. In 1987 he was one of the former radicals whom Peter Collier and I recruited for the "Second Thoughts Conference" we held at the Grand Hyatt in Washington, D.C. We had assembled a group of former Sixties radicals who were fed up with the anti-American passions and totalitarian romances of the left and were ready to say goodbye to all that. The intellectuals grouped around *Dissent*, whom Michael Lind now counts as his comrades, were among the most vocal in attacking our second thoughts about the Sixties as overwrought and even renegade.

The second reason for my interest in Lind's political conversion was a long-running dialogue between Radosh and myself about whether we should have wound up as conservatives at all. Radosh was, in fact, still on the editorial board of *Dissent*, though more in name than anything else at the time of Lind's conversion. He had been banned by *Dissent's* editor, Irving Howe, from writing in its pages because of his opposition to the Sandinista dictatorship. Having forbidden Radosh to write on this subject, Howe then pressured him to resign from the *Dissent* board. Howe stopped short of actually removing Radosh because another board member, Marty Peretz, shared Ron's views and Howe was reluctant to antagonize Marty, who was one of the magazine's funders.

Although hated by the left for his courageous book *The Rosenberg File* – which showed that Julius and Ethel Rosenberg had indeed been part of a Communist espionage effort—and for his writings against the Sandinistas, Radosh still thought of himself as a "social democrat." He had voted for Bill Clinton in the 1992 election. He was ambivalent about being situated in the conservative camp where left-wing critics had effectively placed him by their constant vilification. I had no such ambivalence. The image of the right that the left had manufactured—authoritarian, bigoted, mean-spirited, "Neanderthal"—was an absurd caricature that had no relation to the way I saw myself or my new comrades-in-arms. Conservatism to me was liberal, a commitment to the values and principles of individual liberty embodied in the American founding. I had rejected the leveling illusions and totalitarian longings of the left. I had no apologies for what I had become. My only political regrets had to do with the durability of the politics that Radosh and I had once espoused and now rejected as dangerous and destructive. When Radosh alerted me to the appearance of Lind's article, the subtext of his call was a question: "Is Lind right about intellectual conservatism? Should you be having third thoughts?"

And so I came to regard Lind as a sort of *Doppelgänger.* I wanted to see how the intellectual world was going to treat him for his apostasy. I had been prepared for what happened to Peter Collier and myself when our own rejection of half a lifetime of leftism became public. I had expected the attacks from the Left. I knew that we and Radosh would be smeared as renegades, CIA spokesmen and worse. But only Collier foresaw the real punishments that were in store for us; in particular, the penalties that the left would exact on our intellectual and literary careers. At the time Collier and I published our declaration of independence in *The Washington Post* and were called "Lefties for Reagan," we had not been active in the movement for nearly a decade. After our disillusionment, we had allowed a decent interval to elapse before reentering the political arena; we had not betrayed or exploited the confidences of recent friends. We thought the long gestation—a calculated gesture to preserve our political options—would preempt the attacks on us as renegades and traitors. In this regard we were hopelessly naïve.

During the ten-year interval, we had written a series of bestselling biographies and several celebrated magazine articles, some of which were optioned by Hollywood producers. We were hoping to carve out new careers as literary figures. But when our apostasy became public, the retribution was swift and without limit. Before our declaration, the biographies we had written were regularly given front-page treatment in the Sunday *New York Times Book Review*, which described them as "hypnotically fascinating," "irresistible" and the like, and put them on its list of the year's top ten books. But once we openly discussed the reasons for our rejection of the left and admitted to voting for Ronald Reagan, all that changed. Our next biographies were relegated to the back of the *Book Review*; while *Destructive Generation* was derisively dismissed, by a reviewer who had once raved about us, as the work of political "extremists."

Despite our best efforts not to be typed as political conservatives, we found that we were now unwelcome in the pages of *The Times*, *The Atlantic*, *Harper's*, *The New York Review of Books* and even *The New Republic*, where we had hoped to find a home. Our first biography, *The Rockefellers*, had been nominated for a National Book Award but now we realized that we would never be in line for literary prizes again. Nor were the issues that we raised in our apostasy the source of much attention or interest in these intellectual journals. We had been founders of the New Left, had written some of its basic political texts, and had edited *Ramparts*, its flagship publication. Yet our defection was treated as venal in motive and our commitments dismissed by writers like Garry Wills as "marginal" to the movement and the Sixties. None of the above-mentioned magazines took seriously the arguments we and the other members of our second-thoughts group had raised at the conference.

There was a further irony in all this, which added to my curiosity about the fate of Michael Lind. Perhaps no greater caution exists for a leftist tempted to leave the faith than the charge of "selling out." To those who have it, the radical commitment seems to be less a political than a moral choice. Leaving the political faith is thus as inconceivable as leaving a religious one. Only pathological behavior—taking money or some other material benefit—could explain to a leftist the decision to adopt an opposing political stance; no decent person could ever make such a choice in the absence of some kind of payoff. Even in the post-Communist world, the average leftist remains in this way a vulgar Marxist despite all. The fact that Peter and I had actually lost opportunities for personal gain as a result of our change-of-heart was incomprehensible to our former comrades, who accused us of selling out.

The penalties we paid were a lesson for me in the pervasive control the left exercised over the culture's commanding heights. Lind's successes in the aftermath of his *Dissent* piece now completed the course. Prior to his apostasy, Lind was a nonentity in the conservative movement. He had no claim to importance other than the fact that he had been sponsored and befriended by important conservatives like William F. Buckley Jr. and Irving Kristol, whose hands he then proceeded to bite. But once he did his about-face, this obscure junior editor of an obscure magazine (circulation 4,000) became an intellectual hot property. Whereas Collier and I found ourselves unwelcome in the literary culture after our *Washington Post* piece, lead articles and cover stories by Lind suddenly appeared within months of each other in *The New York Review of Books, The Atlantic, Harper's, The New York Times* and *The Washington Post.* He was made a senior editor successively of *Harper's, The New Republic,* and *The New Yorker;* he was signed by New York publishers for three lucrative book deals, including an account of his apostasy, based on the *Dissent* article, called—what else?— *Up from Conservatism: Why the Right Is Wrong for America.*

The transformation from right to left had paid off handsomely. In fact, it seemed less a conversion than a career move. Lind actually got all the rewards our former leftist comrades had falsely accused Collier and me of getting; but he drew no suspicion about his motives. I was curious to see if his book lived up to the billing—if he had the goods as well as the goodies.

Up from Conservatism comes with a flap copy that describes Lind as "a former rising star of the Right," which he was not, and a blurb from Gore Vidal describing the book as "a fascinating look—from the inside—at that web of foundations and other interested people, corporate and simply dotty, that now shape most of what passes for political commentary." In his blurb, Vidal also compares Lind to Alexis de Tocqueville.

My first interest, in the *Dissent* article and the book, was the reason for Lind's break with the conservative movement I had joined. They would provide an opportunity to check on any illusions that might have insinuated themselves into my new political directions. In writing our own *explications de vie,* Collier and I had been careful to point out that for us there was no sudden revelation on the road to Damascus, no single moment or event that unraveled the skein of our former political selves. The change in our perspective had occurred through many events in the course of many years.

If there was a single chain of events that encapsulated the process of our second thoughts, it was the war in Vietnam, which provided what we referred to as the shaping metaphor for our generation's view of the world. It was the tormented aftermath of that war that became our point of no return. As the Soviets moved into the vacuum created by America's defeat, it was clear to us that the Cold War was ultimately a zero-sum game. When America lost, so did humanity and the cause of freedom, even in Vietnam. More people were killed in Indochina in the first three years of the Communist peace than had been killed in thirteen years of the anti-Communist war. Those victims were a direct result of the antiwar movement's efforts. The survivors had been swallowed by a socialist police-state even worse than the corrupt regimes that it replaced. Salting those wounds, the left showed a lack of concern for the victims that was matched only by its continuing malice towards America. But what finally turned us away from the left was not only the evil it had done. It was its inability to look at its deeds and make a moral accounting, to steer an altered course that would keep it from contributing to similar tragedies in the future.

In *Up from Conservatism,* Michael Lind reveals that in contrast to us he actually did experience a Damascus-style revelation on the way to his new career. His epiphany came from the 1991 publication of a book called *The New World Order* by Pat Robertson, which detailed "a conspiracy theory blaming wars and revolutions on a secret cabal of Jewish bankers, Freemasons, Illuminati, atheists, and internationalists." Confronted with this threat from Robertson, who had founded a new and powerful organization called the Christian Coalition, "the leaders of intellectual conservatism—William F. Buckley Jr., Irving Kristol, and Norman Podhoretz, instead of protesting, chose unilateral surrender." Those intrepid souls who criticized Robertson, like Lind himself, were "denounced as 'liberals' and even 'Marxists.'" The result, according to Lind, was an "exodus of the major young intellectuals formerly associated with the right," himself among them. The overall consequence of these events, as Lind tells it, was that "American conservatism is dead. . . . Today the right is defined by Robertson, Buchanan, and the militia movement."

Any reader who was not a liberal zealot or otherwise predisposed to hate and fear the right, and who was reasonably acquainted with the conservative movement in America, might be tempted to close Lind's book right there. The characterization is so off-the-wall and self-discrediting that further exploration of the author's thoughts would seem hardly necessary. Consider for example the remark about an exodus of "the major young intellectuals" of the right following the alleged surrender to Robertson. This flourish may add a frisson of importance to his own departure, while seeming to support his claim about the death of conservatism. But where is the evidence? I actually did a double-take on reading the sentence, since I was unaware that any such defection besides his own had taken place. This despite the fact that my personal interest in such a development would have been great.

Later Lind identifies "the major young intellectuals" as actually only three: Jeffrey Herf, Bruce Bawer and Jacob Heilbrunn. Herf was, in fact, one of the featured speakers at our Second Thoughts Conference in 1987 and is still a friend. It is news to me that Jeffrey Herf ever thought of himself as a Republican, let alone a conservative. He has second thoughts about the Sixties left, but he has always been a Democrat and on the left side of the spectrum. At our conference, he particularly outraged Hilton Kramer by defending some of what the New Left had done and by describing himself as a "feminist." Bruce Bawer is a book and film critic who actually remains a conservative.[1] Jacob Heilbrunn is a Harvard graduate student who was briefly at *The National Interest* and is known only for the article he wrote about Pat Robertson in liberal *New Republic,* which he co-authored with Michael Lind. Whatever his politics, he is hardly a conservative "star."

As though sensitive to the indefensible nature of his thesis, Lind repeats it endlessly throughout his book: "The 'right' now means the overlapping movements of the 'far right'.... [same paragraph] The only movement on the right in the United States today that has any significant political influence is the far right...." Lind summarizes the philosophy of this right in the following words: "The fact remains that a common worldview animates both the followers of Pat Robertson and Pat Buchanan and the far-right extremists who bomb abortion clinics, murder federal marshals and country sheriffs, and blow up buildings and trains. That worldview is summed up by three letters: ZOG. ZOG stands for 'Zionist-occupied government,' the phrase used by far-right white supremacists, anti-Semites, and militia members for the federal government."

Nor is it just hateful philosophy which conservatives share. "In the manner of the southern right from the Civil War until the civil rights revolution, which operated both through the Democratic Party and the Ku Klux Klan, or the modern Irish Republican movement, with its party (Sinn Fein) and its terrorist branch (the IRA), the contemporary American far right has both public, political wings (the Christian Coalition and Project Rescue) and its covert, paramilitary, terrorist factions." Naturally, Lind doesn't name any of these factions or attempt to link terrorist and paramilitary groups with their alleged fronts, like the Christian Coalition,

---

[1]At present Bawer is actually a writer for the David Horowitz Freedom Center.

which (unlike Sinn Fein) has denounced such violence. For Lind, whose book is an exercise in slander, the accusation is all that matters.

Lind doesn't explain how William F. Buckley, Jr.—who 30 years ago drummed anti-Semites and John Birchers out of the mainstream right and whose most recent book is about the anti-Semitism of Pat Buchanan and others—"surrendered unilaterally" to those hateful and menacing forces. Nor does he attempt to explain how Norman Podhoretz, accused by Lind's new anti-Semitic admirer Gore Vidal of being an Israeli agent, could be brought to do the same. Lind's claim is simply that Pat Robertson's Christian Coalition is electorally so powerful that conservatives like Buckley and neo-conservatives like Podhoretz are reluctant to challenge him for fear of jeopardizing the Republican agenda.

The absurdity of Lind's argument is breathtaking. If Robertson shared such extremist worldviews with Pat Buchanan and were acting on them within the Republican Party, why would he and his Christian Coalition support Robert Dole in the Republican primaries and not Buchanan? Lind refers to Robertson as "the kingmaker" of the Republican Party. What does that mean if not the ability to determine the party's candidate? And if that were the case then why not himself, since he has run as a candidate before? If the far right had been the only "significant political influence on the right," why didn't Robertson engineer his own nomination, or at least give it to another right-wing outlier like Phil Gramm or Bob Dornan? If fear of losing Robertson was enough to intimidate Buckley, Podhoretz and the neo-conservatives from confronting his alleged anti-Semitism, why were they so ready to attack his alleged cohort Pat Buchanan as an anti-Semite and even "fascist" (as both *The American Spectator* and Bill Bennett called him), at a time when Buchanan was winning 30 percent of the vote in two presidential primaries? And where is the evidence that Buchanan, who has become almost a darling of the left, believes in the ZOG?

It needs to be said, since Lind does not bring it up in his book, that when Lind's original attacks on Robertson were taken up by the general media Robertson responded publicly. Both in interviews and in paid advertisements in *The New York Times*, Robertson expressed his personal anguish and dismay at the implications that others had found in his works. He denied any intention to identify Jews as social conspirators; he apologized to the Jewish community for any offense his book may have given, pointing out that nowhere in his book were the Jews explicitly singled out for blame; and he recalled his longstanding efforts on behalf of Israel, which included marshalling crucial votes in Congress during the 1973 and 1990–91 Middle East wars, where Israel's survival may be said to have hung in the balance. He concluded his *mea culpa* by declaring that he was proud to be a strong supporter and dependable friend of both Israel and the Jews. Rather than fear, this testimony and the facts behind it explain why Buckley and Podhoretz were quick to descend on Buchanan—who refused even to consider that his notorious outbursts might give anyone offense—but left Robertson relatively (only relatively) unscathed.

Robertson's behavior in explaining himself, it should be said, contrasts dramatically with that of leftwing political anti-Semites like Lind's blurb-writer Gore Vidal, not to speak of Louis Farrakhan, who unlike Robertson actually preaches a virulent anti-Semitism and has been embraced by forty congressional members of the Democratic Party that Lind has chosen for his new ideological home.

When he gets around to actually analyzing Robertson's text, Lind reveals just how manipulative a polemicist he can be. In composing *The New World Order*, Robertson or his researcher did make an egregious decision to draw on tired conspiracy-theories from anti-Semitic texts. But what is interesting about his use of those texts is that in his own book, where he cited them, he removed most of their specific references to Jews, and particularly to the Jewishness of principals involved in the alleged conspiracies—a peculiar quirk, to say the least, for an anti-Semite, let alone for the kind of neo-Nazi menace that Lind has conjured. Nor is Lind unaware of Robertson's editorial process. Indeed, Lind actually draws his readers' attention to it in claiming that Robertson's omission of ethnic particulars is *further* evidence of his anti-Semitism: "Throughout *The New World Order,* as I shall show in further detail below, Robertson uses 'German' or 'European' where his anti-Semitic sources have 'Jewish.'" Because this seems to convey a certain innocence in Robertson's references, Lind quotes a passage from Robertson's text and inserts in brackets the offending connections Robertson has removed:

> Later the European powers [i.e., bankers like the Rothschilds] began to see the wealth of North America as a great treasure, and some of them still wanted to get their tentacles into America's economy [note the 'octopus' metaphor, a staple of anti-Semitic and anti-capitalist rhetoric]. They eventually did so not by force, but by investing their money here, by sending people [i.e., Jewish bankers like Paul Warburg and Jacob Schiff], and by buying land.

This is a bizarre way to demonstrate that an author is anti-Semitic.

The crucial questions to ask about what Lind calls "The Pat Robertson Scandal," are these. First: are Robertson's politics actually governed by these conspiratorial views? And if so, how did he come to be an early supporter of Bob Dole? Second: are they shared by Ralph Reed, the director of the Christian Coalition, whom everybody, including his liberal opponents, agree is a shrewd strategist and supple intellect operating in the political mainstream? Third: are they shared by the 1.8 million members of the Christian Coalition, which as even Lind is forced to admit is a direct-mail coalition and not a party or cult in the manner of the Posse Comitatus, the John Birch Society, or the Nation of Islam?

Lind makes no effort whatsoever to assemble evidence that would illuminate or answer these critical questions, and thus to ascertain whether Pat Robertson's conspiracy views are anything more than one man's hot air. In other words, Lind's "analysis" is completely empty of any real-world referents or implications.

What Lind does for effect is to lump Robertson with David Duke, who unlike Robertson was a card-carrying member of the

Ku Klux Klan and the neo-Nazis. Lind also asserts, without argument or evidence, that the Christian Coalition is identical to the John Birch Society. He takes Buckley's unwillingness to attack Robertson publicly as evidence for the historic capitulation of mainstream conservatism to the anti-Semitic, racist far right. But the kooky doctrines of John Birch Society leader Robert Welch were demonstrably separate from the GOP mainstream. Welch publicly attacked Dwight Eisenhower as a Communist, and his members followed suit. Lind does not mention a single occasion during the six years of the Christian Coalition's existence when its policies have reflected a conspiratorial mentality or an anti-ZOG agenda.

A section of this silly and squalid book that fascinated me was Lind's effort to explain the world of intellectual conservatism, an environment with which I am quite familiar. Lind's chapter on the subject, "The Triangular Trade: How the Conservative Movement Works," is as dishonestly constructed and argued as the rest of his book. The title itself is an open smear: "One might speak of the interaction of money, ideas, and activists on the right as a 'triangular trade, like the Eighteenth Century cycle of rum-slaves-molasses." According to Lind, part one of this trade is the grass-roots faction that he identifies as the Goldwater-YAF right, linked in McCarthy-like sweeps to the John Birch Society, *The National Review*, and all the dread demons, anti-Semites, bigots, militia storm-troopers and killers of federal agents whom he seems to invoke on every other page. The second leg in the trade is the "corporate right," which turns out be the hoary specter of Wall Street and Big Business. The business elite, according to Lind, has "acquired its own intelligentsia in the form of libertarians," specifically the Cato Institute, which in Lind's fantasies draft all the tax-cuts-for-the-wealthy-legislation that incite Richard Gephardt and David Bonior to their fits of egalitarian outrage. In sum, according to Lind: "The strategy of the modern Republican party is based on a division of labor, with the grass-roots right serving as an electoral coalition, and the libertarian right as a governing elite."

According to Lind, this arrangement presents a problem for Republicans because the libertarians regard the grass-roots Goldwaterites as fascists, while the Goldwater fascists regard the libertarians as betrayers of their authoritarian dreams. To make this alliance work, an "umbrella ideology" is provided by the third part of the triangular trade—the neo-conservative "brain trust," a network of intellectual think-tanks. The purpose of the think-tanks is to compel conservative intellectuals, through monetary bribes, to shill for the Republican agenda.

I will pause here for the benefit of readers who may not have any personal contact with the intellectual right, in order to shed some anecdotal light on this picture, which is as remote from the realities of contemporary conservatism as Pluto is from the sun. Thus, for example, my friend Marshall Wittman, a former New Leftist—onetime head of the Waco, Texas Free Angela Davis Committee and also a Jew—was until recently the legislative director of the Christian Coalition in Washington and thus in Lind's typology a crypto-fascist anti-Semite. Marshall is now at the Heritage Foundation, which is the biggest policy think-tank on the right but passed over in Lind's text because it is not libertarian and so its role in formulating the Republican agenda would completely refute his thesis.

Another friend, Shawn Steel, is a veteran of the Goldwater campaign, a former YAFer and grassroots activist. He is treasurer of the California Republican Party and finance chair of conservative Republican Dana Rohrabacher's campaign organization. He is also on the board of the Center for the Study of Popular Culture, part of Lind's neo-conservative "brain trust." Both Steel and Rohrabacher are devout libertarians, farther from being "fascists" than any of my former comrades on the left including all of Lind's new friends. Both have been particularly active in recruiting Asian-Americans to the Republican cause. Neither is an isolated example. A reunion of Goldwater activists, which I attended, was held in Orange County during the presidential primaries four years ago. Every significant right-wing Republican from the California congressional delegation and legislature was present to honor Howard Ahmanson, whom the *Los Angeles Times* has described as the "king of the religious right" in the state, but who opposed, for example, Prop 187, California's anti-illegal immigration initiative. Nearly every one of the 27 speakers, led by far-right Representative "B-1 Bob" Dornan, supported the moderate George Bush over the far-right Pat Buchanan for president. So much for Lind's guide as to how the conservative movement and the Republican Party work.

In fact, Lind's analysis amounts to little more than the kind of crackpot conspiracy theory he pretends to deride. Indeed, Lind's book reminds me of nothing so much as the Bircher tracts of the Sixties like *None Dare Call It Conspiracy*. According to Lind, "The modern conservative brain trust originated in a scheme hatched in the 1970s by William E. Simon, Irving Kristol, and others." The alleged plan was to make conservative intellectuals, hitherto an independent-minded, quirky, and diverse community, a controlled monolith that would function as a reliable tool of the Republican Party. "By the early 1990s, thanks to the success of the Simon-Kristol initiative, almost all major conservative magazines, think tanks, and even individual scholars had become dependent on money from a small number of conservative foundations." By this point, the puppet-masters Simon and Kristol are being referred to by Lind as the "Wall Street corporate raider" and the "ex-Communist-apparatchik." For the record, it is worth noting that Irving Kristol's connection to the Communist Party is this: in 1938 he spent a year in a Trotskyist—read *anti*-Communist—splinter group, arguing with the apparatchiks and demonstrating what a poor candidate for any Leninist Party he was.

Smears like this are not coincidental to Lind's argument; they *are* his argument. He writes: "The conservative movement these ex-radicals [like Kristol] crafted was therefore one that adopted the characteristic institutions and strategies of Communism while purveying an anti-Communist (not merely a non-Communist) message." The Communist Party imposed conformity on its intellectuals through ideology and terror. Kristol's party, according to

Lind, imposes an identical uniformity through the dispensation of monies under the control of a few right-wing foundations. "What passes for intellectual conservatism is little more than the subsidized propaganda wing of the Republican Party. Public dissent on matters of concern to the U.S. business elite is not tolerated."

This is a pathetic rant without a scintilla of evidence to back up its claims. Joshua Muravchik and Ben Wattenberg, to name just two fellows at the American Enterprise Institute (AEI), signed a public ad supporting Bill Clinton in 1992, without losing their jobs or suffering any other consequences. Currently there are at least three conflicting and hotly-debated conservative positions on immigration reform, an issue of obvious concern to the business elite. The head of one conservative think-tank has been hired by Silicon Valley computer firms to promote open immigration, while other "brain trust" members call for greater restrictions. Jack Kemp and Bill Bennett, whose Empower America qualifies as a unit of the "brain trust," flew to California to oppose the immigration-restriction ballot proposition, which was the principal platform of the Republican governor's election campaign, supported by the heads of all of California's conservative think tanks. Almost every conservative journal has published vigorous debates on this issue. It would be hard to imagine that kind of political diversity on the Democratic side of the political spectrum on any issue so important.

The grand puppet-master himself, Irving Kristol, is correctly described by Lind as censorious on cultural issues. But then Lind doesn't explain how it is that congressional Republicans have led the fight against the V-Chip and censorship on the Internet. The range of issues on which conservatives disagree is almost endless. *The National Review* recently published a cover feature by Bill Buckley calling for the legalization of drugs, to the dismay of Bill Bennett and most of the conservative intellectual community, including the editorial board of *The National Review* itself. An even more instructive incident took place last spring over the publication of Dinesh D'Souza's *The End of Racism*. While the

D'Souza book was funded in part by one of Lind's demonic right-wing foundations, it was publicly attacked and damaged by two foundation-funded intellectuals and charter members of the conservative brain trust, Glenn Loury and Robert Woodson. So much for the party line.

Since Lind's strategy is reflexively one of tar-and-feather, D'Souza and Charles Murray get extra punishment as they have already been targets of vicious liberal attacks. Murray is indisputably one of the leading social scientists in America but he and D'Souza are portrayed by Lind as intellectual whores, "subsidized conservative publicists," hired to promote the political agendas of the Republican party. "If this seems too harsh a judgment," Lind writes, "suppose that Murray's research had convinced him that in fact Head Start programs did work, and needed to be substantially expanded—and that to do so he recommended higher income-taxes on the rich. One need not be a complete cynic to think that he might have trouble getting grants in the future from conservative foundations, or renewing his stay at AEI."

If complete cynicism is not required, a dose of ideological blindness or just plain stupidity helps. How could anyone overlook the fact that Murray and D'Souza are best-selling authors and national celebrities who can command six-figure book contracts and lucrative speaking fees and thus are quite able to support themselves, in the unlikely event that AEI should decide to terminate them for ideological deviations? Murray would not even have to make that choice because there is enough diversity in the conservative universe to support conflicting views. In fact, Murray left another conservative think-tank and went to AEI precisely because the first did not want to support his work on *The Bell Curve,* while AEI was willing to do so. So much for Lind's conservative monolith.

As if Lind's penchant for the political gutter and his disregard for the simple truth were not sufficient, when *Up from Conservatism* turns to a brief autobiographical moment, what is revealed is that Lind is a poseur and phony as well. The man who has exploited his minor-league political metamorphosis for great personal gain reveals that he was never a conservative at all, and did not rise "up from conservatism." In his own words, which appear midway through his text: "My political journey has been far less dramatic than a switch from left to right. My political views have scarcely changed since college."

Lind's views, it turns out, are and have always been those of a centrist Democrat whose political hero is Lyndon Baines Johnson. Notwithstanding this unswerving political allegiance, Lind insinuated himself into the conservative movement while still at Yale, accepted a job at *The National Review* and proceeded mole-like for ten years to burrow through conservative institutions—the Heritage Foundation, the Bush Administration, *The National Interest*—taking advantage of conservative patrons all along the way, only to turn them, for personal gain, into the unlikely villains of his intellectually vapid, self-promoting tract.

Shortly after Peter Collier and I first entered the conservative world, Norman Podhoretz warned me: "When you were on the left, you got away with everything. Now that you're on the right, you'd better be careful because they won't let you get away with anything." Michael Lind has made the reverse crossing. Indeed, *Getting Away With Everything* would have been a good title for this reprehensible, gutter-sniping book.

8

Still Lying After All These Years

Perhaps the most famous statement about the Sixties, an era we seem unable to escape, is a quip attributed to its own Pied Piper, the late Timothy Leary: "If you remember the Sixties, you weren't there." Unhappily, it is an observation that applies not only to burnt-out acid-heads like Leary, but to the hard-wired political activists and humor-free Marxists who once guided the Movement on its destructive mission to remake America as well.

To me it is this generally overlooked phenomenon that has been the biggest surprise of all. Who would have thought that New Leftists, having made a cult of authenticity in their youth, would become such hypocritical ass-kissers of that *Zeitgeist* in middle age? It cracks me up whenever Tom Hayden or Angela Davis or Noam Chomsky or *The Nation*'s editors are described by their media friends as liberals—Chomsky as a "Jewish liberal," no less—and the same veteran radicals embrace the label as though it belonged to them. Holy My Lai! Remember when the LBJ liberals were the enemy and we were the In-Your-Face, Up-Against-the-Wall-Motherf—-er revolution-aries? Apparently none of them wants to.

A few years back, I found myself on a panel at Georgetown University debating the historian Michael Kazin on the subject of the Sixties and Vietnam. Kazin was maintaining to undergraduates who hadn't even been born at the time that "all we wanted was to

This article was published July 30, 1998 on frontpagemag.com; http://archive.frontpagemag.com/Printable.aspx?ArtId=22637

give peace a chance." It was a phrase, of course, from a famous tune by John Lennon and a kind of anti-Leninist manifesto at that. For that was the hour of the Weathermen bombers, and the party-line slogan among leaders of the "anti-Vietnam" protest movement, like Kazin himself, was "Bring the War Home." "Give Peace a Chance" was namby-pamby liberalism, the politics we hated most. Nixon wanted peace. We wanted the Vietnamese revolution to triumph. In those days, Michael Kazin was not a liberal at all but an SDS revolutionary and proud of it. As head of the Harvard chapter of SDS, Kazin had led the famous chant at the 1969 national SDS convention: "Ho, Ho, Ho Chi Minh, NLF Is Gonna Win!" It was a response to the chorus on the other side of the hall, where Progressive Labor Maoists were screaming, "Mao, Mao, Mao-Tse-Tung, Dare to Struggle, Dare to Win." That was what Kazin's New Left was about. But when I reminded him of it at Georgetown he refused to acknowledge the truth, preferring instead to repeat the self-serving lie.

Memory can play tricks on all of us, but Kazin's failure to correct himself showed that this was no false memory. It was more like a fallback position. After all, no one wants to remember the glory days of youth as a time of support for a bloody Communist aggressor and desertion of one's country in time of war.

Not *Salon*'s Joe Conason, for sure. In a July 4th column attempting to show that American leftists are really patriots, Conason summed up the "progressive" attitude towards the war against Communism this way: "The criminal excesses of the Cold War in Vietnam and elsewhere, so eagerly indulged by the right, alienated many Americans on the left from their country for a time." Sure, Joe, it was the "excesses" of a war to save the rest of the world from the cruelest and most oppressive empire in human history that caused dim-witted (if well-meaning) leftists like yourself to side with the Communist enemy in Vietnam, Korea, Cuba, El Salvador, Nicaragua, China and Central Europe.

It is mealy-mouthed and cowardly evasions like this that distinguish the present pathetic left from the Sixties originals, whose candor was their only redeeming feature. A famous *Ramparts* cover, showcasing a ten-year-old with Vietcong flag in hand, explained the position of radicals thus: "Alienation is when your country is at war and you want the other side to win." Alienation, Joe, is where the left begins, not where it is pushed by some alleged excess.

This year we are marking the 30th anniversary of 1968 and one of the darker periods in American history. The commemorations have produced some bald manifestations of the bad-faith syndrome, and have also provided a revelation or two. At a Freedom Forum conference on 1968, *Life* magazine editor and former Sixties activist Robert Friedman claimed that most student protestors were not simply trying to avoid the draft (as they most assuredly were) but were "motivated by something beyond that was weighing on us."[1] Folksinger and former Sixties activist Mary Travers (of "Peter, Paul and Mary") explained the "something" as idealism. Then she said this:

> I think sometimes that that was the last generation who believed in the American dream and its myths. These kids had gotten involved in the civil-rights movement and they were on the side of the angels, they were going to make America the country that it's always said it was.

Referring to oneself in the third person is a characteristic dissembling, but here it is only the beginning of the baloney. Come off it, Mary. Your diapers were red. Your father was a hack novelist for the Communist Party, USA. When other kids were going to Frank Sinatra concerts, you were headed for the Party's annual May Day parade to march against Wall Street warmongers and show your solidarity with Stalin's peace-loving commissars. You didn't believe in the American dream. You lusted after a Communist utopia

---

[1] In fact the "antiwar" movement disappeared as soon as Nixon replaced the draft with a lottery and announced that he was winding it down. There were virtually no antiwar demonstrations during the last four-and-a-half years of the war, because there was no draft.

midwifed by armies of bearded guerrillas or carried on the wings of a MIG-21. Why all the liberal folderol? Why can't you just tell it like it was?

Another Freedom Forum panel featured the ex-president of SDS and ubiquitous academic pundit Todd Gitlin, author of a history of the Sixties called *Years of Hope, Days of Rage.* (Even the title is classical New Left b.s.; it was years of rage and days of hope.) In his book Gitlin claims that "most New Left radicals were, in the end, reluctant revolutionaries." In fact, the opposite is true. According to Gitlin, however, it was only the terrible war and the assassinations of leaders like Kennedy and King that convinced leftists like him that revolution was the answer. "With King and Kennedy dead, a promise of redemption not only passed out of American politics, it passed out of ourselves."

On that panel, Gitlin faced his ideological enemy Maureen Reagan and experienced repressed-memory syndrome, recovering a crucial moment he had blocked. Maureen Reagan brought up the other radical movement of the Sixties, the 1964 Goldwater campaign, recalling that Goldwater did not want America to get involved in a land war in Asia and had opposed the escalation of a war that Democratic Party liberals had launched. At the time America was only providing military "advisors" and had not committed its armies to Vietnam. Where was Gitlin in this pivotal presidential debate over whether America should get into the war?

> Gitlin: I didn't vote for president in 1964.
> Reagan: Ah.
> Gitlin: I was then involved in what we felt was a movement that was going to try to change the terms of American society.

Well, Todd, that's a delicate way to put it. Far from mooning after Kennedy and King—liberals whom you and your radical comrades disdained—you were engaged in a subversive movement to overthrow the whole damn American system: values, culture, traditions, political institutions, economic arrangements, everything. Like the rest of us, you knew better than anyone over 30 what was good for everyone else. Remember? You were on a mission to destroy Amerikkka and replace it with some Marxist utopia that couldn't work—as even you now probably realize. You were too busy with your revolutionary agendas to bother about a little thing like keeping America out of an Asian war. And now you cannot even remember it.

Here are some things you and Mary and Joe and all the other arrogant nostalgists for those times should remember. First, Vietnam. Whether America should have attempted to save South Vietnam from a brutal conquest by Communists is perhaps a problematic issue. Perhaps it cannot be resolved. But here's an issue that is clear: after America was forced to withdraw from Southeast Asia because of the turmoil that leftists like you promoted at home, two million innocent peasants were slaughtered by your Communist allies—more than had been killed in all 13 years of the war that Kennedy and Johnson and Nixon had waged to prevent the bloodbath from happening. By the way, if you want a measure of what you have inflicted on the peasants of Vietnam, think of South Korea, which was rescued from a similar fate by U.S. Cold Warriors who were not obstructed by antiwar protestors like you. South Korea is now one of the richest nations in the world and its leading dissident has been elected prime minister, although in 1950 it was a dictatorship and its per-capita income was lower than Cuba's. In contrast, twenty years after the Communists conquered Vietnam, that country of New-Left dreams is a ruthless dictatorship and one of the poorest nations on earth, because that it is what Marxist progressives do: they ruin economies, which they haven't got a clue how to run, and make people unbelievably poor in the process. Cuba, the New Left's favorite socialist paradise, is poorer than it was in the Fifties and is ruled by the longest-surviving dictator in the world.

Second, the Sixties is not a time that decent Americans should remember with affection. It may have been a great party, who can doubt it, but the hangover has been horrific—and who can doubt that? The Sixties pioneers promoted drugs and promiscuous sex while delegitimizing authority, law, and the moral restraints that keep the human beast at bay. The results of counter-cultural agitations were massive drug, crime, and AIDS epidemics that together have taken a greater toll in young American lives than all the wars of the Cold War that the counter-culture opposed. On top of that, the Sixties spawned a politics of racial division—black power, racial preferences, identity-politics—that has practically undone the achievements of Martin Luther King, Jr. and the entire civil-rights movement—nonviolence, integration, and universal moral, ethical, and intellectual standards for all. Your new politics of race has pushed us down the path toward racial separatism and national disintegration.

Instead of applying the tainted brush of socialist realism to the Sixties and painting it in the false colors of idealism and hope, it would be far better to think of the decade as a cautionary tale and a reminder that we are not necessarily smarter than our parents— most certainly not wiser. If there is a generation not to trust, it is probably the one *under* 30, which hasn't had time to test its ideas or to have sobering second thoughts.

9

Repressed Memory Syndrome

N ostalgia is in the air. A generation of balding boomers is busy remembering the 30th anniversary of the year 1968. In their imaginations it is a time of lost inno-cence—a moment when impossible dreams were brutally cut short by assassinations and repressions that left them stranded on the shores of a conservative landscape.

A summary expression of such utopian regrets appeared recently in a *Salon* article by Stephen Talbot, who is also the pro-ducer of the recent PBS documentary *1968: The Year That Shaped a Generation.*[1] The narrative line of this film was shaped by radi-cals of the era like Todd Gitlin and Tom Hayden. This choice of authorities was predictable for the veteran of a movement that promotes itself as an avatar of "participatory democracy" but also closes off debate in its ranks with a regularity worthy of the Com-munist states it admired. Thus Talbot excludes from his cinematic paean to revolutionary youth any dissenters among those who were there.

Dissenters like me; for I am one of those former radicals who does not share Talbot's enthusiasm for 1968 or his view of it as a fable of Innocents at Home. One explanation may be the fact that I am ten years older than Talbot, and I know about the state of our

---

This article was published on August 31, 1998, http://archive. frontpagemag.com/Printable.aspx?ArtId=22635
http://www.salon.com/1998/09/08/news_108/
[1]See Stephen Talbot, "Days of Rage," September 1, 1998, http://www. salon.com/1998/09/01/newsc_3/

"innocence." Yet Gitlin and Hayden are also pre-boomers. An age gap cannot really explain the differing views of what took place. Oh sure, like Gitlin and Hayden I would prefer to recall the glory days of my youth in a golden light, but for me the era has been irreparably tarnished by actions and attitudes which I vividly remember and they prefer to forget.

The myth of innocence begins with President Lyndon Johnson's announcement in March 1968 that he would not run for reelection. Talbot was 19 years old and draft-eligible. "We were all like Yossarian in Catch-22," he recalls. "We took this very personally. They were trying to kill us. But now Johnson had abdicated. We were free. It felt, quite simply, like a miracle."[2] The miracle, of course, was the democratic system that we had declared war on. Contrary to what Hayden, Gitlin, Talbot and all the rest of us were saying at the time, the system worked—and we should have defended it instead of trying to tear it down. Talbot does not notice or reflect on this fact.

And, of course, "they" were not trying to kill "us." Even in retrospect, the narcissism of the boomer generation is still a marvel to behold. The attention of Johnson and Nixon after him was actually on the fate of Indochina, where they were committing American forces to prevent the bloodbath and oppression that were in store for the Vietnamese should the Communists win the war. In the event, more people—more poor Indochinese peasants—were killed by the Marxist victors and friends of the New Left in the first three years of the Communist peace than had been killed on all sides in the 13 years of the anti-Communist war. That's a fact which has caused many veterans of those years to reconsider our "innocence"—but not Talbot or the other nostalgists he cites.

In their memory, innocence was brutally ambushed when forces allegedly inherent in the System conspired to murder the agents of our hope: Martin Luther King, Jr. and Bobby Kennedy. "I

---

[2]See Stephen Talbot, "The Year of Dreaming Dangerously," July 22, 1998, http://www.salon.com/1998/07/22/news_83/

experienced King's assassination as the murder of hope," writes Talbot, speaking for all of them. Gitlin, whose history of the Sixties first announced this theme, remembers his thoughts at the time: "America tried to redeem itself and now they've killed the man who was taking us to the mountaintop." There is something extremely distasteful in this false memory of Gitlin's; for, as Gitlin well knows, in 1968 neither he nor Hayden nor Talbot nor any serious New Left radical was following King. Here's an indicator: not a single white student activist leader or antiwar spokesman was in Memphis demonstrating alongside King at the time that he was killed. In fact, not one known activist in the New Left was following King when he was killed. Two years earlier, while King was still very much alive, he had been unceremoniously toppled from the leadership of the civil-rights struggle by the radicals of the Student Nonviolent Coordinating Committee, led by Stokely Carmichael and H. Rap Brown, whose agendas of black power, racial separatism and violent struggle had replaced King's nonviolent integrationism in the imagination of the left.

Gitlin was far from the idealistic liberal he portrays himself in his book or as a talking head in Talbot's film. Like everyone else in Students for a Democratic Society, he had stopped voting in national elections as early as 1964 because, as the SDS slogan put it, "The revolution is in the streets." As New Leftists viewed them, the Republican and Democratic parties were the Tweedledum and Tweedledee of the corporate ruling class. Activists who saw themselves as revolutionaries against a "sham" democracy were not going to invest hope in a man whose agenda was integration into the system, and who refused to join their war on the Johnson administration.

Tom Hayden's attempt to formulate a doctrine of original innocence involves fewer untruths than Gitlin's but is no less dishonest. Instead of flat untruths, Hayden manipulates facts. "At that point," he says of the King assassination, "I had been so knocked out of my middle-class assumptions that I didn't know what would happen. Perhaps the country could be reformed and Robert

Kennedy elected president. Perhaps we would be plunged into a civil war and I'd be imprisoned or killed." But the reality was that any "middle-class assumptions" held by Hayden or other SDS activists had been chucked into the garbage-bin years before. Three out of four drafters of the 1962 Port Huron Statement, SDS's charter, had been red-diaper babies, offspring of Communist Party members and Marxists. The fourth was Hayden himself, who by his own account had learned his politics in Berkeley in 1960—eight years before the King and Kennedy assassinations—at the feet of "red-diaper babies and Marxists." (Hayden names Communist Party member Michael Tigar in particular.) By 1965, Carl Oglesby was proclaiming publicly that it was time to "name the System" that New Leftists wanted to destroy. The name of the System was, of course, "corporate capitalism," analyzed in pretty much the same terms as in the texts read by Communist cadres in Moscow, Havana and Hanoi.

In 1968 Hayden was already calling the Black Panthers "America's Vietcong" and planning the riot he was going to stage at the Democratic Convention in Chicago in August. Hayden's attack on the Democratic Party convention is conveniently misrepresented as a "police riot" in Talbot's film, Gitlin's book, and Hayden's own disingenuous memoir, *Reunion*. Civil war in America was not something that might be imposed on the SDS revolutionaries from the outside or above, as Hayden insinuates. Civil war was what they were trying to launch themselves. In his 1970 book *The Trial*, Hayden actually called for armed civil war.

Talbot's mythology continues: "Out of the ashes of the riots in the wake of King's murder, new hope came in the form of Bobby Kennedy, who (in less than four years, and after reading Camus) had undergone a profound transformation from Vietnam hawk and aide to Sen. Joe McCarthy to dove and spokesman for the dispossessed." Sure, and President Clinton is a virgin.

It is true that Bobby Kennedy had made a feint in the direction of the antiwar crowd and a gesture or two for César Chávez. It is also true that Hayden attended Kennedy's funeral and even wept a tear or two. But those tears had little to do with Hayden's political agendas, which were more accurately summed up in Che Guevara's call to create "two, three, many Vietnams" inside America's borders. Hayden's tears for Kennedy were personal, and he paid a huge political price for them. After the funeral, SDS activists wondered out loud, and in print, whether he had "sold out" by mourning a figure whom they saw not as a champion of the cause but as a Trojan horse for the other side.

With Kennedy and King dead, the stage was set for what Talbot calls "the inevitable showdown" in Chicago. And here a glimmer of the truth enters his narrative. "Both sides, rebels and rulers, were spoiling for a confrontation." But then, almost as quickly, he reverts to political correctness: "Chicago's Mayor Richard Daley made it possible. He denied permits for protesters at the Democratic Convention." Thus, according to Talbot, the denied permits made confrontation inevitable.

The epigram that Talbot employs for the article he wrote about '68 to go with his film—"Demand the Impossible"—explains far more accurately why it was Hayden, not Daley, who set the agenda for Chicago and was therefore responsible for the riot that ensued. True, the police behaved badly, and they have been justly and roundly condemned for their reactions. But those reactions were entirely predictable. After all, it was Daley who just months before had ordered his police to "shoot looters on sight" during the rioting after King's murder. The predictable response of Chicago's police was an essential part of Hayden's calculation in choosing to organize protests against the Democrats in Chicago in the first place.

In a year when any national demonstration would attract 100,000 protesters, closer to 3,000 actually showed up for the Chicago blood-fest. That was because most of us realized there was going to be bloodshed and didn't see the point. The two-party system was a sham; the revolution was in the streets. Why was Hayden focusing on a Democratic Party convention? In retrospect, Hayden was more cynical and proved to be shrewder than we were. By destroying the presidential aspirations of Hubert Humphrey, he broke the power of the anti-Communist liberals in the Democratic Party and paved the way for a takeover of its apparatus by forces that dramatically shifted the party to the left.

One reason the facts surrounding the Chicago riots have been obscured by the left is that the nostalgists don't really want to take credit for getting Richard Nixon elected. As a matter of political discretion, they are also willing to let their greatest coup—the capture of the Democratic Party—go un-memorialized. Instead they prefer to ascribe this remarkable development to impersonal forces that apparently had nothing to do with their own agendas and actions. Talbot summarizes: "'While the whole world [was] watching,' [Daley's] police rioted, clubbing demonstrators, reporters, and bystanders indiscriminately. The Democratic Party self-destructed." Well, actually, it was destroyed.

When the fires of Watergate consumed the Nixon presidency in 1974, the left's newly-won control of the Democratic Party produced the exact result that Hayden and his comrades had worked so hard to achieve. In 1974, a new class of Democrats was elected to Congress which included antiwar activists like Ron Dellums, Pat Schroeder, David Bonior and Bella Abzug. Their politics were left as opposed to the anti-Communist liberalism of the Daleys and the Humphreys; and their first act was to cut off economic aid and military supplies to the regimes in Cambodia and South Vietnam. Though it is conveniently forgotten now, this cutoff occurred two years after the United States had signed a truce with Hanoi and all American troops were withdrawn from Vietnam.

"Bring the Troops Home" may have been the slogan of the so-called antiwar movement but was never its ultimate goal. The ultimate goal was a Communist Vietnam. Anti-Communist regimes in Saigon and Phnom Penh fell, and the killing fields began, within three months of the cutoff. The mass slaughters in Cambodia and South Vietnam from 1975 to 1978, which took place as a result of the withdrawal of aid, was the real achievement of the New Left and could not have been achieved without Hayden's sabotage of anti-Communist liberals like Humphrey and Daley.

While Talbot forgets the *dénouement*, he does get the significance of the war correctly: "The war in Vietnam and the draft were absolutely central. I remember a cover of *Ramparts* magazine that captured how I felt: 'Alienation is when your country is at war and you hope the other side wins.'" This is a softened version of what we actually felt. As the author of that cover line, let me correct Talbot's memory and add a detail. The *Ramparts* cover featured a picture of a Huck Finn-like seven-year-old—our art director Dugald Stermer's son—holding the flag of the Vietcong, America's enemy in Vietnam. The cover line said: "Alienation is when your country is at war and you *want* the other side to win." (italics added) *That* represented what we actually believed—Hayden, Gitlin, Steve Talbot and I. It is not that important to me what lessons my former comrades now draw from our service to the wrong side in the Cold War. I just wish they would remember it as it happened.

I also wish they wouldn't make themselves retrospective supporters of the latter-day struggle against Communism, whose true warriors and champions—however distasteful, embarrassing, and uncomfortable it must be for them—were Richard Nixon and Ronald Reagan, the leaders they most resented and despised. Go over the 50 years of the Cold War against the Soviet empire and you will find that every single political or military program to contain the spread of this cancer and ultimately to destroy it was opposed by those who now invoke the "spirit of '68"—the anti-Communist rebellions in Czechoslovakia and Eastern Europe—as their own.

"Assassinations, repression, and exhaustion extinguished the spirit of '68," Talbot concludes his story. "But like a subterranean fire, it resurfaces at historic moments." Citing socialist writer Paul Berman, the originator of this myth, Talbot argues that "the embers of '68 helped ignite the revolution of 1989 that brought liberal democracy to Eastern Europe and ended the Cold War."[3] The distortion of memory is one thing for Berman, who belongs to a minuscule faction of the Left that was indeed anti-Communist—even if Berman himself supported the Black Panthers and went on to praise the deputy chief of the Sandinista secret-police as a "quintessential New Leftist." But it is particularly unappetizing in Talbot, who made films into the '80s celebrating Communist insurgents as they busily extended the Soviet sphere in Africa. America, bless its generous heart, has already forgiven Steve Talbot for that. So why lie about it now?

Of course, the New Left was critical of the Soviet Union—and so at various times were Khrushchev, Castro, and Ho Chi Minh. But its true enemy was always democratic America—a hatred that was never merely reactive, never truly innocent, and remains remarkably intact to this day. The worldview of this left was aptly summarized by I. F. Stone's adoring biographer, who reported approvingly Stone's belief that "in spite of the brutal collectivization campaign, the Nazi-Soviet Pact, the latest quashing of the Czech democracy, and the Stalinist takeover of Eastern Europe ... Communism was a progressive force, lined up on the correct side of historical events." Indeed.

Berman, Gitlin, and now Talbot have mounted this preposterous last-ditch effort to save the left from the embarrassments of its deeds by trying to take credit for helping end a Communist system that in spite of everything the left had aided and abetted throughout its career. From its beginning, the New Left disparaged the threat from the Communist enemy as a paranoid fantasy of the Cold War Right. The unseemly attempt to retrieve an honorable past from such dishonorable occasions might be more convincing if any of these memorialists were able to recall a single left-wing demonstration against Communist oppression in Vietnam, the Cambodian genocide, the rape of Afghanistan or the dictatorships

---

[3]Paul Berman, *Two Utopias*, 1997

in Cuba and Nicaragua. Or if one veteran leader of the New Left had once publicly called on the Soviets to tear down the Berlin Wall, as Ronald Reagan actually did. Support for the anti-Communist freedom fighters in Afghanistan and Africa and Central America during the 1980s came from Goldwater and Reagan activists on the Right, like Grover Norquist, Oliver North and Dana Rohrabacher, whom progressives despise for that very reason.

It would be nice if we could use this 30th anniversary of the events of 1968 to end the cold war over our past, and start restoring a sense of the tragic to both sides. But to do that, the nostalgists of the left will first have to be persuaded to give up their futile attempt to rewrite what happened and to start telling it like it was.

10

Fidel, Pinochet & Me

T he arrest of Chile's counterrevolutionary general, Augusto Pinochet, and the approach of the 40th anniversary of the Cuban revolution, together bring into focus two cele-brated battles of the Cold War in which members of my generation took passionate sides. As one who went into these battles on one side and came out on another, I have mixed but ultimately clear emotions about this history and the events that shaped it.

Being in the left imbues one with a sense of having chosen the moral side in all such conflicts. Belonging to the camp of morality and progress becomes a kind of second nature, and compensates for the fact that most, and ultimately all, of these battles are nec-essarily lost. It used to be said among us, for example, that as revo-lutionaries we were destined to lose every battle but the last. We did not join the progressive cause to support history's winners but to stand up for its losers: the powerless, the victimized, the oppressed. Our political commitment was about weighing in on the side of social justice. It was a good feeling.

When it came time to relinquish those political commitments, it was for that very reason far easier to identify what was wrong with the left and to draw back from it than it was to move in the direction of the right and plant my feet on new political terrain. As a matter of fact, I withdrew from all politics for nearly ten years

This article was published on November 23, 1998, http://archive.front-pagemag.com/Printable.aspx?ArtId=24297;
http://www.salon.com/1998/11/23/nc_23horo/

before changing course. As I was stepping back from the left, repelled by crimes that progressives had committed and catastrophes they were responsible for, I had a nagging feeling about certain political events and historical figures associated with this past. One of the figures was Pinochet who now, as an invalid at death's door, is being hounded by the left which wants him arrested and tried for crimes 30 years past.

In our progressive version of Chile's history, we saw the restoration of democracy in Chile as having produced a historical anomaly, a Marxist elected to power in 1970. This Marxist, Salvador Allende, had even been allowed by the ruling forces to form a government and begin a program of social reform. We knew, of course, that this could not last. Ruling classes never give up their power without a fight; that was one of our basic maxims. Sooner or later there would be a counter-revolution, probably a military coup. The only question was when. In making this calculation we had our eye on Washington, the capital of the world imperialist system. In political statements we issued, we invoked the cautionary memory of the Bay of Pigs, the failed CIA attempt to topple Fidel Castro in the third year of his revolutionary regime. This was the true face of American power, whose policies were orchestrated by multinational corporations with investment stakes in the Third World. It was only a matter of time before their interests asserted themselves.

As predicted in our script, the coup against Allende came in 1973. The regime was toppled, and in the heat of the battle Allende committed suicide. The generals' coup had been led by Pinochet, who became the nation's military dictator. Thousands of progressives were rounded up; some 5,000 were executed. The military dictatorship was made permanent. Chile's democracy was dead.

We knew, of course, that the CIA was behind these events. Richard Nixon and Henry Kissinger could not tolerate another revolutionary example in the hemisphere. The International Telephone and Telegraph Corporation (ITT) had big investments; its influence reached far into the Nixon Administration and the American intelligence community. It was all straight out of Lenin.

Even though I was a defector from the left, I did not want to be any part of such developments, even retrospectively. It was one thing to reject the left; it was quite another to embrace what appeared to be this kind of right—one that trampled over defenseless people, making their lives even more miserable than they had been. Nor was there any particular reason for me to do so. It was perfectly possible to have concluded that the schemes of the left were utopian and could result in great social disasters without jumping to an opposite conclusion: that the sadism of military dictators was a proper or even preferable alternative.

Another reflex familiar in the thought-patterns of progressives like myself was to avert one's eyes from bad news when it came from the left. Too much was at stake in each revolutionary enterprise, which we saw as a harbinger of human possibility. The enemies of promise would use every socialist failing to kill the socialist dream, and thus hope itself. Because these habits die hard, while I was on the left I had paid less and less attention to the fate of the Cuban revolution that had inspired Allende and the Chilean progressives. For many years I knew Castro's revolution had been going from bad to worse but I ascribed its problems mainly to the machinations of the two evil empires, Washington and Moscow.

At the end of the Seventies, I went to see a documentary about Castro's revolution made by Cuban filmmaker Nestor Almendros, who had left the island in 1963. Almendros was an Academy Award-winning cinematographer whose credits included *Sophie's Choice, Kramer vs. Kramer* and *Days of Heaven.* His documentary, *Improper Conduct,* focused on the Cuban government's treatment of homosexuals as a metaphor for its treatment of all social and political deviance. It was a stunning indictment of what the revolution had become. One scene was an interview of a black Cuban exile filmed on a street in New York's Harlem. The exile was a flamboyant homosexual in his early 20s, dressed in a tangerine satin shirt open to the sternum and white flared trousers. The interviewer asked him whether he liked the freedom he had found in America and in Harlem. With a broad smile, he answered he did. The interviewer asked why. He said, "I am free here. In Cuba I could be arrested just for being dressed like this, and put in jail for six months." The interviewer asked: "How many times were you arrested?" The Cuban answered: "Seventeen."

The young man was not a political person. He was one of those ordinary Cubans on whom history had been inflicted, and with it the drama that socialist intellectuals had created. If this was what the revolution represented to a Cuban like him, what did that say about the ideals to which I had been so devoted? The island now had a lower per-capita income than in 1959, when Castro took power. The political prisons were full. Hundreds of thousands had fled. Hundreds of thousands more were waiting to flee. Castro had turned Cuba into an island prison.

Ten years after I saw Almendros's film, an election was held in Chile. Pinochet was ending his military rule and restoring Chilean democracy. A national referendum, authorized by Pinochet, would be held to pronounce judgment on his own regime. Even the left would have the right to field a candidate. Pinochet had always justified his military regime as a temporary measure in much the same way that Castro had defended the revolutionary dictatorship. It was necessary to defend the regime, restore stability, and create the economic foundations of a true democracy. But Castro's "temporary" dictatorship was still in place, and Cubans had no democratic freedoms.

Under the 15 years of Pinochet's rule, Chile had prospered so greatly that it was dubbed the "miracle economy," one of the two or three richest in Latin America. It provided a stark contrast to Castro's achievement. In 1959, when Castro took power, Cuba had been the second richest economy in Latin America, but in the 25 years since then it had become one of the three poorest. While Pinochet was holding his referendum, Castro was approached by socialists in Europe to hold a similar election that would create a democratic regime in Cuba. He refused.

The results of Pinochet's referendum were instructive. If Pinochet had won, he would have become the new president of a democratic Chile. But Chileans rejected Pinochet and elected a more moderate candidate who was not of the left. True to his word, Pinochet stepped down. His dictatorship had indeed been a temporary measure to restore Chile's stability, prosperity, and democracy.

Those developments prompted me to look again at the events that had taken place after Allende's election and his attempt to institute radical programs that led to a civil war and the coup. I had long since become suspicious of the idea that a CIA intervention explained this result. The CIA surely had a finger in the pot, but it had become clear over time that there were real limits to what the CIA could accomplish. It had not, for example, been able to overthrow Castro despite 30 years of trying. It could not even oust the Marxist dictator of a mini-state like Granada, or a drug lord in its own employ like Panama's Manuel Noriega. Those removals had needed military invasions. And Chile was not a tiny island or an isthmus nation but a relatively large country, with a long-standing democratic tradition.

An article that appeared in *The Wall Street Journal* shortly after Pinochet's recent arrest summarizes what I discovered. "Salvador Allende reached the presidency of Chile in 1970 with only 36 percent of the vote, barely 40,000 votes ahead of the candidate of the right. In Mr. Allende's 1,000 days of rule, Chile degenerated into what the much-lionized former Chilean President Eduardo Frei Montalva (father of the current president) called a 'carnival of madness'.... The Chilean Supreme Court, the Bar Association, and the leftist Medical Society, along with the Chamber of Deputies and provincial heads of the Christian Democrat Party, all warned that Allende was systematically trampling the law and constitution. By August 1973, more than a million Chileans, half the work force, were on strike, demanding that Allende go. Transport and industry were paralyzed. On Sept. 11, 1973, the armed forces acted to oust Allende, going into battle against his gunslingers. Six hours after the fighting erupted, Allende blew his head off in the presidential palace with an AK-47 given to him by Fidel Castro."

Forty years of history have left us with a perspective on two regimes. Castro bankrupted his country, tyrannized its inhabitants, and is now the longest-ruling dictator in the world. Pinochet presided over his own ruthless dictatorship for fifteen years, created a booming economy, and restored democracy to Chile. If one had to choose between a Castro and a Pinochet, from the point of view of the poor, the victimized, and the oppressed, the choice would not be difficult. As an American conservative, however, I don't even have to do that. It was Chileans, not Henry Kissinger or Richard Nixon, who made the real decision to remove Allende and put Pinochet in power. Unlike the American left, which actively and passionately supported Fidel Castro and denied the realities of the oppressive state, the American right's sympathies for Pinochet were muted, and did not involve blindness to the stringencies of his rule. In short, Pinochet's dictatorship does not compromise any conservative expectations in the way that Castro's dictatorship refutes the visions of the left.

Imprisoning Pinochet while he is on a foreign trip to seek medical help is one of those bad ideas of progressives that will come back to bite them. Consider the prospect for Castro when he ventures abroad for parallel reasons. Yet, on second thought, perhaps the idea does work from their point of view because what made Pinochet vulnerable to this kind of arrest is that he had voluntarily retired from his dictatorial regime. There is no danger of Castro doing that.

11

*Marginalizing
Conservative Ideas*

P eople who identify with the left often ask the following
question: How is it possible for decent human beings not to
be progressive like us? How can they not share our concern
for social justice or the better world we are attempting to create?
The answer offered by progressives themselves is twofold: that
ignorance clouds their understanding or that social privilege
blocks their human responses. In the eyes of progressives, their
conservative opponents who are not members of the "ruling class"
are prisoners of a false consciousness that prevents them from recognizing human possibility. This false consciousness is rooted in
the self-interest of the ruling class or gender or race, which is
intent on defending the system that secures its privilege. In other
words, opposition to progressive agendas grows naturally from
human selfishness, myopia and greed. To progressives, theirs alone
is the calling of reason and compassion.

The right has questions too. How is it possible for progressives
to remain so blind to the grim realities their efforts have created?
How can they overlook the crimes they have committed against
the poor and oppressed they set out to defend? How can they have
learned so little from the history their ideas have engendered?

The answer is that progressives have a false consciousness of
their own. Being so noble in their own eyes, how could they not be

This article was published on December 01, 1998, http://archive.front-
pagemag.com/Printable.aspx?ArtId=24290. (Adapted from *Politics of Bad
Faith: The Radical Assault on America's Future*)

blind? And their blindness also springs from an insularity created by their contempt for those not gifted with progressive sight. As a result, radicals are largely innocent of the ideas and perspectives that oppose their agendas because their assumptions and beliefs are false. The works of Mises, Hayek, Oakeshott, Sowell, Strauss, Bloom, Kirk, Kristol and other anti-socialist thinkers are virtually unknown on the left, excluded from the canons of the institutions they dominate and absent from the texts they write. This silencing of ideological opponents has led to a situation which one academic philosopher lamented as "the collapse of serious argument throughout the lower reaches of the humanities and the social sciences in the universities." The same judgment cannot be made about the excluded conservatives, who are forced by the cultural dominance of the left to be thoroughly familiar with the intellectual traditions and arguments that sustain it. This is one reason for the vitality of contemporary conservative thought outside the academy, and for the inability of progressives to learn from the past.

Following the collapse of the socialist empire, the marginalization of conservative ideas in the academy has been so pervasive that even those conservatives whose analyses were dramatically vindicated by the events continue to remain hopelessly obscure. As far back as 1922, Ludwig von Mises wrote a 500-page treatise predicting that socialism would not work. Socialist theorists, he wrote, had failed to recognize basic economic realities that would eventually bankrupt the future they were creating. These included the indispensability of markets for allocating resources, and of private property for providing the incentives that drive the engines of social wealth. Moreover, socialists showed no inclination to take seriously the problems their schemes created: "Without troubling about the fact that they had not succeeded in disproving the assertion of the liberal school that productivity under socialism would sink so low that want and poverty would be general, socialist writers began to promulgate fantastic assertions about the increase in productivity to be expected under socialism."[1]

As close as any analysis could, Mises's warning anticipated the next 70 years of socialist history. Under the Soviet Union's central planning, the Kremlin rulers were indeed unable to allocate resources rationally, or to promote technological innovation, or to replace the profit motive with a viable system of non-monetary "social" incentives. As a result, the socialist economy was unable to keep abreast of the technological changes that would catapult the West into the post-industrial era. The socialist economy could not even create sufficient growth to feed its own people. Once the breadbasket of Europe, Soviet Russia became under socialist planning a chronic importer of grain, an economy of forced rationing and periodic famine. The effect of socialist order was exactly as Mises had predicted in 1922: the generalization of poverty and the crippling of productivity, so that Russia was unable to enter the information age and compete economically with the West.

Although history has dramatically confirmed Mises's analysis, and just as dramatically refuted his left-wing opponents, his intellectual contributions are as unrecognized today as they were before the Communist fall. On the other hand, while the intellectual tradition that gave rise to Mises's insights is marginalized in American universities and its paradigm dismissed, Marxism and its variants, which inspired the Soviet catastrophe, flourish. The profusion of Marxists on university faculties is, in fact, without precedent, while Marxist ideas and theories have spawned the principal texts of the new generations. While Mises's writings are invisible, the works of Stalinists like Antonio Gramsci, Eric Hobsbawm, Howard Zinn and Walter Benjamin—which ignore the most basic economic realities of how modern societies function— are familiar to undergraduates. In fields like critical studies,

---

[1]Ludwig von Mises, *Socialism: An Economic and Sociological Analysis*, 1922 edition, p. 182

cultural studies and American studies, and in academic schools like historicism, structuralism, post-modernism, and feminism, the discredited Marxist tradition has become the intellectual well-spring of current academic theory. The comparable schools of conservative and libertarian thought hardly exist within university walls.

It is hardly necessary to add that no serious attempt has been made by progressive intellectuals to re-visit Mises's critique—or to respond with answers that would justify the respect now accorded to the bankrupt intellectual tradition of the left. Given the verdict of history on socialist experiments, Mises's works and others that derive from the tradition of classical liberalism should central texts in any serious academic discourse. Instead they are so marginal to university curricula, it is as if they had never been written.

In contrast to Mises's fate, Stalinist intellectuals like Gramsci, Hobsbawm, and Zinn have become icons of the left-wing professoriate, their writings reissued in scholarly editions, their texts well-thumbed by undergraduates, their ideas developed and refined in doctoral studies. As though the human disasters produced by its ideas had never taken place, the reactionary tradition of the left is now dominant in the American university in a way its disciples would never have dreamed possible 30 years ago

Mises of course is not alone. His disciple Friedrich Hayek, an equally towering intellectual figure and Nobel Prize-winner in economics, is equally obscure in the academic culture. As with Mises, the theoretical edifice Hayek created is as comprehensive as Marx's, and has been vindicated by the same history that refuted Marx's ideas. Yet the name Hayek is all but absent from the discourse of the left, and from the academic curriculum the left has designed. Typically, Hayek's mature works on capitalism and socialism are rarely if ever mentioned in the broad intellectual culture, their arguments never confronted. The average college graduate is acquainted with whole libraries of radical blather, the repackaging by third-rate intellects of discredited Marxist formulas in the works of bell hooks, Frederic Jameson, Derrick Bell,

Andrew Ross, Richard Delgado and Catharine MacKinnon; but that graduate has never opened a text by the most important figures of 20th-century social thought.

An ideological *omertà* is the left's response to its vindicated critics, especially to those who emerged from its own ranks. It is an intellectual version of Stalin's efforts to transform his political opponents into "un-persons," to obliterate their influence and ideas. The historian Aileen Kraditor, once a star in the firmament of the academic left, is a figure less prominent than Mises and Hayek but no less illustrative of the method by which the left deals with its critics. The books Kraditor wrote—*The Ideas of the Woman Suffrage Movement, Means and Ends in American Abolitionism,* and *The Radical Persuasion*—were once routinely cited by Sixties progressives as models of the scholarship radicals produced. But then Kraditor had second thoughts and departed the radical ranks. As a pioneer in feminist scholarship, Aileen Kraditor should have been a prime candidate for high honors in today's academy. But she had the bad judgment to become an anti-Communist and to write a book puncturing the radical illusion.[2] As a result, it is as though she had never existed.

Based on her own experience as a member of the Party during the height of the Cold War, Kraditor's last book set out to describe the intellectual world-view of American Communists. *"Jimmy Higgins": The Mental World of the American Rank and File Communist, 1930–1958* is the definitive study of its subject. Yet despite an explosion of academic interest in the history of American Communism, Kraditor's work is almost never referred to, its insights never engaged by the academic community. Instead, Communists and Communist sympathizers like NYU's Robin D. G. Kelley and Princeton's Ellen Schrecker have become preeminent academic authorities on American Communism, while Kraditor has been made an unperson in the intellectual culture.

---

[2]Aileen Kraditor, *"Jimmy Higgins": The Mental World of the Rank and File Communist 1930–1958,* Praeger, 1988

This politically motivated censorship and self-enforced ignorance insulates the left from uncomfortable encounters with former comrades and necessary truths. Defectors from the radical
ranks quickly discover that their ideas are ignored and their realities erased. It is the way a bankrupt intellectual tradition enforces
its academic rule. The unwritten law of the radical intellect is this:
once the revolutionary idea has been called into question, the
questioner must cease to exist. In a democracy, this extinction
may be accomplished by character smears or ideological exclusion.
But it is required in order to preserve the radical faith. To the religious mind, the thought of God's death is unthinkable.

12

Can There Be
a Decent Left?

Fifteen years ago, Peter Collier and I assembled a group of disillusioned New Leftists for a conference in Washington we
called "Second Thoughts." Those second thoughts had been
provoked by many factors and events, most instrumental among
them the wholesale slaughter of innocents in "liberated" Cambodia and Vietnam by forces that had been supported by the American left. It was not the first sprouting of radical second thoughts.
Generations of leftists before us had been repelled by the similar
crimes of Stalin and Mao and Castro, and had shed their progressive worldviews for more sober and conservative politics. Irving
Kristol, who was on the panel of elders we invited to our conference, observed that second thoughts had begun with the creation
of the modern left during the French Revolution, and had been
repeated many times since. Our second thoughts, he said wrily,
were an instance of what Yogi Berra called "déjà vu all over again."

Now it is déjà vu once more. The events of 9/11 and their aftermath have produced a whole new generation of second-thoughters
in various stages of reassessment. They include such luminaries of
the literary left as Salman Rushdie, Martin Amis and Christopher
Hitchens who this fall joined with their sometime opponents to
defend America's empire against a radical Islamic enemy they
might once have considered a vanguard of the Third World

This article was published on Tuesday, March 26, 2002, http://archive.
frontpagemag.com/Printable.aspx?ArtId=24456
http://www.salon.com/2002/03/28/walzer/. Reprinted in *Left Illusions*,
2004

oppressed. Now the editor of *Dissent*, Michael Walzer has come forward with an articulate question about second thoughts and how far to push them. A philosopher, social critic and lifelong democratic socialist. Walzer has pointedly titled his article, "Can There Be A Decent Left?"[1]

The seriousness of that question can be measured in the fact that insofar as there is a "decent left," Michael Walzer has exemplified it throughout his career. I should interject here that our political paths crossed nearly 40 years ago, when I was a young and combative Marxist in England. I do not remember the substance of our disagreements, and I no longer have copies of *Views*, the obscure leftwing magazine that printed them. But I am certain that he was the more civil of the two of us—and just as certain that he, being to my right, was more correct on the issues.

One could also say that the faction of the left which *Dissent* represents is itself the decent left. During the Sixties *Dissent's* founder Irving Howe symbolized resistance within the left to the totalitarian elements that had come to dominate the decade. Although its editors were seduced in the 1980s into a "critical" defense of the Sandinista dictatorship, they had an otherwise honorable record of having opposed Communism throughout the Cold War, even if they only grudgingly supported, and were often excessively critical of, America's efforts to contain the Communist threat.

It may also be that "decency" more describes Walzer's personal temperament than it does the politics of the *Dissent* community. An obvious manifestation of decency is to respect those you disagree with if they deserve it. As a matter of disclosure, I must interject here that *Dissent* editor Paul Berman once described me in its pages as a "demented lunatic"—as if my sins had been great enough to deserve the redundancy. *Dissent's* other intellectual leader, Richard Rorty, has defined the left as a movement "against

---

[1]http://www2.kenyon.edu/Depts/Religion/Fac/Adler/Politics/Waltzer.htm

cruelty." But his own writings have not been without crude demo-nizations and peremptory dismissals of his conservative oppo-nents as dolts and fascists, whose ideas a civilized progressive is obliged to dismiss. He has even celebrated the left's political dom-ination of university faculties, something he well knows is the result of an ideological purge of conservatives that he would cer-tainly deplore if the roles were reversed.

In bygone eras, political second thoughts tended to focus on the left's active support for nightmare regimes it mistook for earthly paradises, the embodiments of its utopian dreams. By contrast Walzer's doubts originate in his observations about the left's pas-sivity in regard to the defense of America against what he recog-nizes to be a nightmare threat. "Many left intellectuals live in America like internal aliens, refusing to identify with their fellow citizens, regarding any hint of patriot feeling as politically incor-rect," Walzer writes. "That's why they had such difficulty responding emotionally to the attacks of September 11 or joining in the expression of solidarity that followed." In their first responses, Walzer notes, leftists failed "to register the horror of the attack or to acknowledge the human pain it caused." Instead they felt *Schadenfreude,* a German word meaning joy at another's sor-rows, a "barely concealed glee that the imperial state had finally gotten what it deserved."

Even though some of these leftists regained their "moral bal-ance," they still exhibited a myopic attitude when addressing the problem of what should be done. Their sense of being internal exiles in America was again at the root of their response. "That's why their participation in the policy debate after the attacks was so odd; their proposals (turn to the UN, collect evidence against bin Laden, and so on) seem to have been developed with no con-cern for effectiveness and no sense of urgency. They talked and wrote as if they could not imagine themselves responsible for the lives of their fellow-citizens. That was someone else's business; the business of the left was ... what? To oppose the authorities, whatever they did."

Hence the left put its energies into defending the civil liberties of—suspected terrorists. Walzer is himself still unwilling to calling it this bluntly. That would mean finally stepping away from the left, which he is not ready to do. So he applauds the exaggerated concern of the left for, say, the prisoners of Guantanamo, calling it "a spirited defense of civil liberties" and a "good result." But that is a minor hesitation in the face of the larger question he has raised about the way the left sees and feels itself to be an alien presence in its own country. This latter observation is a classic second thought.

In my own passage out of the left nearly 20 years ago, it occurred to me that my revolutionary comrades never addressed to themselves what should be the obvious questions for social reformers: "What makes a society work?" "What will make *this* society work?" In all the socialist literature I had read, there was hardly a chapter devoted to the creation of wealth, the problem of getting people to work or to behave in a civilized manner. Socialist theory was exclusively addressed to the conquest of power and the division of wealth that someone else had created. Was it any surprise that socialist societies had broken world records in making their inhabitants poor?

Michael Walzer puzzles at length over the failure of the left to understand the religious nature of the al-Qaeda enemy. "Whenever writers on the left say that the root cause of terror is global inequality or human poverty, the assertion is in fact a denial that religious motives really count. Theology, on this view, is just the temporary, colloquial idiom in which the legitimate rage of oppressed men and women is expressed." He notes that "a few brave leftists" like Christopher Hitchens have described the al-Qaeda movement as a "clerical fascism." Actually this is a lingering political correctness in Walzer. Hitchens described al-Qaeda as "Islamo-fascists." But Walzer does not seem to grasp the religious roots of radicalism generally, and therefore fails to understand the affinity of American radicals for al-Qaeda and its Palestinian kin.

The indecent left reacted badly to 9/11, Walzer concludes, because it is still under the spell of the Marxist schema. These "ideologically primed leftists were likely to think that they already understood whatever needed to be understood. Any group that attacks the imperial power must be a representative of the oppressed, and its agenda must be the agenda of the left. It isn't necessary to listen to its spokesmen. What else can they want except ... the redistribution of resources across the globe, the withdrawal of American soldiers from wherever they are, the closing down of aid programs for repressive governments, the end of the blockade of Iraq, and the establishment of a Palestinian state alongside Israel?"

This is an accurate reading of the political left. But Walzer is still puzzled: "I don't doubt that there is some overlap between this program and the dreams of al-Qaeda leaders—though al-Qaeda is not an egalitarian movement, and the idea that it supports a two-state solution to the Israeli-Palestinian conflict is crazy. The overlap is circumstantial and convenient, nothing more. A holy war against infidels is not, even unintentionally, unconsciously, or 'objectively,' a left politics. But how many leftists can even imagine a holy war against infidels?"

This question reveals a gap in Walzer's perception of the left that has its roots in his own decency; as well as in the fact that, after all is said and done, he is a moralist and reformer, not a revolutionary. There is, in fact, a large literature examining the religious character of the modern revolutionary left written by authors as different as Berdyaev, Talmon, Voegelin, Niemeyer, Furet and Kolakowski. (I have written about this myself in *Radical Son* and *The Politics of Bad Faith*.) If one looks, it is not hard to see how the left's social melodrama neatly fits traditional Judeo-Christian eschatologies, from which its key texts were derived. Marx, as is well known, descended from a long line of rabbis. There is the Fall from an idyllic communal state, the travail through a vale of suffering and tears, and then a social redemption. There is the passion for moral purity and for the purges—witch-hunts—that result. The left's redemption, of course, comes not through the agency of a divine Messiah but through the actions of a political vanguard deploying its power through the socialist state.

In the last thirty years, but particularly in the last dozen, it has been impossible for leftists to visualize the utopian redemption that one once motivated their mislabeled "idealism." The catastrophe of every socialist scheme in the 20th century has had a devastating effect on leftwing optimism and has replaced it with the corrosive nihilism that makes it impossible for most leftists to defend a country which, compared to the socialist paradises, is a veritable heaven on earth. All that remains of the revolutionary project is the bitter hatred of the society its exponents inhabit, and their destructive will to bring it down. This answers Walzer's question as to how so-called "progressives" could be either so unwilling or so slow to distinguish and defend their own country—a tolerant, secular democracy—in the face of evil.

Peter Collier and I drew attention to this nihilism more than a decade ago in a book we wrote about our second thoughts. We also pointed to its sense of alienation as the defining element of the "progressive" left. As editors of *Ramparts* magazine, we produced a cover that featured a seven-year-old holding the flag of the Vietcong, America's Communist enemy in Vietnam. The cover line said, "Alienation is when your country is at war, and you want the other side to win." Coincidentally, in our book, *Destructive Generation*, we offered as an exemplary instance of this alienation a quote from Michael Walzer: "It is still true," Walzer wrote, "that only when I go to Washington to demonstrate do I feel at home there." The statement made more than a decade ago provides a measure of Walzer's present second thoughts. Like Christopher Hitchens, who published a beautiful tableau of his own transition for *Vanity Fair* after 9/11, Michael Walzer has come home.

Yet, his second thoughts are incomplete. They are inspired by his rejection of the left's nihilism rather than of its visionary goals. In the end, Walzer does not actually answer the title question of his article with a "no," even if he comes admirably close. "I would once have said that we [the left] were well along: the American left has an honorable history, and we have certainly gotten some things right, above all, our opposition to domestic and global inequalities. But what the aftermath of September 11 suggests is that we have not advanced very far—and not always in the right direction. The left needs to begin again."

Those of us whose second thoughts have led us away from the left are naturally skeptical of this optimism. The left has been beginning again since the French Revolution—and again and again. If after all this tragedy if it is "*déjà vu* all over again," why not give it up entirely and save the world another century of grief?

13

The Left and
the Constitution

More than a decade ago, Peter Collier and I wrote a book about Sixties radicals called *Destructive Generation*, which provoked—among other responses—one of the most savage attacks on us that anyone has written before or since. The author of this attack, Hendrik Hertzberg, is now a senior editor at the *New Yorker*. I mention this otherwise trivial fact in the interest of full disclosure, since I am about to address his latest article, which is an attack on the Constitution and eerily related to his earlier assault on Collier and myself.

That assault was inspired by a reference we made in our book to Michael Walzer, Hertzberg's friend and the editor of the socialist magazine *Dissent*. In *Destructive Generation*, Collier and I suggested that a key to understanding the radical agendas of Sixties leftists could be found in the alienation they felt from their own heritage. We offered as an example a cover illustration for *Ramparts*, the radical magazine we once edited. The cover in question featured the photo of an all-American youngster holding the flag of the Communist Vietcong. The cover line said, "Alienation is when your country is at war and you want the other side to win." We linked this extreme statement to what we thought was a more temperate version of the same sentiment by Walzer, who had written that the only time he felt at home in Washington was when he went there to protest.

This article was originally published as "Alienation In a Time of War," Tuesday, August 06, 2002, http://archive.frontpagemag.com/Printable. aspx?ArtId=23390, Reprinted in *Left Illusions*, 2004

This was the trigger of Hertzberg's attack. In his view, we had conflated Walzer—and by implication himself—with the hate-America, Vietcong-loving radicals of the New Left. To him, this was unfair and even outrageous. Not only did he and Walzer not share the pro-Communist allegiances of radicals; they had fought them in ideological combats over this very issue. At the Port Huron founding of SDS, their political colleague Michael Harrington had thrown down the gauntlet to the SDS founders for refusing to take an anti-Communist stand. As socialists, Hertzberg and his friends identified with the left and were often fierce in their rejection of American capitalism and its political governors. But it was also true that they were willing to make peace when the opportunity arose. After the Sixties, Hertzberg had even gone to Washington to write speeches for President Jimmy Carter.

Hertzberg's dislike of being linked to a left that had slipped its patriotic moorings was a product of the select political space he had chosen as his own. As a "democratic socialist" he belonged to a progressive elite, carrying the torch of the true socialist faith against reactionaries on both sides of the political barricades. At a May Day gathering of Socialist Party veterans held in Washington this year, he unveiled this conceit at the core of his faith: "I still believe that the anti-communism of the socialist was a superior kind of anti-communism. A lot of people here are all too familiar with the old, long noble struggle for the good name of socialism: the endless explanations that no, socialism isn't the same as ommunism, and no, socialism isn't some milder form of communism, and yes, socialism is in fact the very opposite of communism. That struggle ... forced you to think clearly ... just what it was you were against and just what it was you were for."

Those outside Hertzberg's faith might not be so easily convinced that he and his vanguard stood for "the very opposite of communism," but his presentation was nothing if not forceful. "You weren't against communism because communism had aspirations of equality. You weren't against communism because communism wanted free medical care for everybody. You were against it because it crushed democracy and terrorized people and ruled by violence and fear, and systematically destroyed the most elementary and indispensable liberties, like freedom of speech."

In other words, being a "democratic socialist" made you an avatar of the best of all possible worlds. It was obviously unforgivable that anyone should attempt to sully your reputation with guilty associations and improper conflations as Peter Collier and I had allegedly done. But then fate intervened, and the terrorist attack on America had recently caused Hertzberg's idol, Michael Walzer, to make the same conflation and the same association. Reflecting on the attacks of 9/11 in a spring editorial for *Dissent*, Walzer came remarkably close to the very perception of Collier's and mine that had provoked Hertzberg's wrath a decade before.

In his editorial, Walzer asked, "Can There Be A Decent Left?" a question provoked by the spectacle of his progressive comrades rushing to judgment against their own country in the wake of 9/11. Walzer wondered about the depths of an alienation that could cause people to refuse to come to the defense of their country even when it was attacked. "Many left intellectuals live in America like internal aliens, refusing to identify with their fellow citizens, regarding any hint of patriot feeling as politically incorrect.... Many of the[ir] first responses [manifested a] barely concealed glee that the imperial state had finally gotten what it deserved." Walzer wanted to know why America should inspire such "resentment" and alienation in radical hearts. "Wasn't America a beacon of light to the old world, a city on a hill, an unprecedented experiment in democratic politics?"

Two months after Walzer posed these questions, Hertzberg responded with an article in the July 29 issue of the *New Yorker*, which the editors billed as "Hendrik Hertzberg on Our Flawed Constitution." According to Hertzberg, while America's democratic values provided an inspiration to the world, America's institutions did not provide a democratic model of governance that others should follow. Once again he was laying down a marker that separated him from the rest of the crowd. To provide a foil for his argument, Hertzberg referred to a book by Robert Dahl that asked the question, *How Democratic Is the American Constitution?*

Challenging America's founding principles is fair enough, even perhaps at a time when both the nation and its ideals are under ferocious attack. But Hertzberg's authorial voice in this article has an emotional edge and a disturbing animus that does not seem so fair. From Dahl's book, for example, Hertzberg cites a negative report card on America's performance in areas like economic inequality, energy efficiency and social expenditures, and then comments: "although Dahl doesn't mention, this, we [Americans] seem to be getting straight A's in world domination."

Hertzberg is quick to preface his assault with the observation that he is not the first to strike at the Founding: "Treating the Constitution as imperfect is not new. The angrier abolitionists saw it, in William Lloyd Garrison's words, as a 'covenant with death and an agreement with hell.' ... Academic paint balls have splattered the parchment with some regularity." According to Hertzberg, on the other hand, such critiques are only permitted to intellectual and political elites. For the unwashed mass, questioning the Constitution remains unthinkable: "But in the public square the Constitution is beyond criticism. The American civic religion affords it Biblical or Koranic status, even to the point of seeing it as divinely inspired. It's the flag in prose." This makes the terrain dangerous for reformers like himself, particularly in the post-9/11 environment. "The Constitution of the United States is emphatically not something to be debunked, especially in the afterglow of sole-superpower triumphalism."

But can Hertzberg really be referring to this country as one in which the Constitution cannot be challenged? Did he miss the feminist clamor over the Constitution's failure to protect women, or the movement for an Equal Rights Amendment that this sentiment spawned? Is he oblivious to the complaint from the right that the framers failed to provide a defense clause for the unborn? Was he comatose in the aftermath of the last presidential election when agitated Democrats, including United States senators and the former First Lady, called on the nation to scrap the Electoral College and alter the way the Constitution has mandated our choice of presidents for over two hundred years?

What really upsets Hertzberg is not any superstitious attachment Americans may have to their Constitution, but his own isolation from the conviction of ordinary Americans that the system has worked pretty well—well enough to make America a "beacon of light" to the rest of the world.

Hertzberg's perverse distance from his countrymen is announced in his opening remarks about the American Founding: "The most blatantly undemocratic feature of the document that the framers adopted in Philadelphia in 1787 was its acceptance—indeed, its enshrinement—of slavery, which in its American form was as vicious and repugnant as any institution ever devised by man." Ever devised by man? What about Auschwitz? The Soviet *gulag*? How about the slavery in Egypt that built the pyramids? How about the institution of virgin sacrifice among the Incas? How about black slavery in Cuba or Brazil? Perhaps Hertzberg is unaware that in Caribbean slave-societies the mortality rates for slaves exceeded the birth rates. Perhaps he is ignorant of the fact that slavery in the United States was the only slavery in the West whose environment encouraged the natural generation of the slave population so that, between the signing of the Constitution and the Civil War, the slave census in the United States increased more than fivefold, whereas everywhere else in the Hemisphere slaves had to be imported annually to make up the manpower deficit caused by attrition.

To write, as Hertzberg does, that the Constitution enshrined slavery is worse than a mere distortion of the facts. Far from glorifying it, the framers avoided even using the words "slave" or "slavery" because the majority of them abhorred the institution and were determined to end it –were convinced in fact it would shortly die of its own reactionary weight.

Hertzberg's distortion of the founders' intentions does not end here. Listing the constitutional compromises they made with slavery, he writes: "Most notoriously, under Article I, Section 2, a state's allotment of seats in the House of Representatives (and, by extension, its Presidential electors) was determined by counting not only 'free Persons' but also 'three-fifths of all other Persons.' This is simply diabolical, because to the insult of defining a person held in bondage as three-fifths of a human being it added the injury of using that definition to augment the political power of that person's oppressors."

Actually the opposite was the case. Far from being either an insult or an injury, the three-fifths compromise weakened the voting power of the Southern slaveholders who had demanded that "slaves should stand on equality with whites." Had the framers counted slaves as five-fifths and not merely three-fifths of a person, they would have maximized the voting power of the slave states.

Hertzberg's distortion of this history is even worse than it appears, because it is based on the suppression of a more basic fact. All the constitutional compromises with slavery were necessary in order to achieve the Union that, within 20 years, would abolish the slave trade and within a single generation would fight a civil war to free the slaves themselves. The only real moral issue involved in the constitutional arrangement was whether the framers should have made any compromise with the slaveholding South. Should there have been a Union at all? On that question the final word belongs to Frederick Douglass, the most renowned free black person in the Republic and a former slave himself. "My argument against the dissolution of the American Union is this: It would place the slave system more exclusively under the control of the slaveholding states, and withdraw it from the power in the Northern states which is opposed to slavery.... I am, therefore, for drawing the bond of the Union more closely, and bringing the Slave States more completely under the power of the Free States."[1]

---

[1]Frederick Douglass, "The Constitution of the United States: Is It Pro-Slavery or Anti-Slavery?" a speech delivered in Glasgow, Scotland, March 26,1860; emphasis added

While Douglass's statement exposes the injustice of Hertzberg's attack, it also understates it. In 1787 the American founders had just completed the only successful colonial rebellion in human history, defeating the greatest empire of the age. If the Northern states had rejected a compromise with the South, it is perfectly reasonable to suppose that the British imperialists who burned the White House in 1812 would have forged an alliance with the Southern slave states and crushed the North. Then slavery would have been institutionalized throughout the continent; there would have been no Civil War; and it is anyone's guess when the slaves might eventually have been freed.

Hertzberg acknowledges the amendments outlawing slavery and guaranteeing equal rights that were incorporated into the Constitution after the South's defeat. He then adds this. "But nothing was done to alter the political institutions that in 1860 had held four million people—one American in eight—in bondage and that, for the next century and, arguably, more, denied millions of their 'free' descendants both equal protection and the franchise." So stated, that is another incomprehensible charge. The enslavement of four million people was not the work of American political institutions but a legacy of the British Empire and the necessity of compromise to hold that empire at bay. As Hertzberg continues his attack, he reveals its logic. Because of America's flawed political institutions, "even so grotesque and obvious an injustice as apartheid in the public schools [in the South] was beyond the ability of the national government to correct. And when, after ninety years, formal, official school segregation was outlawed the deed was done through the exercise of un-elected, unaccountable, unchecked, quasi-legislative judicial power...."

In the end, Hertzberg's disenchantment with the American system is that it is not "majoritarian," but was constructed with a built in system of checks and balances at times thwarting the majority will. In pursuing social justice, the federal government is unable to ignore state's rights, judicial precedents and other governmental restraints that have made America's political history

different from, say, that of revolutionary France. Like other socialists, Hertzberg yearns for a government that can enforce what they
regard as the "General Will" and secure social justice through an
Assembly or Parliament, directly elected by the people—one man
one vote.

One of the institutions currently thwarting this General Will is
the United States Senate. "Once slavery was removed, the most
undemocratic remaining provision of the Constitution was, and is,
the composition of the Senate—its so-called equality of representation, whereby each state gets two senators, regardless of population." While Hertzberg regards this representation as unfair, the
founders devised it specifically to provide a check on the will of
the people, which the founders famously distrusted. The House of
Representatives is the chamber known as the "People's House"
because it is elected once every two years instead of six, and is
composed of members who represent equal portions of the elec-
torate. The Senate was the framers' device to slow the machinery
of popular justice because they recognized that popular injustice—
the tyranny of the majority—was an equally likely result of democratic power unchecked.

Summing up his case, Hertzberg cites Dahl. "Compared with
the political systems of other advanced democratic countries, ours
is among the most opaque, complex, confusing, and difficult to
understand." On the other hand, along with England's equally
complex constitutional monarchy, it is the most stable democracy
that history records. By contrast the advanced democratic countries that Dahl has in mind include France—with its four bloody
revolutions and five Republics—and Germany, of which no more
need be said.

Ignoring these unpleasant facts, Hertzberg insists on a "true"
democracy whose government could run roughshod over communities that don't agree with his political agendas. Consider the
argument he makes against senatorial privilege: "The rejection of
the Versailles Treaty and the League of Nations after the First
World War and then of preparedness on the eve of the Second are

only the best known of the Senate's many acts of foreign policy sabotage, which have continued down to the present, with its refusal to ratify international instruments on genocide, nuclear testing and human rights." Hertzberg concedes that "some will take all this as proof that the system has worked exactly as the framers planned." But then he adds: "To believe that, one must believe that the framers were heartless, brainless reactionaries."

The cat is out of the bag: Americans who disagree with progressives like Hertzberg are heartless, brainless and reactionary. It is precisely this kind of arrogance, not unusual for social reformers, that made the framers fearful of democratic majorities in the first place, and that made them determined to provide checks which would prevent majorities from tyrannizing everyone else.

The founders were not democrats and socialists like Hertzberg. They were conservatives who had a healthy distrust of political passions and who devised a complex system designed to frustrate the schemes of social redeemers and others convinced of their own invincible virtue. If not for the immense, undemocratic power vested in the Supreme Court, schools might still be legally segregated. If not for states' rights, slavery might have spread throughout the nation. If not for the opaque, complex, confusing American framework, the descendants of Africans who were dragged to this country in chains might not today be the freest and richest blacks in the world.

What makes these ancient issues important is that our nation is now under attack. It must confront its enemies in a state weakened by 30 years of cultural assaults from the left that have made many Americans ambivalent about their heritage. Moral ambivalence about one's country can lead to an uncertainty of resolve in defending it. But there is really no historical justification for Americans to be ambivalent about their history and the institutions of their founding. As Michael Walzer and President Bush have both pointed out, this nation is still a beacon of freedom to the rest of the world, and its defense is important not only to us but to them as well.

14

Neo-Communism

A nation's wars are tests of its citizens' loyalties, commitments and political understandings. It was a striking fact of the "antiwar" demonstrations against Operation Iraqi Freedom that leftists were able to mobilize more protesters in three months—from the UN deadline of November 7 to the launch of the war in March—than its predecessor had been able to mobilize in the first six years of the Vietnam War. This was also true of the worldwide protests against America's determination to topple the Iraqi dictator Saddam Hussein.

Both the rapidity and size of the anti-Iraq mobilization indicate that it was not merely—and not mainly—a response to the particular war or to the issues that defined it but the expression of an attitude toward American power itself, with the war as a pretext. Indeed, the rapid growth of protests in advance of the facts that might justify them—e.g., the "quagmire" that Vietnam became, the mounting loss of life without apparent result—shows that the left's attitude towards American power is relatively indifferent to the uses to which that power is put. Otherwise, why go into the streets to save a regime as despicable as Saddam Hussein's? This same phenomenon was on display in the demonstrations after the 9/11 attacks, which mobilized tens of thousands of American college students to oppose an American response *before* America had lifted a finger in response. The purpose of the demonstrations was

This article was published on April 22, 2003, http://archive.front-pagemag.com/Printable.aspx?ArtId=18600

to protest *any* military response that America might consider to the unprovoked terrorist attack.

The same attitude was manifest after the mission to topple the regime had been accomplished with minimal casualties and no significant reaction from the "Arab street" (as critics had assured us there would be). In April 2003—less than a week after United States and British forces had liberated Iraq; after the victors had opened Saddam's prisons, dismantled the torture chambers, shipped vast quantities of food and medicine to the Iraqi population and had begun to assemble the first Iraqi regime in history that would not be a monarchy, military junta, fascist dictatorship or chamber of horrors—at *that very moment* the faculty senate of the University of California, Los Angeles passed a resolution to "condemn ... [the] United States invasion of Iraq." The extraordinary session was convened for the express purpose of making that condemnation. The vote was 180–7 in favor, reflecting just how left the faculty senate of that university had become. The professors also voted to "deplore the doctrine of preventive war the president has used to justify the invasion" and to "oppose the establishment of the American protectorate in Iraq," even though the president had already justified Iraq's liberation under U.N. Security Council Resolution 1441 and no American "protectorate" was ever contemplated.

In other words, 95 percent of the faculty senate at one of America's most prestigious academic institutions espoused the view—without any visible evidence to support it—that its own country was a dangerous, imperialist aggressor, bent on acquiring control of a sovereign nation. The co-author of the UCLA resolution, Professor Maurice Zeitlin, is a leftist I happen to have known for 40 years from the moment we both arrived at the University of California to pursue graduate studies at the beginning of the Sixties. Zeitlin was a Marxist who in 1961 published one of the first books hailing the triumph of the Communist revolution in Cuba (although he and co-author Robert Scheer naturally didn't call it that).[1] In October 1997 Zeitlin spoke at a UCLA symposium on 20th century utopias, praising the dead guerrilla leader Che Guevara who had attempted to incite a global conflagration, calling for the creation of "two, three, … many Vietnams." Zeitlin declared his continuing faith in the cause that Guevara symbolized. "Che was above all a revolutionary socialist and a leader of the first socialist revolution in this hemisphere. His legacy is embodied in the fact that the Cuban revolution is alive today despite the collapse of the Soviet bloc…. No social justice is possible without a vision like Che's."[2]

In other words, for 40 years, the co-author of UCLA's anti-Iraq resolution had remained a "small-c" communist or—as I prefer—a "neo-communist," by which I mean a political radical and determined enemy of America's capitalist democracy. The UCLA resolution is an expression of *those* commitments rather than a reaction to a particular policy or war.

The faculty resolution at UCLA mirrored an equally illuminating event that had taken place weeks earlier at a Columbia University "teach-in" against the war. During this protest led by 30 members of the Columbia faculty, Professor Nicholas DeGenova declared that every honest opponent of the Iraq War should want America to lose. For his own part, he said, he wished for "a million Mogadishus," referring to the 1993 incident in which 18 American soldiers were killed in an al-Qaeda ambush in Somalia.[3] The negative reaction to DeGenova's statement was so strong that other faculty protesters led by Eric Foner, the leftist chairman of Columbia's History Department, immediately distanced themselves from DeGenova's statement. In Foner's words, "We do not desire the deaths of American soldiers."

---

[1] *Cuba, Tragedy In Our Hemisphere,* Grove Press, 1963
[2] Argiris Malapanis, "L.A .Symposium Debates Che and the Cuban Revolution," *The Militant,* November 24, 1997
[3] See the www.frontpagemag.com issue of March 30, 2003.

The immediate effect of Foner's gesture was to obscure how universally DeGenova's view of the war was shared by those present, including Foner himself. That much was made apparent when DeGenova attempted to explain himself in an interview with *The Chronicle of Higher Education*.[4] In that interview, DeGenova categorically denied he wanted American soldiers to die, and explained why he had referred to Mogadishu in the context of Iraq. "I was referring to what Mogadishu symbolizes politically. The U.S. invasion of Somalia was humiliated [sic] in an excruciating way by the Somali people. And Mogadishu was the premier symbol of that." DeGenova's comment was virtually identical to remarks made by Noam Chomsky after the attacks of 9/11.[5] Chomsky, an intellectual leader of the antiwar left, has written a book about 9/11 that has sold over 200,000 copies. In Chomsky's view, the World Trade Center deaths were regrettable but the unprecedented humiliation of the imperialist power—America— was an historic victory for social justice and human progress.[6]

In the *Chronicle* interview, DeGenova explained that at Columbia he had also drawn an analogy between Mogadishu and the "historical lesson" of Vietnam. "What I was intent to emphasize was that the importance of Vietnam [was] that it was a defeat for the U.S. war machine and a victory for the cause of human self-determination." DeGenova did not explain how the slaughter of two-and-a-half million Cambodians and a hundred thousand Vietnamese by the Communist victors after America's defeat, or the colonization of South Vietnam and Cambodia by the Hanoi regime, was a triumph of self-determination. But he did elaborate on the present relevance of the historical distortion. "The analogy between Mogadishu and Vietnam is that they were defeats for U.S. imperialism.... The analogy between Mogadishu and Iraq is

---

[4]Thomas Bartlett, "The Most Hated Professor In America," *The Chronicle of Higher Education,* April 18, 2003
[5]Noam Chomsky, 9–11
[6]Cf. David Horowitz, *The Ayatollah of Anti-American Hate,* a pamphlet of the Center for the Study of Popular Culture, Los Angeles, 2001

simply that there was an invasion of Somalia and there was an invasion of Iraq."

Of course there was no invasion of Somalia. U.S. troops were sent to Mogadishu not to invade the country but to feed starving Somali Muslims. A local al-Qaeda warlord named Aidid was stealing the food before it could reach the Somali people, and Americans were sent to try to capture the thief. But it is safe to say that not a single protester at the Columbia event nor a single signer of the UCLA resolution, nor many of the 14,000 professors who signed a protest petition against the war, would disagree with DeGenova's reading of this history of Vietnam, Mogadishu and Iraq.

These same views are reflected in an antiwar declaration by Michael T. Klare,[7] Five College Professor of Peace and World Security Studies at Hampshire College and four other schools.[8] Klare is also a regular contributor to *The Nation*, where he was an apologist for Soviet expansion and a staunch opponent of American policy during the Cold War. More than a month before the hostilities began in Iraq, Klare wrote an article for *The Nation* titled, "Resist War and Empire." While the UN inspectors were conducting their searches for weapons of mass destruction, while the world was waiting to see if Saddam Hussein would disarm, while the Russians were attempting to get Saddam to step down, and before a single shot had been fired or troop deployed, Klare issued this clarion call: "The peace movement must prepare itself to conduct a long-term struggle against the administration's imperial designs in the Gulf. These plans must be exposed for what they are: a classic appropriation of political power and material goods (especially petroleum) by material force masquerading as a campaign for democracy." Vladimir Lenin could not have chosen the words better.

---

[7]http:// discoverthenetworks.org/individualProfile.asp?indid=1540
[8]Klare teaches in rotation at Hampshire, Amherst, Mount Holyoke, Smith, and the University of Massachusetts (Amherst).

What the prologue to the war and its aftermath reveal is that the facts of the war are not the issue for the "antiwar" left and neither is the war itself. The so-called "antiwar" left is a neo-communist movement that was launched forty years ago under the pretense of being a "*new*" left." It has been at war with the American "empire" ever since. Throughout America's Cold War conflicts with Communists in Eastern Europe, the Soviet Union, China, Southeast Asia, Africa and Central America, and in the aftermath of America's liberation of a billion inhabitants of the Communist empire, this left has been impervious to every good deed America has done and oblivious towards every bad deed its Marxist and now Islamo-fascist enemies have committed. Instead this left habitually attributes bad deeds perpetrated by America's enemies to America itself—hence the search for "root causes" of the hatred directed against America every time America is attacked.

The neo-communist left opposes America's efforts to promote freedom and supports America's declared enemies not because of what America *does,* but because of what they think America *is.* The neo-communist left is impervious to facts because it is a political messianism, in essence a religious movement. Its delusions of social redemption are fed on a rich diet of anti-American myths. Those myths were once generated in institutions funded by the Communist Party and other marginal radical sects. But that has all changed with the long march of the left during the last 30 years through America's institutions of higher learning. The neo-communist left is now entrenched in the liberal arts faculties of America's elite universities, where it is a dominant presence. It has converted America's universities into a political base for its radical and anti-American agendas. In the present war with radical Islam, this poses a problem Americans can continue to ignore only at their peril, and which sooner or later they must address.

15

Neo-Communism II

How to identify the political left? Current usage refers to everyone left of center as "liberal." But what are currently identified liberals "liberal" about except hard drugs and sex? In regard to everything else, they are determined to intervene, regulate and control other people's lives, or redistribute their incomes. Obviously, when terror-hugging radicals like Ramsey Clark and Communist hacks like Angela Davis are referred to as "liberals"—as they routinely are—the obfuscation works to their advantage and against the interests of veracity and democracy. The term "liberal" should be reserved for those who actually occupy the center of the political spectrum; those to the left should be referred to as leftists, which is what they are. This is the easy part of rectifying the political lexicon. A more difficult aspect is how to identify the "hard" left, which is to say not mere fellow-travelers but those who are dedicated enemies of America and its purposes. In practice it is not hard to identify such leftists or to describe them. They are people who identify with hostile regimes like North Korea, Cuba, and China, or who argue that the United States is the imperialist guardian of a world system which radicals must defeat before they can establish "social justice."

Adherents of this anti-American creed variously describe themselves as "Marxists," "anti-globalists," "antiwar activists" or more generally "progressives." Their secular worldview holds that

---

This article was published on May 01, 2003, http://archive.front-pagemag.com/Printable.aspx?ArtId=18423

America is responsible for reaction, oppression and exploitation across the globe, which causes them to regard this country as the moral equivalent of militant Islam's "Great Satan." This explains the otherwise incomprehensible practical alliances that people pretending to be avatars of social justice have made with Islamo-fascists like Saddam Hussein.

Among the intellectual leaders of this left are Noam Chomsky, Howard Zinn, Gore Vidal, Edward Said and Cornel West; among its figureheads Angela Davis and Ramsey Clark; among its cultural icons Tim Robbins, Barbara Kingsolver, Arundahti Roy and Michael Moore; among its political leaders Ralph Nader and the heads of the three major "peace" organizations, Leslie Cagan, Brian Becker and Clark Kissinger; among its electoral organizations the Green Party, the Peace and Freedom Party and the "Progressive Caucus" of the Democratic Party; among its elected officials Congresswoman Barbara Lee (D-California) and Congressman Dennis Kucinich (D-Ohio); among its organizations the misnamed Center for Constitutional Rights and the National Lawyers Guild; among its publications and media institutions *The Nation, Z Magazine, The Progressive, Counterpunch,* Pacifica radio, indymedia.org and commondreams.org. Like the Communist Party in the heyday of the Soviet empire, the influence of the hard left extends far beyond the institutions, organizations and publications it controls.

Yet what to call them? One of the hard left's survival secrets has been its ability to embargo attempts to identify it by labeling as "red-baiters" and "witch-hunters" those who do so, as if simply to name it meant to persecute it. Those same people, on the other hand, think nothing of labeling their opponents "racists" and "fascists," or calling the president of the United States a "Nazi" puppet of the oil cartel. Yet their defense strategy is highly effective in the tolerant democracy they are determined to destroy. I myself have been called a "red-baiter" and "McCarthyite" for pointing out that current "peace" organizations like International ANSWER and Not in Our Name are fronts for the Workers World

Party, a Marxist-Leninist vanguard that identifies with North Korea, and for the Revolutionary Communist Party, a Maoist sect. The facts are obvious and indisputable but their implications are unpleasant, which is what inspires the defamatory attacks.

Notwithstanding this difficulty, a more significant concern is that the term "Communist" in the context of the contemporary left can be misleading. While the Communist Party still exists and is even growing, it is a minor player and enjoys nothing approaching its former influence or power in the left. Even in the hard left, the Communist Party USA is only a constituent part of the whole whereas once, along with its front groups, it dominated progressive politics.

In these circumstances the best term to describe the hard left and its adherents is "neo-communist." The place to begin an understanding of neo-communists, or neo-coms, is the period following 1956, when the left shed its Communist shell to become first a "New Left" and then what might be called a "post-New Left left." In my own writings, particularly *Radical Son* and *The Politics of Bad Faith*, I have shown that the "new left" was in reality no such thing. While starting out as a rejection of Stalinism, by the end of the Sixties the "new left" had devolved into a movement virtually indistinguishable from the Communist predecessor it had claimed to supercede. This was as true of its Marxist underpinnings as of its anti-Americanism and its indiscriminate embrace of totalitarian revolutions and revolutionaries abroad.

At the end of the Sixties the New Left imploded, a victim of its own revolutionary enthusiasms, which had led it to pursue a violent politics it could not sustain. America's withdrawal from Vietnam in the early Seventies deprived the left of the immediate pretext for its radical agendas. Many of its cadre retired from the "revolution in the streets" they had tried to launch and instead entered the Democratic Party. Others turned to careers in journalism and teaching, the professions of choice for secular missionaries. Still others took up local agitations and discrete campaigns on behalf of the environment, feminist issues and gay rights—

without, however, giving up their radical illusions. In the 1980s, spurred by the Soviet-sponsored "nuclear freeze" campaign and by the "solidarity" movements for Communist forces in Central America, the left began to regroup without formally announcing its reemergence or proclaiming a new collective identity, as its Sixties predecessor had done.

At the end of the decade, the collapse of the Soviet empire ushered in an interregnum of confusion for the left, calling a temporary halt to this radical progress. In the Soviet debacle "revolutionary" leftists confronted the catastrophic failure of everything they had fought for during the previous 70 years. Even those radicals who recognized the political failures of the Soviet regime still believed in what Trotsky had called "the gains of October"—the superior forces of socialist production. This leftist faith proved impervious to its rebuttal by historical events. Insulated by its religious devotion to the progressive idea, the left survived the refutation of its socialist dreams. Instead of acknowledging their wrongheaded commitment to the cause, leftists treated the collapse of "the first socialist state," as the death of an albatross whose burden providence had lifted from their shoulders. Having defended the indefensible for 70 years, once it was gone they were simply relieved that they would no longer have to do so.

Turning their backs on their own past, they pretended it was someone else's. They said the collapse proved nothing because it was only the demise of "actually existing socialism," not real socialism. Real socialism hadn't been tried. This subterfuge rescued them from having to apologize for abetting regimes that had killed tens of millions and enslaved tens of millions more—that had broken eggs with no omelet to show for it. Better yet, it relieved them of having to admit that the democracy whose anti-Communist efforts they opposed, and whose actions they condemned, had liberated a billion people from the most oppressive empire in world history. They had no need for second thoughts about what they had done. They just went on to the next destructions, the newest incarnations of the radical cause.

This cosmic bad faith was the foundation of the left's revival in the decade that followed. It was the necessary premise of its reemergence as a leader of the "anti-globalization" and "antiwar" movements that emerged at the end of the Nineties and the onset of the millennium. The progressive left was now ready to resurrect its internal war against America at home and abroad.

If one looks at almost any aspect of this movement—its acknowledged intellectual lineage, Hegel, Nietzsche, Marx, Heidegger, Fanon, Gramsci, in sum, the totalitarian tradition—its analytic model for the democracies of the west, hierarchy and oppression—its redemptive agenda, social justice imposed by state-enforced leveling—and its enemy, imperialist America—one would be hard put to find a scintilla of difference from the Communist past. Of course leftists themselves will concede none of this. Most of them will proclaim their anti-Stalinism and will not defend the Communist systems that have disappeared. But so what? The Soviet rulers themselves eventually denounced Stalin. Were they less Communist for that?

It is appropriate to identify the unreconstructed hard-liners as "neo-communists"—a term that would accurately describe their negative assaults on American capitalism and their anti-American "internationalist" agendas. It may be objected that the term "neo-communist" does not describe a group that identifies itself with the term, but then neither does "neo-conservative." There is no current movement calling itself "neo-conservative," nor do the individuals so designated refer to their own ideas as "neo-conservative." "Neo-conservative" is, in fact, a label imposed by the left on a group of former Democrats, loosely grouped around Senator "Scoop" Jackson, who left the party at the end of the Seventies to support the Reagan administration. They accepted the label after protest and then out of necessity, because the left so dominates the political culture that resistance was futile. But it is no longer used by "neo-conservatives" because, as Norman Podhoretz observed some time ago, "neo-conservatism" is indistinguishable from conservatism itself.

No "neo-conservative" that I know of has challenged Pod-horetz's conclusion. Yet others persist in sticking the "neo" label to conservatives who are seen as foreign-policy hawks. My question is: if the "neo" shoe can be made to fit conservatives, then why not the left as well?

16

Neo-Communism III

Ihave argued that the contemporary left, which denounces American corporations and the global capitalist system, should be called "neo-communist," a term to denote anti-American leftists who demonize the American economic system and identify it as a "root cause" of global problems. An objection to the term is that some members of this left—perhaps many—no longer openly advocate a Communist future. Many call themselves "anarchists" and would be eager to denounce the late Soviet state. I have already provided one answer to this objection. There is no group that identifies its politics as "neo-conservative" either. There are no "neo-conservative" organizations, official or unofficial, and there is no "neo-conservative" policy or plan. Yet there is little objection to the use of "neo-conservative" to describe what others consider a readily identifiable political position.

The resistance to the term "neo-communist" derives from a misunderstanding of the nature of a political left that is actually proud of its Communist intellectual heritage, and still supports socialist "solutions" and the revolutionary idea that created the totalitarian states. It needs to be borne in mind that there are always, and inevitably, two sides to the revolutionary coin. The first is negative and destructive, and leads to the drive to undermine the beliefs, values and institutions of the old order, which must be destroyed before a new one can be created. The second

---

This article was published on May 02, 2003, http://archive.front-pagemag.com/Printable.aspx?ArtId=18398

component of the revolutionary vision is positive and utopian—
the image of a future that condemns the present and encapsulates
the idea of a redemptive fate.

For half a century now, ever since Khrushchev's revelations
about the crimes of Stalin, the left has been driven by its negative
agendas. This is even more the case since the implosion of "actually existing socialism." Leaders of the contemporary left have put
forward no serious plans for the post-capitalist future. More important, none of the energies that drive them are inspired by such
plans. The left's inspirations are mainly negative and nihilistic,
and have been so for nearly fifty years.

Even in its more innocent beginnings, the new left defined
itself by negatives as "anti-anti-Communist." It was a "new" left
because it did not want to identify with Communism. But it also
did not want to oppose Communism, because then it would have
had to support America's Cold War. "Anti-anti-Communism" was
code for anti-Americanism. What the left wanted was to oppose
America and its "sham" democracy.

There is a sense, of course, in which the left has always been
defined by its destructive agendas. Its utopian vision was just that:
utopian, a vision of nowhere. In practice, socialism didn't work.
But socialism could never have worked because it was based on
false premises about human psychology and society, and gross
ignorance of human economy. In the vast library of socialist theory, and in all of Marx's compendious works, there is not a chapter
devoted to the creation of wealth—to what will cause human
beings to work and innovate, or to what will make their efforts
efficient. Socialism is strictly a plan of morally-sanctioned theft. It
is about dividing up what others have created. Consequently,
socialist economies create poverty instead of wealth. This is an
unarguable historical fact, but has not prompted the left to have
second thoughts. Because its positive agendas are unworkable, the
left is appropriately characterized by its negative critiques and
destructive agendas. Everything else, everything it claims to
intend, everything it may in fact intend is so much utopian hot air.

In the first article of this series I identified several exemplars of the neo-communist left, one of whom has since responded. Maurice Zeitlin is a professor of sociology at the University of California, Los Angeles, and the co-author of a faculty resolution condemning, after the fact, America's liberation of Iraq. Because the resolution was drafted and passed after the liberation of Baghdad, its agendas were clearly aimed at America and not at the reality in Iraq.

I have known Maurice Zeitlin for more than 40 years, since we were both New Left radicals in the 1960s. In my article, I pointed out that Zeitlin had recently hailed the late Che Guevara at an academic conference, calling him "a leader of the first socialist revolution in this hemisphere." He had asserted that "[Guevara's] legacy is embodied in the fact that Cuban revolution is alive today despite the collapse of the Soviet bloc," and also that "No social justice is possible without a vision like Che's."[1] I concluded that it was Zeitlin's neo-communist agenda, and not any specifics of the war in Iraq, which had inspired the post-hoc UCLA faculty resolution condemning the U.S. action. Zeitlin responded to the article in a terse and angry email which he sent to my assistant, Elizabeth Ruiz, referring to me in the third person. This email affords a further look into the mind of the neo-communist left.

In my article I had mentioned that Zeitlin and Robert Scheer, an *L.A. Times* columnist with similar politics, had written one of the first books celebrating the Communist revolution in Cuba. In his email Zeitlin expressed irritation because I hadn't mentioned in the article that I had edited Scheer's book. ("You can tell Davey for me that he might have mentioned in this column that he edited the book by myself and Scheer on Cuba—and we thanked him in the acknowledgments.") Zeitlin appeared to think that this fact implicated me in his radical politics in a way I had not already owned in my autobiography *Radical Son*. He said of me: "To think

[1]Argiris Malapanis, "L.A. Symposium Debates Che and the Cuban Revolution," *The Militant*, November 24, 1997

that I saved him from an enraged audience and protected his right to speak at the *L.A. Times* Festival of Books a few years ago."[2] I have also written about this incident.[3] "Saved" is a little excessive for the remarks Zeitlin made in defense of my right to express myself. Book-readers are not the most violent of audiences and in any case the event was being televised on C-SPAN. The point Zeitlin seemed to make is that since he defended my free speech at UCLA, he cannot be called a "neo-communist."

Why not? Didn't Communists defend the principle of free speech in America when they stood up to Senator McCarthy? Communists are great defenders of freedom in the democracies they want to overthrow. It enhances their opportunities to subvert the system. Didn't Lenin defend the right to vote in democratic Russia before abolishing it as soon as he took power?

In the second brief paragraph of his email, Zeitlin made his objection to my article clearer, and made explicit his concern to defend his good intentions: "[David] knows damn well that I have long opposed execrable regimes like Hussein's, years before, indeed, Bush even knew who Hussein was. He also knows that I wrote severe criticisms of the restrictions on rights in revolutionary Cuba in *Ramparts*, when he was its very editor and still gung-ho for Fidel...."

This *cri de coeur* begs the most important question: What does it mean to oppose Saddam Hussein's "execrable regime" and at the same time oppose the effort to change it? Or to condemn the regime-change *after* the fact, when Iraqis are rejoicing in the streets? What are intentions worth when actions contradict them? Are Zeitlin's critiques of Castro harsher than Khrushchev's criticisms of Stalin? Did Khrushchev cease to be a Communist because he criticized Stalin?

Zeitlin was indeed critical of the Cuban revolutionary regime, and was critical even earlier than he indicates. He is correct as

[2]From Maurice Zeitlin to Elizabeth Ruiz, April 22, 2003
[3]"Calibrating the Culture War" in *The Collected Conservative Writings of David Horowitz*, Volume 3

well that as a fellow-leftist I did not want to see such criticisms aired—even though I might not have described myself at the time as simply "gung ho for Fidel". The fact is that I published Zeitlin's critique. But Zeitlin could have cited a much more impressive instance of his new-left independence from the Communist past. In 1960 Zeitlin had visited Cuba and interviewed Che Guevara, who was then the second most powerful man in the dictatorship. We published the interview in the first issue of our Berkeley magazine, *Root and Branch*, which was one of the political journals that launched the new left. (Robert Scheer was also an editor.) The rest of us were both shocked and impressed when we read the interview and realized what Maurice had done.

He had not just interviewed Guevara, already a radical legend. He had challenged Guevara's policies and in effect called into question his revolutionary credentials. Maurice had asked Guevara about the role he thought the trade unions should play in a socialist country, specifically Cuba. Should they be independent— as new-left socialists like us wanted—or would they be appendages of the state, as Lenin and Stalin had made them? Maurice reminded Guevara that the elimination of independent unions, which were the organizations of the revolutionary class, had paved the way for the Soviet gulag. Guevara was angered by the question and by Maurice's temerity in raising the question; he refused to criticize the Soviets, abruptly changing the subject.

Forty years ago, Zeitlin had put Guevara to the test and Guevara had failed. Zeitlin's interview revealed that Guevara was himself a Stalinist. We all recognized the significance of what Guevara had said. Yet to our shame we continued to support the Cuban regime, knowing that it was destined to be a totalitarian gulag because that was the *intention* of its creators. Maurice did write a subsequent critique for *Ramparts*. But, like us, he continued to support the regime and to attack the United States and its efforts to restore freedom to Cuba. Later, when I had second thoughts about my political commitments and departed the political left and comrades like Zeitlin, I wrote about my regrets for defending a regime that had become the most sadistic dictatorship in Latin American history. Except for Ronald Radosh and other "second thoughters" who have also turned their backs on the left, I don't know any former comrade still of the left, like Zeitlin, who has done the same.

The left's silence over the unforeseen consequences of its political commitments underscores the pitiful impotence and ultimate irrelevance of good intentions. What does it matter that we *wanted* to create a "new" left or a *"democratic* socialism" if we did not put our actions behind these desires? If we did not apply the same standards of judgment, and action, to socialist tyrannies that we did towards others? What were our "critiques" worth if we were prepared to continue our support for such regimes, or to remain part of a movement that actually defended them? What are Zeitlin's critiques worth if he preserves the myth of Che's leadership and maintains the viability of the socialist idea? If the bulwark against Communist totalitarianism—the United States—remains his main enemy?

Forty years later, the results of our defense of the Cuban revolution are indisputable. Cuba is an island prison, a land of regime-induced poverty, of misery and human oppression greater by far than the regime it replaced. Yet despite his criticisms Maurice Zeitlin is still defending the Cuban "revolution" along with its patron saint, Che Guevara. As a UCLA professor he is now teaching a new generation of college students, who have no memory of this past, that Guevara is an inspiration for the future, in other words to idolize the very predator that Zeitlin himself had justly criticized 40 years earlier! In view of this record, what do Zeitlin's parenthetical condemnations and critical asides matter? Zeitlin's career reminds me of an Irwin Shaw story called "The Ninety-Yard Run," about a college football star whose great play in his senior college year turns out to be the high-point of his life, and the rest downhill all the way.

In defining the term "neo-communist" and applying it to leftists like Zeitlin, I was careful to be specific. I defined a neoommunist as "a political radical and a determined opponent of America and its capitalist democracy." What I had in mind was not just a political outlook, but an outlook reflecting a profound feeling of alienation from America and a hostility towards it that only someone who was or had been a radical himself could really understand. In attempting to describe this attitude, I have elsewhere employed as an example a line we once used in *Ramparts* magazine, the flagship publication of the new left. On the cover of our issue we had placed a photograph of a seven-year-old holding the flag of the Communist enemy in Vietnam. The cover line said, "Alienation is when your country is at war and you want the other side to win."[4] That was the way we felt, and we felt that way because our outlook led us to look at the United States as the imperialist leader of world reaction, which meant that anything that caused America's defeat would benefit mankind.

In the 1980s, I was provided a personal insight into Maurice Zeitlin's own profound alienation from his country—a country that had provided him with intellectual freedom, a six-figure income, and opportunities to travel all over the world doing research and writing Marxist tracts at American taxpayers' expense. When the incident in question occurred, I had not seen Maurice nor heard from him in more than 20 years, since our days together in the radical Sixties. I had no idea whether he had had second thoughts like mine or whether he was still on the left. Our paths crossed, so to speak, because of a newspaper report about another Sixties radical named Margaret Randall who was applying for the reinstatement of her American citizenship, which she had renounced years before. She was being supported by a chorus of comrades, who claimed that in resisting her request the State Department was trampling on her civil rights.

This news item so outraged me that I wrote a letter to the *Los Angeles Times* urging the authorities to deny her request. The

---

[4]*Ramparts*, April 1969

reason Randall no longer had her citizenship was that she had joined a movement of local terrorists in Mexico City who were attempting to sabotage the 1968 Olympic games. When the street-battles were over and many lay dead, she publicly renounced her American citizenship and attacked her homeland as a "fascist" state. She then went to live in Communist Cuba and work there as a teacher, indoctrinating Cuban schoolchildren in the Communist creed. In my letter to the *Times,* I urged officials to demand that Randall apologize to her country before reinstating the citizenship she had renounced. Being an American, in my view, meant accepting a social contract that included a commitment to democracy and individual freedom. I thought Randall should be treated like new citizen-applicants, who are required to make a formal commitment to the country and its principles before being receiving its citizenship. What is America if it is not a nation of citizens committed to these common ends?

Zeitlin read my letter to the *Los Angeles Times.* His reaction, which I learned through a mutual friend, was: "I wonder how low Horowitz will sink next?" That came as a shock to me, because I remembered his bold defense of freedom to Che Guevara years before, and I was unaware of his political evolution since. The remark told me more about Zeitlin's political commitments than I cared to know.

The purpose of the term "neo-communist" is to identify a movement that regards the United States as the root cause of international evil on grounds that it is the guardian of the international property system. In the eyes of radicals, this makes America the bulwark of "social injustice" around the world. These propositions have profound implications for one's loyalties and commitments. They explain how individuals who claim to honor peace, justice, equality and freedom can interpose themselves between America and a monstrous fascist like Saddam Hussein.

In an earlier article in this series, I referred to Nicholas DeGenova, the Columbia professor who made himself notorious by wishing for "a million Mogadishus"—a million American military defeats. The outrage at his remarks was a response to his wish for American military casualties. But this was to miss the forest for the trees. As DeGenova himself explained in defending his remarks afterwards, what he meant was not that a lot of Americans should be killed—the left always imagines it can separate support for America's troops from support for America's wars—but that the defeat of America itself would be a victory for humanity. This is the essence of the neo-communist vision. It explains how leftists like Maurice Zeitlin can condemn America's liberation of Iraq, despite the fact that they recognize that Iraq's regime is "execrable" and that the Iraqi people have been freed from a tyranny. The defeat of America is a defeat of "U.S. Imperialism," the oppressor of peoples all over the world, and thus a victory for "social justice."

A key to understanding the mentality of the left is that it judges itself by its best intentions, while judging its opponents—America chief among them—by their worst deeds. Or by the fantasies of what their worst deeds might be. By imagining a perfect world of social justice that leftists will surely create, they can make America's most positive achievements look bad. If a world can be created in which everyone would be fed and have shelter and medical attention, then the fact that they don't can be attributed to America, because America is the guardian of the international "status quo." From this vantage, every good that America has achieved can be seen as a social obscenity. It may be the case, for example, that America has raised unprecedented millions out of the ranks of poverty into a comfortable middle-class existence. But a neo-communist sees this achievement as one that is realized at the expense of a million greater achievements. A historical good that America has accomplished is thus turned into a malevolent deprivation, an evil deed. By extension, when the left acts to weaken America or defend America's enemies, it is really advancing the cause of social progress.

In the past the Communist left was driven by the illusion that the Soviet Union was actually a "workers' paradise" and that true socialism had been achieved. Communists who defended Stalin's oppressive state believed that Russia was really a paradigm of human freedom. Neo-communists know the execrable nature of regimes like Iraq's but defend them against American arms nonetheless. Unlike Moscow, Baghdad is not their socialist mecca. In order to sustain their antagonism to America's intervention in Iraq, they must disconnect their intentions from their actions and their actions from the results. In the past, Communists believed in what they did. Today, neo-communists justify their deeds with the excuse of good intentions. Isn't it what all utopians do? If you believe in a future that will redeem mankind, what lie will you not tell, what crime will you not commit to make the future happen? Which is why progressives have committed so many atrocities in the last half-century and lied to everyone, especially themselves. The Communist mantra, "the ends justify the means," is exactly the rationalization that neo-communists use to defend their alliances with reactionary Islamic radicals and fascist regimes. Using good intentions to justify bad deeds is the first requirement of a utopian faith.

17

Discover the Networks

[PREFATORY NOTE: *DiscovertheNetworks.org*, a website I created, is an encyclopedia about the post-Communist left. In its seven-year existence, it has been visited by millions of individuals, many of them writers and broadcasters who have turned the insights afforded by it into books and on-air analyses. When the website was first posted on February 15, 2005, it was visited by 250,000 individuals in its first two days and aroused a furious controversy on the political left. The focus of the left's attacks was a one-page index of some of the figures included in the database, illustrated by thumbnail-size photos. Protesters objected to the apparent linkage of American leftists and Islamic terrorists like Osama bin Laden, even if the link was merely a juxtaposition on the index-page. I understood that such a juxtaposition, even without any overt linkage, could lead to unsubstantiated conclusions but was not about to remove bin Laden or other Islamists from website since there were already *de facto* alliances between the left and Islamist organizations such as the Muslim Brotherhood and Hamas. Moreover, anti-Western utopianism was a fundamental political bond between these forces, which had already led to the formation of what I had described as an "unholy alliance" in a book of that name the year before. Nonetheless, to accommodate any legitimate concerns, I decided to divide the offending index-page into five columns representing five categories of leftists. In this way the

This article was published on March 02, 2005, http://archive.front-pagemag.com/Printable.aspx?ArtId=9412

website now distinguished, for example, radical and moderate leftists, accommodating some of the criticisms—though not, it should
be said, to the satisfaction of the leftists, who still complained.
The article that follows is my defense of the new index and an
explanation of why it made sense. The photos were eventually
removed to forestall copyright claims, after we had been harassed
by several of these. With the photos gone, there was no point in
retaining the page itself, since it was merely an attempt to encourage readers to enter the database. The article that follows was my
defense of the categories we had introduced for the page that no
longer exists, and is included here because it analyzes the factions
of the left as I perceived them.]

If you visit the "Individuals" search-page in DiscoverTheNetworks, you will see that we have separated the leftists included
there into five columns, identified as "totalitarian radicals,"
"anti-American radicals," "leftists," "moderate leftists" and
"affective leftists." The latter includes mostly entertainment figures whose political commitments are emotionally rather than
intellectually based in a way I will analyze below. We have
arranged the grid this way even though we think it feeds certain
illusions, to accommodate those who expressed anguish over the
original format where no such distinctions were made. Their
anguish focused on the fact that the original grid contained radicals characterized by a spectrum of views from the totalitarian left
to the democratic left, and that it also included Islamic radicals
along with Hollywood entertainers, Democratic Party legislators
and academics.

It is particularly ironic that one of the most outraged critics of
regarding this aspect of the site was a professor named Michael
Bérubé, whose blogs can be found here.[1] For among academics the
links are the clearest, since the university is the most obvious

---

[1]http://www.michaelberube.com/

political base of the hard left. Sami al-Arian, a figure in the grid, ran the Palestinian Islamic Jihad whose most recent feat was the assassination of the former premier of Lebanon. Al-Arian ran this operation from the University of South Florida, where he was a professor of engineering. After his terrorist activities had been exposed by *The Miami Herald*, and while he was being pursued by the FBI, al-Arian was defended by the American Association of University Professors as a persecuted Palestinian. Venerable leftist institutions like Salon.com and *The Nation*, the ACLU and the Center for Constitutional Rights joined in his defense. Just before his arrest, al-Arian had been the featured speaker at a Duke-sponsored symposium on "Terrorism and Civil Liberties," where he was presented as an expert on civil liberties. More recently, the AAUP and academic leftists have joined in protesting the State Department's decision to bar Tariq Ramadan from joining the "Peace Studies" faculty at Notre Dame. "Peace Studies" itself is an academic field that teaches "one man's terrorist is another man's freedom fighter" and that—in the phrase used by academics Noam Chomsky and Robert Jensen—America is the world's "greatest terrorist state." This is just the tip of the iceberg concerning relationships between leftist professors on American faculties and Islamic radicals conducting a *jihad* against the West.

On the one hand, there was an element in the criticisms against us that could not be so easily dismissed. Moderate leftists who were also included in the grid are obviously patriotic Americans with no relation to Islamic radicals. It did seem unfair to include them. On the other hand, we were trying to make a point that political analysts who are commonly referred to as "liberal" or "populist" are often simply leftists. They are redistributionists and statists, and their networks of support extend into the heart of the "progressive" movement.[2]

---

[2]One of the "moderate" leftists included in the database was then Senator Barack Obama. Little was known about him at the time. For documentation on Obama's lifelong career in the radical left, see Stanley Kurtz, *Radical-in-Chief*, 2010.

The answer to these dilemmas came to me in a conversation with John Gorenfeld, a writer assigned to cover DiscoverTheNetworks by his editors at *Salon.com*. *Salon*, despite its defense of Sami al-Arian and similar lapses, is part of what we describe in the new grid as the "left" sans the adjectives "totalitarian" and "anti-American." Not quite moderate but not quite radical either, the editors of *Salon*, according to our taxonomy, are leftists of patriotic and democratic intent. I wrote a column for Salon for two years and would do so again if invited. I assure you that such a relationship would not be possible with hard-left venues like Counter-Punch.org, alternet.org, the *Progressive* or *The Nation*.

In today's conventional political lexicon, the term "moderate leftist" is equivalent to "liberal." We have not used "liberal" as a designation because part of the agenda of DiscoverTheNetworks is to challenge the use of the word "liberal" to describe people who are leftists. To do so obscures the seamless network of the left. Redistributionism, support for racial preferences, and a complacent acceptance of the existing political monolith on academic faculties are not attitudes that can reasonably be called liberal. They are the product of a successful campaign by leftists to conduct "a long march through the institutions" by assuming the political coloration of liberalism in order to escape accountability for the leftist past and in order more easily to advance their radical agendas in the American mainstream. The leftist slide of the Democratic Party is a by-product of this campaign.

Another ambition of the DiscoverTheNetworks website is to unmask the radical agendas of *faux*-liberal organizations and individuals like the misnamed Center for Constitutional Rights. This organization was founded by totalitarian radicals and has merged with the National Emergency Civil Liberties Committee, a communist front. Its politics are aligned with Castro's uba and Islamo-fascists. The convicted terrorist lawyer Lynne Stewart is a protégée and icon of the Center, as is Stanley Cohen, the lawyer for Hamas.

The term "affective leftist" requires some explanation, and I am grateful to Peter Collier for the description that follows.

"These are people in positions of influence who are *bien-pensant* in the extreme. In spite of their social status, they see themselves 'in opposition'—a legacy from the 1960s when the notion of 'The System' as a malign code word for America was born. They are also involved in post-radical chic, glorifying people who 'authentically' represent oppositional ideas in a way they would not have the courage or really even the political inclination to do themselves. To these people, as opposed to serious leftists, political 'ideas' are the intellectual equivalent of a fashion statement, always adjusting to meet current trends, always meant as a sort of code to tell the world that they are good people. Obviously, I'm talking here about people like Katie Couric and Robin Williams and almost all of Hollywood. Some Hollywood people like Sean Penn with his Communist lineage are harder core and should be distinguished from this category; but there aren't that many of them, and in any case as actors their politics are largely emotion-based as well. These affective liberals have as their bottom-line definition the fact that they want to feel that they are on the right side rather than any real commitment to a vision (or anti-vision) for the country. They are for 'freedom' when it is freedom to kill third-term fetuses or engage in same-sex marriages or stuff coke up their noses; they do not define freedom as anything to do with captive peoples around the world having the chance to escape the tyrannies that constrain them. They like Fidel because he is a thorn in America's side and a sort of dime-store existentialist, and they rhapsodize about his spreading of literacy in Cuba without considering the fact that at the same time that he teaches people to read he tortures writers like Armando Valladares whose books he doesn't like."

Those who are still unconvinced about the principle of inclusion that governs this database are invited to read my book, *Unholy Alliance: Radical Islam and the American Left,* written alongside the construction of DiscovertheNetworks.org, whose taxonomy reflects its perspective. *Unholy Alliance* describes the "mind of the left" in its journey from Stalinism to the present day.[3] It sets this analysis within the frame of 9/11 and the war in Iraq. It shows how the "antiwar" left, was formed, how it created "solidarity" links to Islamic radicalism, how it shaped the Democratic Party's 2004 election campaigns and how it determined the unprecedented defection of mainstream "liberalism" from the war itself.

The purpose of DiscoverTheNetworks is informational, not polemical. It seeks to describe the political left, and thus clarify the terms of the political debate. For example, it is impossible to understand the recent leftward turn of the Democratic Party if the entire left from Noam Chomsky to Jimmy Carter is subsumed by the term "liberal," which is the way the culture's arbiters—e.g., *The New York Times,* the network news bureaus—currently frame this subject. If Noam Chomsky and Angela Davis are referred to as liberals—as they are in these media outlets—how does one understand the politics of Joe Lieberman? The conflation of liberal and radical agendas, of leftwing politics and liberal dispositions, is a misnomer that makes crucial political conflicts incomprehensible. There is a battle raging in the Democratic Party between a moderate left and a radical left, between an authentic centrism and "progressivism." This conflict cannot be detected, let alone understood, when viewed through a lens as ill-defined as "liberalism" in its current usage. Joseph Lieberman is liberal; MoveOn.org is not.[4]

Having revised our database to reflect the varieties of leftism, we welcome further comments and observations. But past a certain point such revision would support familiar delusions of the left about its record of the last fifty years. The progressive left supported Communist enemies of freedom during the Cold War. Many progressives did so "critically," deploring the lack of freedom in the Soviet bloc countries, while explaining it away as the

---

[3]This section of the book is included in Volume 2, *The Left,* of this series.
[4]This battle is now over. The ouster of Joseph Lieberman was one milestone, the presidency of Barack Obama another, in the transformation of the Democrats into a leftwing party

result of America's Cold War "aggressions" against the socialist world. The same explanations are still offered for the Cuban dictatorship's domestic failures and repressions: The American blockade did it. These same leftists, while rhetorically critical of the Soviet bloc, were busily applauding the totalitarian camp for "restraining" American "imperialism." They dedicated themselves to weakening America's Cold War efforts by launching campaigns for unilateral disarmament and the like. Yet when the Soviet system collapsed, they pretended not to have done what they had done, or felt what they had felt. They washed their hands of "actually existing socialism" and accepted no responsibility for their complicity in its crimes.

We have some concern that the attitudes reflected in this false innocence are encouraged by descriptions that distinguish factions of the left in our new grid. In creating the categories of leftists who are neither anti-American radicals nor totalitarians we may seem to be absolving "moderates" from responsibility when they work in coalitions with radicals who are anti-American and totalitarian, or when they fail to reject those radicals. Political commitments are not only reflected in ideals and hopes; they are also measured by oppositions, partnerships and actions. Antiwar leftists of the Sixties may have described themselves as "anarchists" and democratic socialists, but the effect of their activities was to establish brutal police-states in Cambodia and Vietnam that slaughtered masses of innocents.

Contemporary leftism is, in fact, largely a nihilism. Since the collapse of socialism—and really since the collapse of the international Communist monolith in the wake of the Khrushchev report—the left hasn't had a coherent unifying agenda. It has been split into many protesting factions balkanized by "identity politics" and with no common remedies for perceived ills. This is a fallout from the failure of Marxist class politics, which subsumed all radical agendas concerning race, gender and ethnicity into a universal formula of socialist revolution. According to the formula, the elimination of private property and the rule of the working class would create a universal brotherhood of man that would resolve all serious social conflicts, including those of race and gender. Few leftists believe this anymore, which is why they are unable to form a shared and coherent vision of the liberated future. What is left is nihilism—anti-globalization, anti-racism, anti-sexism, anti-homophobia.[5] As a result, according to a recent article by an academic Marxist, the "twin pillars" of leftwing unity are now its hostility to Israel and to the United States.[6] It is a negative inspiration that explains the unholy alliance between American and Islamic radicals, despite all their obvious differences. The enemy of my enemies is my friend.

The importance of the negative in understanding the forces that create the left can be seen most clearly in regard to the war in Iraq. Most leftists who are not of a totalitarian persuasion deplored the Saddam regime. Nonetheless they acted to save it. The bottom-line in politics is not what your good intentions are, but the consequences of your actions. Opposition to the Iraq War forged a *defacto* partnership between left-wing critics of Saddam and Islamic radicals who supported him. Osama bin Laden himself recognized this in a *fatwa* on al-Jazeera TV just before American and British troops entered Iraq: "The interests of Muslims and the interests of the socialists coincide in the war against the crusaders."

The current revision to the "Individuals" grid on Discover-TheNetworks stresses the positive intentions of leftists, which can be misleading. In the war for democracy in the Middle East, the left—and this means the *entire* left, totalitarian, anti-American and "moderate"—has either been AWOL in supporting the war or has been pulling for the wrong side—against the liberation of Iraq, and against the establishment of democracies in the Middle East. There are some exceptions. Christopher Hitchens and

---

[5]And recently, anti-Islamophobia
[6]http://discoverthenetworks.org/Articles/The%20European%20and%20American%20Left.htm

Richard Gephardt both qualify as moderate leftists who supported the war against Saddam and thus the war to make the Iraqi elections possible. There were others. But the majority of leftists—the majority of the Democratic Party—were on the wrong side of this battle. In politics, it is the side you're on that matters. So even if we have provided a grid that shows these important distinctions, we have not considered it necessary to remove from the database any of the individuals we originally included.

18

Keeping an Eye on the Domestic Threat

One of the most frequent questions I am asked about my journey to the right is why I did not stop somewhere in the middle, by which the questioner usually means the "conservative" end of the Democratic Party. In fact, I remember very clearly why I did not. At the time, which was just before the 1984 election, Ronald Reagan and the Republicans were trying to hold the line against a Communist offensive in Central America, while Democratic senators led by Tom Harkin, John Kerry and Christopher Dodd were conducting their own private diplomacy in Central America attempting to cut deals with the Communists. Back home the Democratic House was seeking to cut funds to the anti-Communist forces on the ground. I had turned my back on the left because of the support it gave to the Communists in Indochina; I was not about to throw in my lot with them when they were enabling another Communist conquest.

I was put in mind of these events by a recent report on the *Newsweek* website. "Senate Intelligence Committee Chair Dianne Feinstein and other prominent Senate Democrats have accused spies at the Homeland Security Department of basing official intelligence reports on dubious open-source material. Inquiries ... indicate that at least some of the data that Feinstein and her colleagues deemed 'questionable' came from a website set

---

This article was published on March 16, 2010, http://frontpagemag.com/2010/david-horowitz/keeping-an-eye-on-the-domestic-threat-2/print/

up by outspoken conservative activist David Horowitz to catalogue negative information about the political left."

It was a reference to DiscovertheNetworks.org. According to
Newsweek, Senator Feinstein's immediate concern was "a profile
of an unnamed but prominent American Islamic leader [...] produced by Homeland Security's intelligence office during the latter
years of the Bush administration. The report was requested by the
Department's civil rights office, whose officials were preparing to
meet with the Islamic leader. But instead of sending the civil
rights office a quick bio of the individual in question, Homeland's
intelligence office issued a 'finished' intel report that was circulated to other intelligence agencies and, eventually, to Congressional oversight committees."

In other words, Senator Feinstein and the Democrats were
objecting to the scrutiny of a prominent Islamic leader scheduled
to meet with the Bush Administration, even though leaders of
prominent "mainstream" Islamic organizations such as CAIR
have been convicted of terrorist activities, while others have been
linked by the FBI to a formally-organized network of the Muslim
Brotherhood, the fountainhead of Islamic terrorism. The letter
from the Senate Intelligence Committee, which was the focus of
the *Newsweek* article, complained that the Department of Homeland Security "used 'certain questionable' source material to glean
'derogatory' information about [a particular] Muslim leader,
including information from an unidentified source 'with obvious
political motivation whose stated purpose is to "identif[y] the individuals and organizations that make up the left."'" The senators
added that the source also included information on "'numerous
members of Congress and two former Presidents of the United
States.'"

The source was censored from the Intelligence Committee letter, but *Newsweek's* Mark Hosenball was able to identify it via a
Google search as Discoverthenetworks.org: "The website is one of
a number of anti-left and anti-Islamic websites operated by the
David Horowitz Freedom Center, a Los Angeles-based assortment

of conservative political organizations founded and headed by David Horowitz, a 1960s-vintage far-left organizer who migrated sharply to the political right."

When Hosenball interviewed me, I told him that I had no knowledge of the Homeland Security matter but hoped that intelligence officials were consulting DiscovertheNetworks regularly—for the sake of the country. He quoted me as saying that the political left, including some members of Congress—the one I named was Barbara Lee, head of the Congressional Black Caucus—have "a long history of . . . actively working with and collaborating with America's enemies." I also assured him that the material on DiscovertheNetworks.org, which can easily be checked, is factual.

Of all the projects of the David Horowitz Freedom Center during a 22-year history—its university campaigns, the scores of books its principals and contributors have authored, the hundreds of lectures they have given and the thousands of articles its websites have published—I regard the creation of DiscovertheNetworks as its single most significant achievement with the most far reaching long-term impact. This is not because it is a "catalogue [of] negative political information about the political left," as *Newsweek* claimed. It is rather a map describing the origins, activities, agendas, funding and interlocking networks of a movement whose collective goal is the destruction of American capitalism and pluralism, of the framework America's founders created more than 200 years ago.

Ever since making my political conversion I have been aware that the American public is dangerously naïve about the nature and purposes of the American left; although mercifully this innocence is rapidly coming to an end. The extent of it is reflected in an incident twenty years past, when I gave a speech to the Cardinal Mindszenty Foundation in St. Louis. Cardinal Mindszenty was a hero of the anti-Communist cause, and the Mindszenty Foundation was as conservative an organization as was likely to host me. In my days as a radical I would have described myself as a "Marxist revolutionary," but when it came to my introduction, my host presented me as "a former peace activist and civil-rights worker." How familiar is this? Sworn enemies of American capitalism and American democracy such as Angela Davis and Michael Moore are universally described by mainstream media as "liberals" even though they are Marxists. The campaign to prevent America from toppling Saddam Hussein was portrayed in the mainstream media as a "peace movement" even though its leaders were self-described supporters of Korean dictator Kim Jong-Il and other Communists; they had not organized a single "peace" demonstration in front of the Iraqi embassy to demand that Saddam Hussein cease his defiance of 17 UN arms-control resolutions and allow inspectors to visit his weapons sites.

DiscoverTheNetworks strips the veil from thousands of radical groups that fly under false flags and evade detection by referring to themselves as peace movements, civil-liberties organizations and campaigns for "social justice." Now, for the first time, the left's history, its agendas and commitments are displayed for a public that has not made the study of the left a lifetime occupation. The most alarming aspect of the *Newsweek* report is the fact that the Bush Homeland Security Department had to refer to our research to warn the White House of the dangers a prospective visitor might pose, because the department did not have the information in its own files.

PART III

Slander As Political Discourse

I

Paul Berman's
Demented Lunacy

W hen a man begins his review of your life by calling you a "demented lunatic," as Paul Berman does in his bizarre comments on my autobiography *Radical Son* in the Winter issue of *Dissent*, the expectation that he will misrepresent you in ways both small and large is high. Berman doesn't disappoint. To avoid unnecessary tedium, and because *Radical Son* is readily available, I will confine this reply to two of his distortions.

Berman portrays me as a Leninist, not only in my adolescence in the 1950s, but also as a New Left activist in the 1960s, and even in conservative middle-age, now that I have progressed in his view from being a "fanatic" of the left to one of the right. As Berman sums me up: "I think [Horowitz] feels that a ruthless disregard for truth and facts is the practical way to proceed on all political questions.... " Readers of *Radical Son* will know that my feelings are precisely the opposite. My break with Lenin's duplicitous politics was triggered by a sort of epiphany that occurred in 1953 and is described on page 78 of my autobiography. I was all of 14 at the time, and was walking across the Triborough Bridge on my way to a demonstration in behalf of the Rosenberg spies. During the walk, I was being instructed by a political mentor in the very Leninist doctrine to which Berman alludes, "that it was necessary to lie in order to advance the revolutionary cause." I instinctively rebelled at this idea. "How could we make a virtue of lying, and still

This article was published on January 8, 1998, http://archive. frontpagemag.com/Printable.aspx?ArtId=24351 advance the cause of truth? Would the Rosenbergs lie about their innocence? In my heart, I . . . felt that Lenin's instruction to be dishonest was wrong." It is a theme that runs throughout my book, and has guided my political life.

This very anti-Leninist rebellion is what defined my politics as a New Leftist in the Sixties. During that time I avoided joining any of the Leninist sects then proliferating in the movement. The same urgency not to evade or suppress the truth in the service of a political idea is what later caused me to risk my life, and lose most of my friends for telling the truth about the Black Panthers, an action that Berman also distorts by falsely suggesting that Kate Coleman and others preceded me in exposing the Panthers' crimes which, as he knows, is the opposite of what happened. I was the silent source for Coleman's courageous article. I still live with an element of risk, perhaps far greater than any Berman has experienced, as a result of my efforts to bring the truth to light.

Berman attaches great significance to an article of mine that appeared in *Soldier of Fortune* magazine in January 1987, "an episode in his publishing career that [Horowitz] evidently wishes to suppress." This is a Berman invention. Here is how he embellishes the episode in the course of adversely comparing my career to that of another second-thoughter, André Glucksmann: "Now was [Horowitz's] moment at *Soldier of Fortune*. He became a simple-minded fanatic [sic] the mirror image of his worst (and not his best) moments on the left." The piece he is referring to was actually a "Speech to My Former Comrades on the Left" (published in this volume as "*Semper* Fidel") that I gave at a Berkeley teach-in on Nicaragua, held on April 4, 1986. The speech was reprinted under that title in *Commentary* in June 1986. Berman himself replied to it in *The Village Voice* in August 1986, six months before its appearance in *Soldier of Fortune* under the title "The Intellectual Life and the Renegade Horowitz."[1] Following its

---

[1] "The Intellectual Life and the Renegade Horowitz" referred to in "Why I Am No Longer a Leftist" in the present volume.

appearance in *Commentary* the article was picked up by many journals, including the *Utne Reader* (a left-wing *Reader's Digest*). *Soldier of Fortune* was one of the journals that requested reprint rights. I granted the rights, without exception, to every magazine (and textbook editor) who requested them. Had I realized the uses to which future detractors might put this liberality, I might have been more selective. But the idea that I embraced the politics of *Soldier of Fortune* at that time, or any time, is absurd.

2

In Defense
of Matt Drudge

The oddest feature of the affair that pits White House flack Sidney Blumenthal against Internet gadfly Matt Drudge is probably the most revealing: the failure of the press to defend one of its own. Last August, Blumenthal filed a $30 million libel suit against Drudge for reporting a rumor that Blumenthal was once involved in a spousal-abuse court case and then failing to reveal his unnamed sources, even though Drudge quickly retracted the claim. I should state at the outset that I am the co-chair of the Matt Drudge Defense Fund, which is raising money to support his legal case.

Matt Drudge is an entrepreneur who made his web-based Drudge Report a national media player. While media conglomerates, in their glass-towered fortresses, deploy battalions of scribes across the globe, Drudge operates alone from his Hollywood apartment on a salary of $36,000 a year. Such a mismatch should have made Drudge the underdog favorite in a case that would seem to pit a White House Goliath against an Internet David. But it hasn't. One obvious reason is that little Matt Drudge kept scooping the big guys on stories ranging from alleged White House scandals to Republican politics and network television changes. Drudge also played right into the hands of a journalistic establishment that resents this upstart new medium, the Internet. His apparent recklessness in reporting a rumor he couldn't back up evoked images of

November 17, 1997, http://archive.frontpagemag.com/Printable.aspx?
ArtId=24382
http://www.salon.com/1997/11/17/nc_17horo/

journalistic irresponsibility and informational chaos generated by a free medium many find threatening.

The fact that Drudge is an Internet libertarian rather than a statist liberal doesn't help his case, either. Sidney Blumenthal, on the other hand, began his career at the socialist tabloid *In These Times*. From there he went to such bastions of official liberalism as the *New Republic* and the *Washington Post*. His time at the *Post* was an up-and-down experience; he did a brief stint reporting foreign policy before being sent (some say demoted) to the less weighty Style section. He then shifted to *The New Yorker* where political soulmate Rick Hertzberg had become the new managing editor. After Blumenthal was made White House reporter, the sycophancy of his stories about Bill and Hillary Clinton and his constant playing down of the mushrooming Whitewater scandal made other reporters at the *New Yorker* wince. Yanked from his beat, Blumenthal finally got what he really wanted: a job at the Clinton White House, as a senior communications advisor. There was a chorus of hoots to send him off from his colleagues in the press; *The New Republic* suggested the Clintons owed him back pay for services already rendered.

This is the man who has taken a holier-than-thou attitude to the offending Matt Drudge for reporting a "Republican" rumor he was unable to back up. No matter that Drudge immediately retracted the item when it was first challenged and apologized for it in an interview with the Post's Howard Kurtz. Blumenthal wanted sources and when Drudge refused, as any other self-respecting journalist would have, Blumenthal slapped him with a $30 million suit. For good measure (and for its deep pockets) Blumenthal also named America Online as a defendant, since it had a contract to run the Drudge Report on its network.

Blumenthal's attorneys compiled a 137-page summary of the charges, throwing in chunks of columns from Howard Kurtz and other comments from Blumenthal friends they thought incriminating to Drudge, and circulated the lawsuit to the entire media and anyone else who requested it. Since lawsuits often contain damaging but unsubstantiated charges, lawyers, as a rule, forbid their clients from distributing such filings, even to friends, to avoid the prospect of libel suits in return. The aim is clear: not merely to nail Drudge but to warn other critics of the Clinton establishment, including those online, to beware.

Despite such attempted intimidation, not to mention the rather low esteem in which he is held by the profession, Blumenthal has up to now been able to rally the press to his cause. When asked about Drudge in a *Christian Science Monitor* survey on Internet reporters, Joan Konner, head of the Columbia Journalism School, sneered: "Drudge isn't a reporter, he's your next-door neighbor gossiping over the electronic fence." Forgotten in their dismissive rush to judgment about Drudge are some of the low-ball hits Blumenthal has administered against people he didn't like, calling former vice-presidential candidate Geraldine Ferraro a "Mafia princess" in a *New Republic* cover story, or referring to Midge Decter as a "dog" in his book-length takedown of the neo-conservative movement. As for accuracy, in a piece he wrote about me in the *Washington Post* he managed to mangle three separate details about my life in the space of three sentences.[1]

The press would be well advised to put aside its snobbish disdain for cyberspace journalism and consider the consequences of abandoning Drudge to the mercies of Blumenthal and his legal juggernaut. Is there a reporter in any corner of the media who has never made a comparable mistake? Or is Drudge being turned into a whipping-boy for media's *ancien régime* fearful of the subversive and the new? The cry has gone out: *the Internet must be brought under control.* At the same time, online content providers like AOL have been warned: Don't mess around with upstarts. This fight isn't just about Matt Drudge; it's about the battle for Internet freedom. And if the Internet loses, guess who's next?

---

[1]See "The Serial Distortions of Sid Vicious," Chapter 4 below.

3

Target of a
Witch-Hunt

An old writer-friend of mine called the other day to say that he had been advised by a senior editor of *The New Republic* not to have anything to do with my partner Peter Collier and myself because we were "Nazis." The reason? We had organized a fund to defend Matt Drudge, the Internet gadfly who broke the story of the President's dalliance with Monica Lewinsky and is being sued by White House aide Sidney Blumenthal, the actual architect of Hillary Clinton's "vast right conspiracy" charges. Every day, now, I get calls from the press about my connections to two points on Blumenthal's charts, Matt Drudge and philanthropist Richard Scaife, who were targeted, for example, in a recent *Newsweek* story. In *The Nation* this week, the Center for the Study of Popular Culture, the institution that Peter and I created, is itself featured as an element in Blumenthal's web.

How does it feel to be the focus of a witch-hunt? Actually, it feels quite familiar. I grew up in the Cold War Fifties in a family of American Communists. The FBI used to linger on the streets of our neighborhood, charting people's comings and goings. My parents lost their jobs as high-school teachers because they would not answer the question "Have you ever been?" Or at least could not answer it honestly. Once in a junior high-school auditorium, when I was 13, a group of toughs whom I didn't know put a drapery cord

Originally published as "The Drudge Affair and Its Ripple Effect, " January 01, 1998, http://archive.frontpagemag.com/Printable.aspx?ArtId=24331
http://www.salon.com/1998/02/23/nc_23horo_3/

around my neck and started shouting "String him up, he's a red!" So I know the drill. Unfair as the treatment of my family and some of our Communist friends was during the McCarthy era, there was a large element of truth in the conspiracy charge itself. My parents were indeed Communists, willing enlistees in a disciplined and secretive movement that did take its orders (and its money) from Moscow and was indeed dedicated to the overthrow of American democracy and the undermining of its security vis-à-vis the Soviet Union. My parents, their friends and most of those who fell into McCarthy's net harbored these loyalties and subscribed to these goals. Yet most people agree, and I am one of them, that McCarthy's witch-hunt was a smear-campaign that injured some people who were innocent of any connection to the actual Communist conspiracy and others who, while connected to the conspiracy, were guiltless of any criminal behavior. McCarthy's true target was not Communists, who were already under FBI surveillance, but his political opponents in the Democratic Party. The Democrats, it should be said, were a rich target since they went out of their way to protect the Communists—Alger Hiss being the most obvious example. Which is why they despised McCarthy and decried his "witch-hunt."

Why then the seeming tolerance by so-called liberals for the current White House inquisition, whose purpose is to smear and destroy its political critics? As anyone can see, there was no conspiracy surrounding the events which evinced the First Lady's accusation. Although it was publicly unknown at the time she made the accusation, her husband had indeed strayed from his marriage vows on the floor of the Oval Office. There is no Communist Party of the right with secret codes and top-down discipline that has the ability to give marching orders to anyone. If Monica Lewinsky was planted in the White House, Democrats did the planting. It was *Newsweek,* no conservative publication, that developed the Lewinsky story. Drudge only made it public. Richard Scaife, who is villain #2 in Blumenthal's conspiracy web, funded investigations that suggested the suicide of Vince Foster might have been involuntary. But then the special prosecutor, Ken Starr, who is villain #1, issued a summary report refuting the speculations that Scaife had funded, while supporting the original suicide report. What kind of a conspiracy is this?

As for my miniscule role in this matter, I had hardly been aware of Drudge's existence when I first heard of the Blumenthal suit and offered to introduce the Internet reporter to a lawyer. The lawyer I chose, Manny Klausner, is a well-known civil rights advocate with long-standing and very public ties to the Libertarian Party. My Center for the Study of Popular Culture also has long been interested in free-speech issues, and has defended feminists and Afro-centrists as well as conservatives on First Amendment issues. Its legal arm spearheaded the battle against speech codes on college campuses some years ago. We even attained some notoriety when we forced a Vice-Chancellor at the University of California to undergo "sensitivity training" in the First Amendment after he banned a fraternity for producing a T-shirt the PC crowd didn't like. We were even criticized by George Will in one of his *Newsweek* columns when he didn't get the satire. So we were active in defending free speech well before the punitive White House suit against Matt Drudge. Our interest did not, in other words, flow from our involvement in a vast conspiracy to discredit President Clinton with false rumors of infidelity as Mrs. Clinton claimed.

It is true that we do get funds from two foundations funded by the Scaife fortune, in addition to 20 others and 15,000 individuals. [Note: Unclear here whether those 20 groups & 15,000 receive money from Scaife, or whether they fund you.] But why is Richard Scaife, whom I have met and talked to twice in my life, being demonized as though he were the mastermind of a plot against the White House? Why is the Center for the Study of Popular Culture, which has sought only to defend a journalist from what it perceived as a punitive and chilling attack, being dragged into the plot? The answer should be obvious from witch-hunts of the past. It is to deflect attention away from the real issues that separate the

White House from its critics. It is to conjure fantasy-demons in order to smear and cripple those critics. The question that should be asked is why, given the black record of witch-hunts of the past, are Democrats so tolerant of this latest version?

The editor of *The New Republic* who called Peter and me Nazis because of our defense of Matt Drudge was an old friend named John Judis. After writing a defense of Drudge, which appeared in *Salon* magazine, I received a call from my writing partner and *Heterodoxy* co-editor, Peter Collier. He himself had just had a call from our mutual friend and fellow second-thoughter, Ron Radosh, whose article on his old Communist summer camp appeared in *Heterodoxy*. Radosh had contacted Judis to suggest he read the article. Judis replied he wouldn't read anything printed in *Heterodoxy* anymore, saying that we were "Nazis" (a charge he withdrew when confronted). The occasion of his wrath was the fact that I had set up a defense fund for Matt Drudge. Peter promptly e-mailed Judis the following message:

> John:
> Drudge, *Heterodoxy*, Susan Estrich, Kinsley, Nazis. Yikes.
> Collier

Collier's references were to the fact that Susan Estrich and Michael Kinsley had also defended Drudge. This prompted a reply from Judis:

> I assume your letter was prompted by a conversation I had with Ron Radosh this afternoon, since I haven't talked to you in ages. You need to know a little background. Ron brought up *Hetero-doxy*. I said, as I have said before to him that I was pissed off about Horowitz's defense of that scumbag Drudge. Radosh attributed my position to my being friends with Sid Blumenthal, and instead of blowing up at him as I should have (the implication is that the only reason I defended him on the George Washington thing was because he was a friend of mine),[1] I started railing

---

[1] The incident referred to was an attempt by leftists to keep Radosh from a faculty position at George Washington University. Judis generously and

about Nazis. I don't think Horowitz is a Nazi, but I do think that his position is detestable. I wrote him a letter at the time but it was returned because he no longer lives at the address to which I sent it. Assuming you are in cahoots on this stuff, I'll send it to you and you can forward it to him if you desire.
John

What follows is the letter to me that was never sent, which Judis e-mailed to Collier:

11/19/97
Dear David:
This morning, a mutual friend or ours urged me to read your articles on Sid Blumenthal and the *Drudge Report*.[2] Rather than responding simply to him (I think I said something to the effect that I'd rather eat dogshit), I thought I would tell you what I thought of your leading the defense of Mr. Drudge.

Let me make the point indirectly through two anecdotes:

1) When the Drudge report first came out, one of my friends called me that afternoon to ask whether I'd seen it and what I knew of Sid's private life. This person, who didn't know Sid, assumed the report was true. I read it myself, and reading about court records, wondered, too, whether Sid hadn't concealed a part of himself from me all these years. Afterwards, I talked to several people who knew Sid and Jackie socially better than I did who thought the report was preposterous, but until the hoax was fully revealed, I still had lingering doubts. The point is this: there is no slander so insidious or so subversive to a person's reputation and character as a charge of wife-beating, especially when backed up with claims about court records. It can lead a friend of twenty years to harbor doubts about them. That's why law schools use this kind of charge as a model for slander and defamation.

2) After the hoax was revealed, I suggested to one of the editors at *The New Republic* that they run a short about it, noting,

---

courageously provided testimony in Radosh's behalf. Radosh was eventually allowed to teach at the school.
[2]See "In Defense of Matt Drudge," Chapter 2 above.

among other things, the connection to AOL, but this editor, knowing Mike Kelly's animosity toward Sid (at least the equal in ferocity of your own) hesitated to suggest it.[3] To my surprise, Kelly brought it up himself and insisted on running a short. His one concern was that even mentioning such a charge in the course of explaining it was a hoax could lend credence to it. In this case, Kelly was willing to put aside his feelings toward Sid because it was a question of principle—of someone attacking someone's reputation in the most scurrilous manner and using the new power of the Internet to do so. Kelly also believed, as I do, that it was important to sue in this instance, because it is important to establish a precedent so that other would-be journalists are deterred from following the example of Mr. Drudge and so that publishers, such as America-on-Line, are deterring from promoting these kind of scumbags.

I'd draw a very sharp contrast between your conduct and Kelly's. The mark of a moral person is the ability, upon occasion, to transcend one's own resentments and hatreds, as well as one's loves and enthusiasms. Kelly was able to do it. You are not. The main difference between your defense of Drudge in the Nineties and your defense of Huey Newton or *Los Siete* during the Sixties is that in the latter cases, you still had a smidgeon of principle.[4] I detest what you are doing.

Yours,

John

Peter replied to this e-mail from John:

2/14/98

John:

I put the letter of 11/19 in the trash receptacle of my e-mail program. If you want to send it to David, go ahead. He will send you

---

[3]Michael Kelly was editor of *The New Republic* at the time.

[4]*Los Siete de La Raza* (The Seven of the Race). A group of Chicanos accused of murdering a policeman. They were a cause célèbre of the Sixties left and *Ramparts,* the magazine that Peter Collier and I edited. *Los Siete* were acquitted and subsequently several of their members were re-arrested and convicted of other crimes, including murder. (See my autobiography, *Radical Son.*)

one, I'm sure, by return mail that will be equally morally uppity and probably even more (and I have to say, more justly) contemptuous.

He will accuse you of ignoring how the item was published and retracted. He will point out that there is an illuminating sequel in the events that monopolize the news today. He will note that Blumenthal is a loathsome individual figure who is doubtless, at this very moment, blackguarding someone, somewhere, somehow, since that is his only discernible talent.

If I know David, he will take you to task particularly for the last paragraph of this still-unsent letter of yours, which won't be difficult, since you've given him a target as big as a barn with what could easily be interpreted as a morally imbecilic proposition about supporting criminal gangs in the Sixties being some sort of misguided principle that can still be said to travel well, in extreme rhetorical instances such as the case at hand, in the Nineties.

"Innocently" supporting murderers in the Sixties: morally ok. Less innocently supporting an Internet gossip-monger in the Nineties: morally criminal. This is a weird moral calculus, my friend.

And after all these bitternesses are exhumed, then where will we all be? Nowhere. Worse than nowhere. Which is why I didn't forward your letter to David.

Some things are better off left unsaid.

Cheers,

Peter

Peter and I then had a conversation, and I asked him to retrieve John's e-mail from his trash, and send it to me. I then replied to John myself:

2/14/98

Dear John,

I have Peter's trash of your e-mail of November in which you explain why you have washed your hands of me, and "detest" what I do, apparently because I have come to the defense of Matt Drudge. This makes me a conspirator, apparently, in the plot to wound Sidney Blumenthal through unkind and inaccurate words that misrepresent the person you presume him to be. Peter has also sent me the reply he wrote in my behalf, and while I concur in his observations, they seem nonetheless incomplete. For me the attack in your letter also broaches basic issues about the nature of our political discourse and I am, therefore, also answering you in my own voice.

Over the last ten years I have kept in touch with you, partly for old times' sake, and partly because I thought you were a man of integrity and would keep faith with the past we shared. Though we no longer shared agendas, I thought there might even come a time when you might provide testimony against the powerful attacks and distortions of my life and Peter's that have been a direct consequence of our political defection. As you can see, this touches directly on the issues you raise about the misrepresentation of your friend at the hands of Mr. Drudge. For Peter and I have been the target of far more relentless distortion and more calculated slander than Sidney Blumenthal. In terms of actual wounds inflicted by mean-spirited and vicious misrepresentations of self, as of damages incurred, your friend does not begin to know what pain is. Or, evidently, how to deal with it.

In view of your attack on me now, it is something of an irony that I thought you might be up to the task of one day defending me against political slanders. I was perhaps misled by the fact that you were willing to entertain any overtures at all from me, when almost everyone Peter and I had known and befriended in the community of the left had turned on us with an irrational hatred. (Let it be said, that I am still grateful for this generosity.) The passion of these newly minted enemies was so intense that we could no longer count on those who had witnessed what we had done to respect the integrity of a single fact that we had shared, if that fact should come under attack. Were Peter and David holy rollers of the ideological sects, partisans of mindless extremes? It was left to us, and to others who had second thoughts, to remember that we were not. Consider how total this attack on our reality has been. While an almost universal hatred has been directed at Peter and me by our former comrades since our politics changed, *we* are the ones accused by *them* of malice; of having acted out criminal fantasies in the past and of being driven only by our hatred of old friends in the present.

But your personal tolerance of me was not the only factor that encouraged my misplaced trust. I was also impressed that in your own writing you made a significant effort to be fair to intellectual opponents on the right like Bill Buckley whose biographer you became. You made a modest specialty of conservative intellectuals and even of "renegades" from the left like James Burnham and Whittaker Chambers. I respected this, and it encouraged me to hope that this spirit of fairness might one day prompt you to be a witness to our truth and thus counter-act the politically motivated efforts to defame us, and thereby dismiss anything we had to say. Only this month, for example, your friend Paul Berman has described me as a "demented lunatic" in the foremost intellectual journal of the left, and as someone who was a Leninist fanatic before his second thoughts and remains one today; lies on both counts.

From the time Peter and I announced our political "second thoughts" in a piece in the *Washington Post* some thirteen years ago, and then organized a conference of other "second thoughters," we were greeted by a wall of hate erected by our former comrades. Your friend Sidney played a significant part in creating that wall. In a signature piece on our conference that appeared in the *Washington Post,* he caricatured us as political buffoons and right-wing extremists. It was the beginning of a campaign to marginalize us in the culture and as human beings. In the same article, Sidney portrayed me as a callow narcissist who had abandoned his principles and his children to flee to the fleshpots of Beverly Hills. Every word he wrote was false, but there was no way for me to respond or to clear my name.

And that was just the beginning. Over the last ten years, the attacks on Peter and myself have relentlessly continued. We have been portrayed as murderers (by your friends Hertzberg and Berman), as political criminals, as racists and homophobes, and always as shrill and monomaniacal ideologues to whom no self-respecting intellectual should pay the slightest serious attention.

This is the culture war John. And it has been successfully waged against us in the very precincts that you roam. Peter and I have written the only books by members of the Sixties left that challenge its myths. They are primary sources for the period as well as analytical texts about its meanings. But in college curricula you will rarely find references to *Destructive Generation* or *Second Thoughts About the Sixties*. The tenured left has seen to that. Instead you will find texts by Sixties loyalists, Angela Davis, Todd Gitlin, and even Huey Newton. Racist anti-Semites like Stokely Carmichael will visit these same campuses as well-paid speakers, and radical ideologues will be invited to serve as commencement speakers. We get no such invitations. This campaign of political libel conducted by Sidney and your friends has not silenced us as they intended but it has not been without success either.

Now I will tell you something that you will not believe, but it is true nonetheless. I don't harbor any personal malice towards Sidney Blumenthal, and that is not the reason I came to the defense of Matt Drudge. For myself, the immediate pain that Sidney inflicted in his caricature in the *Post*, was washed away when I was able to write my own story in *Radical Son* and thus correct his misrepresentation. Moreover, the malice towards Peter and me and the general misrepresentation of our politics is so generic to the left that it would be foolish to load responsibility on one man. If Matt Drudge had deliberately libeled Sidney for political ends and revealed a malicious intent to destroy him in the process, I assure you I would not have come to Drudge's aid.

Nor would I hesitate to have done what Michael Kelly did in printing a correction of the Drudge error. The fact is, as Peter has pointed out, that Drudge did this himself and did so immediately on being informed of his mistake. And his retraction was reported throughout the press and to a far greater audience than the original error.

What then is the purpose of Sidney's $30 million lawsuit? Surely not to send a warning to other writers as you suggest. The suit and the retraction already perform that function. My own piece in *Salon* about the affair was censored in several of its parts simply because the editors were afraid of a similar suit. I reported, for example, that Sidney had been shifted to the Style section of the *Post* when his editors became unhappy about his journalistic methods. This was factually true, but still too risky for *Salon's* editors in the climate Sidney and his lawyers have created. Is this an atmosphere that you, as a writer, want to encourage?

You want to make a claim of special heinousness for Drudge's offense. You write that there is no slander so insidious or subversive of character as the charge of wife-beating. Really? More insidious than Berman's charge that Peter and I were complicit in the murder of our friend, and then sought to shift the blame to others?

Or, let's take your claim about wife-beating charges at face value. Have you considered the case of Don Sipple, the Republican pollster charged with wife-beating by your friends at *Mother Jones?* Perhaps you'll remember that this was the immediate provocation of Drudge's own sin. *Mother Jones* also accused Sipple on the basis of "court records" and did not, like Drudge, qualify the charge as "rumor." Drudge reported the rumor about Blumenthal as one that Republicans were going to surface in order to revenge and neutralize the charge against Sipple. Unlike Blumenthal, who suffered no material damages, Sipple actually lost his job, and had no friends at *Newsweek,* the *NY Times, Time* and the *Washington Post* to report and support his side of the story.

Do you have any idea of what the basis for the charge against Sipple was? The impression given in the media was that he had been convicted of beating his wife in a court of law. When I looked at the original article in *Mother Jones,* it was somewhat of a shock to discover that the charge was actually an unproven claim made by a scorned ex-wife in the course of a bitter custody battle. I have no idea of the truth of this charge, but neither does *Mother Jones* or you. Yet a man has been seriously damaged as a result. Where is your outrage over the insidious subversion of Don Sipple's life?

Here is what is so perverse in your anguish over Sid. Unlike Sipple (or Peter and myself), Blumenthal commands enormous influence and power as a Presidential aide with a large network of friends in the press. He was able to reach millions with his side of the story immediately. In context, such pain as he incurred, though I am sure it was serious, was minimized. By contrast, ten years ago, when I went to Richard Harwood, the ombudsman of the *Washington Post,* to point out the lies that Sidney had written about me, Harwood shrugged his shoulders sympathetically, and suggested I write a letter to the editor. He did remove the offending column from the *Post'*s weekly national edition, a small but gratefully acknowledged gesture. On the other hand, your Sid, now cognizant of the facts and wholly unrepentant, made sure that the slander would reach a wider audience by reprinting the lies he had written, uncorrected, in a book of his collected articles called *Pledging Allegiance.*

Certainly no one in politics is immunized from name-calling, gross misrepresentation and unfounded accusation. That is deplorable but it is also the territory, and has been for a long time. In such an environment, all anyone can ask is to be able to respond to the slanders that are made and correct them. Occupying so high a political ground, Blumenthal had powers of correction that most of us lack. He should be the last to whine. That you and Blumenthal seem so refreshingly thin-skinned only reveals how protected you are, as members of the left, by a media sympathetic to you, and by the relative civility of the conservative press.

In the end, Blumenthal's suit has only one agenda: to destroy Drudge, to run him out of the business, to discredit him, and shut him up along with all the other Clinton thorns from Gennifer Flowers to Paula Jones. In these battles the White House is a Goliath from which you would normally keep your distance. So, why your animus against the Internet David? The error Drudge made in passing on the rumor about your friend hardly reflects a pattern in his journalism. He is so innocent of such smears and of the suits that can attend them that he didn't even have an attorney until I put him in touch with one.

The same cannot be said for your friend. Sid has no doubt the best legal advice money and his proximity to the Clintons can secure. His lawyers showed no qualms about circulating a 137-page suit, filled with unsubstantiated charges against Drudge to the entire media (a practice that invites a libel suit in return). Moreover, he is supported by an armada of prominent left-wing journalists for whom liberal distortion and personal abuse are the *lingua franca* of their craft; Joe Conason, Christopher Hitchens, Frank Rich, Eric Alterman, Alex Cockburn, and Robert Scheer.

It is Sid, isn't it, whose new career is that of the Clintons' shadow McCarthy, architect of the "vast right-wing conspiracy" charge that Hillary dropped on TV the other morning and that has reporters calling me daily. In the reigning paranoia that Sid has stoked in his job as Clinton spear-carrier, I have become part of his infamous conspiracy chart because I set up a fund to pay Drudge's legal bills. This ugly claim is what Maureen Dowd identifies as the Clinton "doomsday strategy" and what Stephanopoulos described as the determination "to take everybody down with him," interns, witnesses, journalists—by exposing their dirty secrets to the public. I'm sure the 941 FBI files the Clintons illegally appropriated will come in handy for such purposes.

It was only a year ago that Peter and I hosted an event in Los Angeles you attended as our guest. The meeting was warm with nostalgia, and for our part we made every effort to put you at ease, in the environment you were entering. Yet, cordial as our relations seemed to be, you didn't call me or even bother to make sure that your letter was put in my hands. You chose instead to attack me behind my back, and to warn our mutual friend Ron Radosh of the contagion involved in any contact with us, that *Heterodoxy* was now off limits if he wanted respectability. "Don't write for *Heterodoxy*. I won't read it. I'd rather eat dog shit," is how you put it.

And so, you have developed your own way of dehumanizing Peter and me, and of becoming part of the *Kulturkampf* against us. This must be why you have abandoned your usual judgment in embracing a scoundrel like Blumenthal (or at least his scoundrel acts). And this is why, while championing Sid, you have never thought to correct the insidious slanders directed at us in the magazines you write for and among the audiences you reach. An assessment of our work that recognized its seriousness and that corrected the caricatures of our character and allegiances would have been a natural sequel to your pieces on previously despised defectors like James Burnham and Whittaker Chambers. The difference is that they are safely dead and we are not. For the people you call your friends and whose praise and plaudits you seek, Peter and I are radioactive—political untouchables, as we have been for the nearly twenty years since those first lies from Blumenthal's pen. What lawsuit is going to give us redress from that?

David

I never heard from Judis again.

4

The Serial Distortions of Sid Vicious

As readers of Christopher Hitchens's point-by-point refutation of virtually every "factual" comment that Sidney Blumenthal (the former special assistant to President Clinton) made about Christopher in his new book *The Clinton Wars* will already know, Sid is such a compulsive prevaricator that he gives ordinary liars a bad name. Sid is also litigious and therefore I will take this opportunity to invite him to sue me for any libelous statement in the article that follows. I have no concerns about Sid filing such a suit because in matters of libel, truth is a bulletproof defense.

Sid has written about me twice. In both instances—and they are related—there are more factual misrepresentations than there are sentences in his texts. Moreover, the misrepresentations are wittingly made, and therefore lies, and also malicious. I haven't sued Sid (and won't) because as everyone knows (and as Sid would have learned had he not dropped his vindictive tort against Matt Drudge) one has to prove damages—loss of income or a job—as well as actual malice in order to win. Another consideration is the fact that libel laws exert a chilling effect on the democratic exchange of ideas and should therefore be used only as a last resort.

I have myself once or twice used the threat of a suit to deter particularly scurrilous charges and to forestall the kind of damage such suits were made for. In the 1980s, Alex Cockburn spent a lot

---

*This article was published on May 30, 2003, http://archive.front-pagemag.com/Printable.aspx?ArtId=18034

of time at cocktail parties spreading the rumor that I was a CIA agent. I have never had contact with a CIA official or operative that I am aware of, or worked for any government agency or—with four exceptions—any employer but myself. The exceptions are a one-year stint as a teaching assistant at the University of California, two years as a lecturer in a University of Maryland College program in England in the 1960s, the Bertrand Russell Peace Foundation during the same period and for a year after, and a little over a year with *Ramparts Magazine,* in 1968, before Peter Collier and I took it over in 1969. For the last six months, I have been on contract as a Fox News contributor. This exhausts my paychecks from others for the last 45 years. During the rest of the time, I have been a self-employed author and also head of a foundation I created.

Sidney Blumenthal's first outburst of literary malice was directed at me in a profile he wrote as a reporter for the *Washington Post* in 1987. The article was headlined, "Thunder on the New Right," and purported to be a report of the coming-out conference Peter Collier and I organized in 1987 for new-left radicals who had grown tired of supporting totalitarian causes, as Sidney evidently had not. Oh, I am aware that Sidney thinks of himself as a "third way" liberal and a small "d" democrat. But at our Second Thoughts Conference we did not propose conservative or "rightwing" agendas and did not think of ourselves in those terms at the time. This was a label that Sid pinned on us. In fact our conference featured several self-professed liberals. One of them, David Ifshin, had been the general counsel of the Mondale campaign and was a well-known Democrat. In our interview with Sidney (and with other reporters) we made a big point of the fact that our only political litmus for the event was that "second thoughters" (as we called ourselves) be anti-Communist and anti-Sandinista, since Nicaragua was the current battleground country in the still-active Cold War. Sidney's attack, therefore, was a matter of the enemies of his friends being his enemies. Why else would he have attacked us so viciously?

In addition to the big lie he told about our conference as the gathering of a rightwing conspiracy—a term he was to coin later for Hillary Clinton—Sidney added three other specific falsehoods about me: "When Horowitz abandoned radicalism, he also left his wife and three children, escaping into conservatism and Beverly Hills. 'When I was a Marxist, I was puritanical,' he said, 'then I got loose.'"

In fact, I had four children not three; I abandoned radicalism in 1975 at a time when I was married (my marriage ended in 1978); I never left my children; never lived in Beverly Hills and never made the statement Blumenthal attributed to me. When I lodged a complaint with the ombudsman of *The Washington Post* he removed the slander from the national edition of the paper. But when Sidney reprinted the same piece in his book *Pledging Allegiance*, all the slanderous and false statements remained intact.

I felt the sting of Sidney's personal slanders for a long time afterwards. I did not have the access to powerful media like *The Washington Post* to reach the same audience. These days, Sidney rarely appears on television without bemoaning "the politics of personal destruction," which a practice he attributes to the demonic right. This is the White House operative who invented the term "vast rightwing conspiracy" to allege that conservatives had made up the president's affair with Monica Lewinsky, and who led the charge in defaming the female victims of the president who had the courage to come forward.

The Second Thoughts Conference that Peter Collier and I organized was a notable success, although it was slandered by half a dozen leftwing journalists, including Alex Cockburn, Christopher Hitchens, Eric Alterman, Jim Sleeper and Todd Gitlin. Twenty years later Peter and I learned from Hitchens that Blumenthal had called each of these worthies prior to the event, and summoned them to attend in order to attack us.

In his new book, *The Clinton Wars*, Blumenthal returns to my case, because I was the person who introduced Matt Drudge to attorney Manny Klausner, who defended Drudge against Blumenthal's libel suit. In Blumenthal's text, I am described as funding Klausner as well. In this accounting, the Matt Drudge affair is a sinister manifestation of the vast rightwing conspiracy's efforts to overthrow a president. The puppet-master of these efforts, according to Blumenthal, was the philanthropist Richard Mellon Scaife. Two related players are Barbara and Michael Ledeen, whom Blumenthal's lawyer deposed. I willingly stipulate that I am fond of Dick Scaife, a decent American, and that Barbara and Michael Ledeen are old friends. What follows is the entire Blumenthal account of our conspiracy, along with my inter-linear comments:

> In July, the Ledeens' testimony yielded the information that they had arranged through a friend, David Horowitz, for Drudge's defense to be paid for and handled.

It is true that Barbara Ledeen called me and said, "You have to help Matt Drudge," whom I had never met. As Barbara and many other people knew, I had created an "Individual Rights Foundation," which mainly fought speech-codes on college campuses, but also defended a liberal feminist under attack from the politically-correct left and filed an amicus brief for a leftwing racist, Leonard Jeffries, because he was fired for making a public speech, a violation of his First Amendment rights.

I had no other conversations with Barbara or anyone else apart from Klausner, a libertarian, about the legal defense of Matt Drudge. Following Barbara's phone call, I had a lunch with Drudge and persuaded him he needed a lawyer. I then set up a meeting between Drudge and Klausner, who was taken on as counsel. I then created a "Matt Drudge Defense Fund," which raised money through direct mail and Internet appeals to pay Klausner's fees, although healthy proportions of his services were donated. The Ledeens had no hand in these matters whatsoever.

The next sentence of Blumenthal's text describes my interest in the case and is an instance of Blumenthal-phobia, his Rosetta stone for explaining any and all opposition to his political agendas:

> Horowitz shared [the Ledeens'] animosity, in his case because of an article I had reported for the *Post* about a political project of his that became a public embarrassment.

I have already described the Second Thoughts conference and the fact that outside the leftwing press the event was a success. The only "public embarrassment" I experienced was the mendacious headline in the *Post* and specific lies with which Sidney attempted to blacken my reputation, in particular his claims that I had abandoned my family along with my principles and fled to the fleshpots of Beverly Hills.

In the next sentence, Blumenthal elaborates the conspiracy he invented whose evil genie is the redoubtable Richard Scaife:

> Horowitz now headed a conservative group funded by Scaife, and he would serve as a conduit for Scaife's under-writing of Drudge's defense and provision of a lawyer employed by a Scaife-funded front group.

The lawyer employed by the Scaife "front" group would be Klausner and the front group would be my Individual Rights Foundation. In fact, I have had four conversations with Dick Scaife in the 17 years his foundation has provided funds for mine, none of them about Drudge. Nor did Scaife earmark any contribution he ever made to me or my foundation for Drudge. Scaife's funds represent about 10 percent of the total monies that went to support all my efforts at that time. Though I would certainly miss them, if Scaife should decide to terminate his support, their absence would not significantly impact my operation. I am supported by more than 30,000 individual donors along with 15 foundations and am confident that if any among them should abandon me, there will be others to fill their place.

I am not even certain that Dick Scaife is familiar with the specific activities of the Individual Rights Foundation, which was actually funded by his son, David, a liberal, who has not been on speaking terms with him for years. Manny Klausner is the general counsel of the Individual Rights Foundation. Most of the funds that went to Klausner were raised through the Matt Drudge Defense Fund appeals and were contributed by tens of thousands of individuals and no foundations, including Dick Scaife's.

Moreover, most of the underwriting for the Drudge legal effort was contributed by Klausner himself in the form of pro bono hours. The money we were able to raise barely covered the court costs, expenses for depositions, and travel to Washington DC.

Blumenthal makes a big deal in his book (and in all his self-dramatizations) of the fact that Matt Drudge didn't call him to fact check the story that precipitated his libel suit. Here is a passage from the letter his lawyer wrote to Drudge when the story appeared, which is reprinted in *The Clinton Wars*:

> Your action in disseminating these outrageous falsehoods across the country was despicable. You acted with actual malice in that you knew that these allegations were false, but published them anyway. You took no steps to verify your allegations.... Indeed, in your cowardice, you never even bothered to check with Mr. and Mrs. Blumenthal before scattering your lies....

Which is a perfect description of Sidney Blumenthal's own journalistic and political *modus operandi.*

5

The Surreal World
of the Progressive Left

It is not for nothing that George Orwell had to invent terms like "double-think" and "double-speak" to describe the universe totalitarians created. Those who have observed the left as long as I have understand the impossible task that progressives confront in conducting their crusades. Rhetorically, they are passionate proponents of "equality" but in practice they are committed enthusiasts of a hierarchy of privilege in which the highest ranks are reserved for themselves as the guardians of social righteousness. Rhetorically they are secularists and champions of tolerance, but in practice they are religious fanatics who regard their opponents as sinners and agents of civil darkness. Therefore, when they engage opponents it is rarely to examine the facts or refute an argument but rather to destroy the messenger himself and remove him from the field of battle.

Consequently, misrepresentation of facts, distortion of motives and general acts of character assassination are the familiar modes of progressive discourse, as any conservative can attest. The raw material for this verbal malice is stored on data-sites with titles like RightwingWatch, SourceWatch, MediaMatters and MediaTransparency, which provide an armory of abuse to be deployed in conflicts with their opponents. Eventually the sheer volume creates an alternative reality which no progressive would even think to check.

---

*This article was published on January 25, 2008, http://archive.frontpagemag.com/Printable.aspx?ArtId=29654

Of course not all leftists are ideological zealots or at least don't start off that way. Last week we posted an interview with me that was conducted by an intelligent and seemingly reasonable young progressive at Campus Progress named Jesse Singal.[1] Before agreeing to be interviewed by Singal, I asked him to correct a malicious profile of me that Campus Progress had posted as one of the guides it provides to its student activists under a general heading "Know Your Right-Wing Speakers." In its grotesque distortions of my statements and positions, the profile is typical of the caricature that passes for "David Horowitz" in the universe of progressive discourse.

Once Singal offered to correct any errors in the Campus Progress profile, I readily agreed to make myself available for the interview. After a month had passed, however, without any correction, I contacted Singal who assured me it was just a matter of fact-checking and would be changed. It never was, although to be fair Campus Progress did post my rebuttal alongside its smears.[2] I am reprinting it here with my specific rebuttals inserted, as a case study in progressive dishonesty.

Know Your Right-Wing Speakers: David Horowitz
Friday March 30, 2007
David Horowitz seems to relish his role as a former campus left-ist who now gleefully spews angry criticism of academia and the left. Horowitz spent his college years, in the late 1950s, at Columbia University, where he was involved in American Maoist Communist political organizations. He went on to receive his Master's degree at another hotbed of liberalism, the University of California, Berkeley.

I was never a Maoist. I will be happy to produce copies of my attacks on Maoism that appeared in *Ramparts* in the 1960s and

---

[1] http://archive.frontpagemag.com/readArticle.aspx?ARTID=29401;
http://campusprogress.org/archives/index.php/rss/rss/P4780/
[2] http://campusprogress.org/tools/155/know-your-right-wing-speakers-david-horowitz

1970s, or a copy of my book *Left Illusions,* which contains at least one of these articles. At Columbia I was a member of the NAACP, which was the only organization I belonged to in college.

His about-face occurred in 1985 when he launched an assault against his erstwhile leftward compatriots, whom he now calls "violently, fervently committed to their unholy war to tear down American democracy and replace it with their version—an Americanized version—of communism." In his reformed state, Horowitz still describes himself as "a civil rights activist" on his website. His blood, sweat, and tears go into defending that downtrodden demographic, white males.

I didn't do "an about face," as a single act, let alone in 1985. I stopped being active on the left when the Black Panthers murdered my friend Betty Van Patter in 1974. I have described this event, along with the transformation of my politics, at length in *Radical Son* (which is available to anyone who is interested in the actual record). I wrote an article about my disenchantment for *The Nation* in 1979, because even though I had grave concerns about the movement and had ceased to be politically active, the left was still my community. The article was about the left's double standards, and unwillingness to take responsibility for its own crimes and mistakes.[3] In 1984, I cast my first Republican vote for Reagan. I did so because he was opposing the efforts of the Sandinista Marxists to turn Nicaragua into a socialist gulag like Cuba. I had supported Fidel; I wasn't going to make the same mistake twice.

The description of my civil-rights activism as defending white males is a malicious misrepresentation of my attitudes but typical of leftist attacks. To take one practical example I am responsible for millions of dollars flowing into an inner-city organization called Operation Hope, which has Andrew Young and other left-wing Democrats on its board. I received an award from this organization for my efforts. As should be evident to any honest reader,

---

[3]See "Left Illusions" in this volume.

what I've actually written on civil-rights issues (e.g., in *Hating Whitey and Other Progressive Causes*, 1999), my efforts are directed in support of blacks and against their oppression by white progressives who control inner-city councils and school boards.

> *Horowitz's "civil rights" activism has manifested itself in a twisted series of seemingly bigoted and clearly controversial attacks. Included in this list are his August 16, 1999, column in* Salon *entitled, "Guns don't kill black people, other blacks do" and his 1999 book,* Hating Whitey and Other Progressive Causes. *In 2001, Horowitz stirred national controversy when he ran nasty advertisements in college newspapers across the country entitled "Ten Reasons Why Reparations for Slavery is a Bad Idea—and Racist Too." The full-page ads ran in several college papers, causing some to issue retractions and apologies, and others to receive protest from outraged students and accusations of racism. Horowitz capitalized on the latter by declaring an "assault on free speech" by left-leaning students.*

If my article about guns and blacks was actually bigoted, how is it that *Salon*'s progressive editors published it without objection (I was a regular columnist for *Salon* in those days.) In fact the article is not bigoted but is a criticism of the NAACP for suing gun manufacturers because the number-one killer of young black males is gun homicides.[4] My article challenged the NAACP to address the real problems that afflict inner city blacks and cause this violence. Here's a sample paragraph: "If the NAACP and other black leaders want to end the terrible scourge of gun violence committed by young inner-city blacks they should launch a campaign to promote marriage and family formation in the African American community; they should issue a moral plea to the community to stigmatize fathers who abandon their children and parents who have more children than they can afford. Instead of waging war against law enforcement agencies and supporting destructive racial

---

[4]See "Guns Don't Kill Black People, Other Black People Do," in Volume 4 of this series, *Progressive Racism*.

demagogues like Al Sharpton, they should support the Rudy Giu-
lianis and other champions of public safety, whom they now
attack. They should campaign for a tripling of police forces in
inner city areas to protect the vast majority of inhabitants who are
law-abiding and who are the true victims of the predators among
them."

One may disagree with this point of view but only a moral illit-
erate or someone who hasn't read my article would describe it as
bigoted against blacks. My book *Hating Whitey* (which is about
the left's hatred of white people) is an argument in behalf of black
people, not against them. The ad I ran against reparations also originated as a *Salon* article, which was titled "Ten Reasons Why
Reparations for Slavery is a Bad Idea—for Black People—and Racist
too." I thought it was a bad idea for black people because it isolated them from all other Americans including Hispanic immigrants, who were being asked to assume responsibility for slavery
and pay reparations for a system that was ended 135 years before.

> *Campus Progress doesn't join those who say Horowitz doesn't
> have the right to speak. We just think his speech is ill-mannered,
> ill-considered, and ill-informed. It should be met with rational,
> firm, strong arguments and real facts. Horowitz came under fire
> again for a January 26, 2005, posting on the History News Net-
> work website about "Why I Am Not Celebrating" the 90th
> birthday of the esteemed African-American historian John Hope
> Franklin. Franklin is the James B. Duke Professor Emeritus of
> History at Duke University and chairman of President Clinton's
> Commission on Race. Horowitz launched an attack on Franklin
> for his response to Horowitz's anti-reparations ad, denouncing
> him as "a racial ideologue rather than a historian" and "almost
> pathological."*

John Hope Franklin attacked me as someone who was pro-slavery, an easily disproven lie, which Campus Progress repeats:

> *In the piece, Horowitz tried to defend his claim that "free blacks
> and the free descendants of blacks ... benefited from slavery."*

What this fragment of a quote really said was this: Proponents of reparations argue that all of America's wealth is based on slavery and that's why everyone alive today, including Hispanic immigrants whose ancestors weren't living in America during slavery, should pay reparations. My response was that if all Americans today benefit from slavery as the proponents of reparations argue, then blacks alive today are also beneficiaries, which undermines the reparations argument. To represent this as being pro-slavery or as saying slavery was beneficial to blacks is either ignorant or dishonest. For a historian like John Hope Franklin to make such a claim is disturbing.

> Through it all, Horowitz has found a smarmy, backhanded way of misrepresenting himself as a defender of civil rights—he baselessly brands his ideological opponents as "racist" to deflect criticism of his own racially inflammatory remarks.

If I have called opponents racist it is either in response to their attacks calling me racist (to make a point), or a description specific to their racial beliefs. It is not a label I carelessly or baselessly ascribe to my ideological opponents. This is something the left is comfortable doing, as I have just demonstrated.

> A contributor to numerous right-wing publications, Horowitz is the president of the Center for the Study of Popular Culture, a think tank financed by conservative funders that serves as an incubator for right-wing radicals. The group's online journal, Front Page Magazine, began running Ann Coulter's column after her post-9/11 radical anti-Muslim comments got her fired from The National Review. Horowitz is a regular on TV and radio shows, where he mindlessly attacks the supposedly liberal media and denounces it for its "falsehoods."

Ann Coulter was never employed by *The National Review*. They merely dropped her syndicated column. Her remarks about 9/11 were obviously satire. The left apparently has no sense of humor. If Jonathan Swift were alive today the left would accuse him of suggesting people eat babies.

> *Horowitz continues his campaign against supposed "liberal bias" on college campuses through his organization Students for Academic Freedom. According to Horowitz, America's schools are moving towards a "one party academic state" that is governed by a ruthless liberal dictatorship.*

I have never campaigned against "liberal bias, never use the word "bias" (since everyone has one) and wrote—in so many words—in *The Professors* that academics have a right to express their points of view.

> *He regales campuses with tales of liberal outrages, some of which cannot be documented despite diligent efforts by researchers and may never have occurred at all.*

This is false. There have been no such diligent efforts, and I have refuted this canard on many occasions which can be found in the article archive on my website, *Frontpagemag.com*, under "Replies to Critics."

> *Horowitz also authored the "Academic Bill of Rights," a misleading manifesto already introduced in eight state legislatures—and in the U.S. House of Representatives—touting the need for "academic diversity" in university faculty.*
>
> *The Academic Bill of Rights would prohibit professors at both public and private colleges from introducing "controversial matter" into the classroom.*

This statement is false. I have never called for the prohibition of controversial matter in the classroom. I have said that if a controversial issue is being discussed, it is a professor's obligation to make students aware that it is controversial and provide them with critical material so that they hear at least two sides to the question. This is what used to be called a liberal position and has been part of the academic-freedom tradition articulated by the American Association of University Professors since 1915.

> *The bill would shift oversight of college course content away from trained professors and administrators and into the hands of state governments and courts.*

This statement is false. I have never sought such legislation, nor have I ever suggested that government should have oversight of college curricula.

> *While it has not been formally adopted anywhere yet, it has inspired legislative policies toward "intellectual diversity" in Ohio and Pennsylvania. The Inter-University Council of Ohio has reached an agreement with Senate sponsors of the Ohio Academic Bill of Rights to implement key principles of "academic freedom" in Ohio public and private universities.*
>
> *Despite fierce objections from the American Association of University Professors, the National Education Association and the American Federation of Teachers, the Pennsylvania House of Representatives passed a resolution that required a Select Committee to "examine, study and inform the legislature about the condition of academic freedom in the state's universities" on July 5th, 2005.*
>
> *Horowitz smugly declared that if the liberal school boards had not refused to adopt his non-legislative Academic Bill, government intervention would be unnecessary. Horowitz and his overwhelmingly right-wing supporters insist that the grievance procedures in the Ohio Academic Bill of Rights and the Pennsylvania resolution protect all students from discrimination based on political/ideological affiliation. After nearly a year and countless hours of testimony, the committee concluded that there were few if any academic freedom violations in Pennsylvania, and that no legislation was necessary. Horowitz has continuously mischaracterized the hearings.*

The above says very little and what it implies is misleading. The Committee conducted no investigation whatsoever of academic-freedom abuses. It was tasked with inquiring about academic freedom policies. What the committee found was that students had no academic-freedom rights in Pennsylvania and no grievance machinery, so it is no wonder that the administrators who testified said that there were no abuses. The Committee's absurd conclusion was the result of a political coup by the teacher unions and their legislative allies.[5]

> *The Academic Bill of Rights is both redundant and misleading. Most colleges already have rules ensuring free expression (political and otherwise), and Horowitz and his supporters have been able to offer scant evidence of campus political bullying.*

Both these statements are false. The Academic Bill of Rights is not about free expression; it is about what is professionally appropriate in a classroom and preventing professors from indoctrinating students instead of educating them. The evidence of faculty bullying of students is substantial.

> *The Bill of Rights serves as a perfect guise for his true aim: to pressure state-funded colleges and universities to pack their faculties with conservative professors.*

This is absolutely false. The first tenets of the Academic Bill of Rights forbid the hiring or firing of teachers on the basis of their political views.

> *According to Students for Academic Freedom, the group seeks "to get more than 500,000 signatures—10,000 per state—to present to lawmakers, alumni, regents and administrations across the nation" in support of the bill.*

This is news to me. I know of no such plans.

---

[5] I have described in detail what took place in *Reforming Our Universities,* which was published after the above rebuttal was written. Volume 6 of this series, *The Left in the University,* recounts the campaign for an "Academic Bill of Rights" and deals with these issues.

*Leading the "victimize us no more!" call to arms that has
become a trademark of conservative pundits, Horowitz laments
the blacklisting" of conservative students and professors and
calls on his followers to keep a close eye on their professors. He
urges them to help him keep a record of the supposed political
bullying that he says occurs regularly in college classrooms in
his Academic Freedom Abuse Center.*

*The Academic Freedom Abuse Center, housed on the Students
for Academic Freedom website, invites students to report having
their "rights abused" in class. But it only looks impressive until
you start reading the actual claims. Some highlights: One student complains because her professor suggested men and women
might see colors differently. Another is offended she was asked
to watch an "immoral Seinfeld episode." A recent entry in the
database was from an Ohio State student who claims he got a
bad grade on an essay because his English professor " hates families and thinks it's okay to be gay." (Another complaint comes
from an Augustana College senior who is upset her school used
"funds from Student activity fees to bring in the one-sided
speaker David Horowitz.")*

This refers to what is simply a bulletin-board for students and
their complaints. The last comment from the Augustana student
shows that we're fair-minded.

*Campus Progress hopes that students, faculty, campus adminis-
trators, and legislators of all ideological and political stripes will
stand up against these efforts by Horowitz to turn state governments into Campus Thought Police.*

This is a false and malicious claim. Every piece of legislation I
had something to do with was a toothless resolution asking universities themselves to honor their own commitments to academic freedom. They are attempts to thwart the Campus Thought
Police and encourage administrations to put their houses in order.

*Censorship is wrong, whether from the left or the right. Faculty
members ought to be judged on whether their scholarship is*

strong under the standards of their academic discipline and whether they are good teachers—not on whether the views they express meet specific guidelines established by state legislatures.

I agree that censorship is wrong, which is why I have campaigned against it, whether it's conducted by government or by professors who suppress one side of an argument.

In addition to the widely criticized Hating Whitey and Other Progressive Causes, Horowitz has authored such books as Destructive Generation: Second Thoughts About the Sixties, The Politics of Bad Faith, and The Art of Political War, which Bush chief campaign strategist Karl Rove called a "must read."

In a recent "lesson" on his new website, DiscoverTheNetworks.org, Horowitz makes the outlandish claim that most of America's progressive leaders, Hollywood entertainers and civil rights advocates are closely aligned with radical Islamist terrorists known for killing Americans.

Please provide the quote which makes this outlandish claim. I never said any such thing, specifically that most of America's progressive leaders, Hollywood entertainers and civil rights advocates are closely aligned with radical Islamist terrorists known for killing Americans. DiscoverTheNetworks is an encyclopedia of the left. It is not an argument that everyone on the left thinks alike or is in alliance with anyone else on the left. A social democrat headed NATO during the Cold War. That did not make him a conservative. He was a leftist who was an anti-Communist.

He's not kidding around. Though at first glance (not to mention upon further inspection) it seems like a simple-minded ploy to earn chortles among the right at the expense of the left, he warns, "This database reflects links that are not merely caricatures by political enemies but are legitimate indices of a political reality." In Horowitz's political reality, Sen. Barack Obama appears on the same row as terrorist leader Abu Musab al-Zarqawi, and John Walker Lindh, the American Taliban, appears next to the Center for American Progress's very own John Podesta.

The previous comment should suffice to dispel these misconceptions. However, what is being referred to here is a picture-index for the database which no longer exists. The fact that Podesta and Zarqawi are in the same database has no more significance than the fact that they are in the Wikipedia database except that the DiscovertheNetworks database is limited to the political left. I'll wager that no one at Campus Progress would object to a database of the right that included Hitler and Sean Hannity or Phyllis Schlafly so why make a federal case out of this one?

Lately it seems that Horowitz will peddle crazy stories to just about anyone who will buy them. In March, he admitted that one of his favorite examples of the extreme liberal bias among college and university professors, is a story which he had never been able to substantiate,

For months Horowitz and his ilk had been chirping on and on about a University of Northern Colorado professor who, they said, asked his criminology class to explain on a midterm "why President Bush was a war criminal" and then failed a student who explained instead why Saddam Hussein was a war criminal. Anti-conservative bias at its best! Unfortunately, in a March 15th report on InsideHigherEd.com, a spokesperson for the school deflated Horowitz's claims, saying that its information "was inconsistent with the story Horowitz has told about this incident," including the question asked, the grade given, and the reasons for the grade the student received.

To repeat: I never use the word bias let alone the phrase "extreme liberal bias." Second this was not about bias on an exam; it was about compelling students to take one side of controversial issues. Third, what I said was correct. The details are contained in

---

[6] See Volume 6 of this series, *The Left in the University*.

"The Case of the Colorado Exam," available on the Front-pagemag.com website.[6]

> *Meanwhile, the day before InsideHigherEd published its report,*
> *Horowitz had attacked Media Matters for slander on his website*
> *and had stood up for the validity of the story. Horowitz, always*
> *interested in the limelight, continued to beat this horse further*
> *to death, arguing that Media Matters was "creating a mountain*
> *out of the molehill of this particular case (our campaign is based*
> *on hundreds of cases)." Sound familiar? Remind anyone of a*
> *very posthumously abused horse named Ward Churchill—one*
> *crazy in a hundred non-crazies that folks like Horowitz talked*
> *about till they were blue in the face? Seems that Horowitz was*
> *just getting a taste of his own medicine.*

Churchill has hundreds if not thousands of "crazy" faculty sup-porters including the Ethnic Studies Association and the entire Ethnic Studies Department at his University.

> *Speaking of tasting, Horowitz was one of several conservative*
> *speakers who got pelted with food by students during speaking*
> *events in April 2005. On April 6, while delivering a speech to*
> *Butler University students, someone hurled a cream pie that hit*
> *Horowitz smack in the face. Campus Progress in no way*
> *endorses such attempts to curb free speech. Horowitz has as*
> *much of a right to speak his mind as the rest of us, no matter*
> *how weak his arguments or hazy his facts. And we don't like*
> *wasting pie, which is (often) delicious. We do think it's particu-*
> *larly lame that instead of chuckling it off and trying to save face,*
> *Horowitz is pressing criminal charges and is on a mission to get*
> *the perp suspended.*

This is made up. The cream pie was shoved in my face. I didn't press criminal charges. I don't think and never claimed that the "perp" was a student, and never pressed for him to be suspended.

> *On April 29, 2005, while speaking at Columbia University,*
> *Horowitz caused quite a stir when he passed out a pamphlet*

that bore a picture of Noam Chomsky with a turban and beard, under the heading, "The Ayatollah of Anti-American Hate." At least Horowitz has a sense of irony: He was there to lecture students about the importance of "ideological diversity." Apparently, this diversity doesn't apply to lefty American scholars.

I don't get this. I have never called for Chomsky to be fired or to be barred from classrooms. I wrote a pamphlet about Chomsky's anti-American fervor. How is this anti-diversity?

Students are starting to push back against Horowitz's famous untruths and hate speech (and we don't mean with pies). Recently, when speaking to students at the University of Hawaii, Horowitz was interrupted by a student each time he told a lie. Instead of shouting him down, however, the students simply corrected Horowitz's misstatements. Needless to say, the students were then told to "shut up" by Horowitz supporters.

The account of my appearance in Hawaii is pure fantasy. My speech couldn't be started for 20 minutes because of the disruptions of campus fascists—leftwingers who had welcomed Ward Churchill as a conquering hero only a month or so before. There were no interruptions once university officials warned the disrupters they would be removed if they continued.

Also recently, our friends at ThinkProgress had the pleasure of being featured in a FrontPage magazine article by Horowitz titled, "The Multiple Lies of John Podesta and Friends" for filing his precious Academic Bill of Rights under "Radical Right-wing Agenda." Apparently Horowitz doesn't see how equating a progressive and inspiring young leader like Senator Obama with a murderous terrorist would be considered radical.

---

[7]See "Discover the Networks" in this volume.

This is a reference to the misunderstood index in Discover-theNetworks.org, which I've already dealt with and which no longer exists.[7]

These days, Horowitz is continuing his unapologetic, unquestioning defense of the Bush White House while accusing liberals who question the war of being anti-American.

This is false. Todd Gitlin opposes the war. I published an article by Gitlin on Frontpagemag.com and called it "A View From the Patriotic Left." I published another anti-war leftist, Sherman Alexie, and also referred to him as patriotic.

He recently attempted to convince the public that Bush was "exonerated" by the bipartisan membership of the Senate Intelligence Committee for his false statements during the 2003 State of the Union about Saddam Hussein seeking African uranium. Actually, what Horowitz referenced was not part of the Senate report, but rather a sentence from a British government inquiry that wasn't published until a week after the Senate report came out. Meanwhile, he slams liberals who question the war—calling them anti-American in his columns in FrontPage Magazine—but never speaks of his fellow conservatives who likewise are outraged about the mess in Iraq.

This is garbage regurgitated from Media Matters, a website run by a self-confessed compulsive liar, David Brock. I have harshly criticized anti-American right-wingers like Justin Raimondo and Lew Rockwell, as well as presidential candidate Ron Paul, on my website.

Horowitz, envisioning right-wing extremism beyond college campuses, has now launched Parents and Students for Academic Freedom, an organization promoting his agenda in primary and secondary schools. They have partnered with ProtestWarrior, one of the far-right's primary high school organizing groups that specializes in outrageous pro-war propaganda. The site for his new underage crusade prominently features stories from an anony-

mous 11-year-old who complains of such events as when a
teacher asked the class, "What would a Taoist think of Bush?"
After researchers have failed to confirm many of the stories from
university campuses Horowitz has claimed to collect, are we
really supposed to trust his nameless grammar school insider?

This is a repeated slander thrown in my direction by the organized left that opposes my Academic Bill of Rights. I have replied to the so-called researchers of the left in the "Replies to Critics" section of my site. The left declares evidence of abuses to be false, and disregards the refutation of their claims.

Despite Horowitz's continuing inability to prove any systematic
anti-conservative bias, he continues to spew forth accusations.

I have written almost 100,000 words analyzing the curricula of more than 200 college courses which actively indoctrinate students in leftwing ideology, not merely express a leftwing bias. These analyses can be found at www.discoverthenetworks.org in the academia section under Indoctrination Studies.[8]

In 2006, Horowitz published The Professors: The 101 Most Dangerous Academics in America, *attempting to create a McCarthyish blacklist of liberal professors.*

The above statement is false. The book specifically defends the right of leftwing professors to express their leftwing views. It is not a blacklist and it is the opposite of "McCarthyish."

Once again, Horowitz's undoing came by way of fact-check. As
Media Matters documented, Horowitz's condemnations are
based on in-classroom statements by professors in only six of the
cases, and, in 52 cases, was entirely dependent on outside-class-
room activities. Furthermore, an in-depth report by Free
Exchange on Campus, entitled "Facts Count," further eviscer-

---

[8]http://www.discoverthenetworks.org/viewSubCategory.asp?id=522. See also, David Horowitz and Jacob Laksin, *One-Party Classroom*, 2009

ated Horowitz's claims, document-ting an absence of student corroboration (only 13 cases, none of which have withstood further scrutiny), manipulation and distortion of quotes, and in some cases, outright fabrication. Many of the accused professors have responded to Horowitz, often finding the accusations so unsubstantiated as to be comical.

The ludicrous "reports" by MediaMatters and Free Exchange (a wholly-owned subsidary of the American Federation of Teachers) were refuted point by point by Jacob Laksin in "Discounting the Facts," which is available in my article archive under "Replies to Critics."[9] Free Exchange simply ignored the refutation and failed to reply to it.

However blatantly ideological and indefensible, Horowitz appears determined to continue preaching "Academic Freedom" to his dwindling choir. In 2007, an increasingly grumpy Horowitz (see grumpy photo) published Indoctrination U: The Left's War Against Academic Freedom. Despite Professors having been roundly denounced, Horowitz recycles already-debunked misrepresentations, half-truths, and creative exaggerations to rehash his agenda. Horowitz blames those intolerant leftists and indoctrinated drones for dismissing his campaign, brushing past any substantive critiques of his ideological bias and dishonesty. Horowitz appears to have been drowned out by his own petulance, with his book already in the discount bin.

More falsehoods. *Indoctrination U* will sell about 20,000 copies, quite respectable for such a book, and probably several times what Michael Bérubé's *What's So Liberal About the Liberal Arts* (which was written to combat my campaign) has sold. *The Professors* has sold about 50,000 copies. This summary of the

---

[9]Laksin's rebuttal is an appendix in Volume 6: *The Left in the University*, of this series.

contents of my book is no more accurate than the wishful thinking about its sales.

> As even the conservative faithful lose their taste for pundits high
> on provocation and weak on proof, perhaps Horowitz should
> reassess just why nobody is listening to him. (And, no, we're not
> just saying all this because Horowitz recently referred to Cam-
> pus Progress as "the gutter left." But thanks for the mention!)

With this "profile" as evidence, I think it's safe to say "gutter
left" is about right.

> So read up on Horowitz and get ready—he may just be bringing
> his cries of liberal bias to a campus near you! You can track leg-
> islation in state legislatures and find out more at Free Exchange
> on Campus, a coalition organized by Campus Progress, the
> American Federation of Teachers, the Center for Campus Free
> Speech, the ACLU, and others.
>
> Some of our Favorite Horowitz Quotes:
> "Leftism itself is an infantile disorder. In the view of this
> puerile left, the American government is an omnipotent father
> who is to be blamed for everything—and is so blamed in order to
> exculpate the children, leftists like Brown and Sheehan, from
> their responsibility for anything." (9/1/05)
> "Do I think some members of the anti-war movement are in
> actual formal contact with the radical Islamists and advancing
> their agendas. Yes I do. Do I think you and Cindy Sheehan are?
> Only peripherally in that the radical Islamists are integrated
> into the anti-war coalition generally." (to David Swanson, cre-
> ator of MeetWithCindy.org, 8/19/05)
> "You see, the left isn't forgiving or civil. Instead they are vio-
> lently, fervently committed to their unholy war to tear down
> American democracy and replace it with their version—an
> Americanized version—of communism." (3/8/2000)
> "The so-called "peace movement" today is led by the same
> hate-America radicals who supported America's totalitarian ene-
> mies during the Cold War. They marched in support of the Viet-
> cong, the Sandinista Marxists and the Communist guerrillas in

El Salvador. Before that they marched in behalf of Stalin and Mao. They still support Castro and the nuclear lunatic in North Korea, Kim Jong-Il. They are the friends in deed of Osama bin Laden and Saddam Hussein." (4/7/2003)...

—*updated by Niral Shah, Dartmouth College*

PART IV

Two Talks on
Autobiographical Themes

Plus Ça Change:
Fifty Years Gone By

I'm glad to be here with you at this our fiftieth class reunion. In fact (and sorry to remind you of this) we've all reached that point in life where we can appreciate George Burns' crack that at *his* age he was glad to be anywhere.

I am especially pleased to be on a platform with my old teacher, Professor Bernard Wishy, whom I have not seen in fifty years. I have often reflected on the impact a few select teachers encountered early can have over the course of a life. Even though Professor Wishy was an instructor of mine for only a single term in my sophomore year in 1956, he is one of these influential mentors for me.

I vividly recall an exchange in his class with a student who strenuously objected to Freud's *Moses and Monotheism* for reasons I have long since forgotten. What I do recall is Professor Wishy's command of Freud's sources and the texts of his critics, in answering the student, even though it was not his own academic field of expertise. In that exchange Professor Wishy conveyed a powerful message to us—that knowledge was a serious business and that there were no simple answers to the questions that truly mattered.

But the most profound impression he left was his classroom demeanor, which exemplified Columbia's official mission, defined in those days as "the disinterested pursuit of knowledge."

This is a talk given at Columbia at the fifty-year reunion of the Class of '59, June 9, 2009, on a panel titled "Changes in the Fifty Years Since We Graduated." [Some leftwing alumni made a failed attempt to rescind my invitation.] http://archive.frontpagemag.com/Printable.aspx?ArtId=35156

Professor Wishy was a scholar, not a proselytizer. We never knew when he might be playing devil's advocate, and taking positions he didn't himself hold in order to shake us from our reflexive assumptions. I don't recall him ever expressing his personal beliefs in the classroom, whether political or religious or otherwise. I don't know how he voted in the 1956 election, or whether he was of the opinion that religion is an illusion as Freud maintained.

Instead, the point of his teaching was to illuminate the process by which one confronts an intellectual argument, understanding that in order to do so one must be acquainted not only with the facts but with the arguments that have preceded one's own. He was there, in other words, to teach us *how* to think and not to tell us *what* to think—therefore to respect the divergent opinions of others. I am afraid this is a vanishing ethos in our culture and a dying pedagogical art in our university classrooms today.

In short, what Professor Wishy taught by example was respect for the difficulty we experience as ordinary mortals in arriving at the truth concerning life's most vexing questions. This was not a lesson I absorbed easily. I was too filled with my own youthful certitudes for that. Nonetheless, I kept the memory of Professor Wishy's classroom with me for the next 20 years until a personal crisis of belief finally allowed me to appreciate what he had taught.

Another influential Columbia teacher was Moses Hadas, a professor of classics who is no longer with us. In one memorable class Professor Hadas drew our attention to the Roman General Scipio Africanus, who wept when his soldiers burned the great city of Carthage because he saw in the flames the future of his beloved Rome. The ancients did not have our view of history as a progress. For them it was a series of cycles, the story of civilizations that rose and fell, came into being and were gone.

In retrospect, it seems odd to me now that Scipio's tears should have made such an impression on a young radical. I arrived at Columbia believing that a progressive future was imminent and that it would transform everything we knew.

Consequently, I viewed my college education not as a step on a personal career path but a preparation for my life mission, which was to participate in a revolution that would change the world. Grandiose as this may sound, it was an audacity of hope shared by all progressives in one form or another, and is still so today.

By contrast, the ancients believed that the world cannot be fundamentally changed, at least not by human beings. At the end of the first chapters of Genesis, an angel with a flaming sword is said to stand at the gates of Eden to prevent us from re-entering because the first man and woman had already demonstrated that it is not within our nature to achieve an earthly bliss.

As a result of the flaws in our nature although we may secure justice in this case or that, injustice we will have with us always. This is why the preacher, Ecclesiastes, said, "There is nothing new under the sun." The French have a similar phrase: *Plus ça change, plus c'est la même chose:* the more things change, the more they are the same.

These statements recognize the fact that the world that so obviously needs repair is a world that we and human beings like us have made. Consequently, our efforts to make it a different world will necessarily fail. This is the religious view of the circumstance we find ourselves in. It is also the conservative view, and it is mine.

Have there been changes since we left Columbia fifty years ago? There have. But from a conservative vantage, none of them have altered the fundamental pattern of our lives—the self-centered and selfish desires, the envy and resentment of others, the resort to dishonesty when it suits our ends, which are the real causes of the social ills we wish to redress.

Some of the changes of these 50 years have been good; others have been bad; some of the good changes have come with consequences that are bad; and regarding some of the changes, there is less to them than meets the eye. *Plus ça change.*

I came to Columbia more than 50 years ago at the tail-end of the McCarthy era as a leftist whose Communist parents had lost their teaching jobs because of their political views. Today, I have returned to Columbia as a conservative.

But in fact the views I hold on the issues that are thought to define these labels such as race and freedom of expression, and my concerns for the poor and those left behind, are no different today from what they were then. The parameters around me have changed, and also my understanding of how things work, but not my fundamental values. Fifty years ago, my radical views caused me to feel like an outsider at Columbia. Returning as a conservative, I find myself an outsider still—and again it is because of my political views.

In the half-century since I graduated, this is the first time that I have been invited to an official Columbia function, and even so the occasion is an alumni reunion not a formal academic event. This exclusion has occurred despite the fact that I am the well-known author of many books, several concerned with university reform; and despite the fact that my son who is also a Columbia alumnus has donated a generous scholarship fund to the college for minority students; or that my granddaughter is currently a Columbia student so that we are in a manner of speaking a Columbia family. Evidently, I have been more loyal to Columbia than Columbia has been to me. Even the invitation to this alumni function had to be sustained against a strenuous resistance by some of my classmates who are professors now at other schools and are apparently of the opinion that my views should be suppressed.

And this attitude of exclusion is a prevailing one among current Columbia faculty. So far as I can ascertain, there is not a single prominent conservative intellectual on Columbia's liberal arts faculty today. The dozen or so books I have written, like those of other well-known conservatives, though widely praised and highly regarded in the world outside Columbia, are more effectively banned in its classrooms than were the books of Marxists 50 years ago, during the height of the McCarthy era.

From a conservative vantage, the changes that have taken place in the last 50 years can be regarded as the result of scientific and technological advances, and do not represent a fundamental reordering of the relations between human beings themselves.

This is the case, for example, with the changes that have taken place in the lives of women, who have moved into a variety of public roles in unprecedented numbers. These developments are quite different than a change in the fundamental relationships between the genders, in male respect for women or in the nature of women themselves.

To the politically incorrect like myself, these new roles and the respect they earn are the result of technological developments that have relieved women of arduous tasks on their end of the division of labor, and of scientific innovations that allow them to control their reproductive cycles and be protected from routine mortality in childbirth.

This conclusion is reinforced by my experience as a student of English literature at Columbia fifty years ago. One of the leading and most honored Shakespearean scholars in the nation at the time was Columbia professor Caroline Spurgeon. Benighted as we may have been back then, I do not remember anyone who thought it odd that Professor Spurgeon was a woman or thoughtless of her work because of it.

Similarly, when I took a course in the 19th-century English novel, five of the twelve authors we read were women, and this was well before the publication of *The Feminine Mystique* and the beginnings of the so-called "women's liberation movement," whose subtext was that men, which would have included my teachers, were their oppressors.

It is true that in recent years we have witnessed the appointments of the first three women secretaries of state, and the first two women Supreme Court justices, with a third now on the way. But these are easily understood as a consequence of technological improvements that afford women new freedom to pursue such careers, rather than the overthrow of an oppressive ruling "patriarchy."

Thus, the Elizabethans I studied in my literature classes were called "Elizabethans" in deference to one of the most powerful monarchs in English history, because long before the women's movement she ruled her era.

In sum, as we embark on the 21st century, women and men are pretty much the familiar genders we encountered in our first days as undergraduates in our Humanities sections reading Homer's 3,000-year-old epic about Helen of Troy, who had the power even then to cause the launching of a thousand ships and the burning of the "topless towers of Illium."

Of course if you were to enroll today in Columbia's Department of Women's Studies you would be taught that we still live in an oppressive patriarchy and that gender differences are "socially constructed" and can be re-constructed, and then eliminated as we reach the highest stage of women's liberation. But this is ideology, not reality.

The fact that this ideology is a required creed for students of Women's Studies reflects not an advance in consciousness but the retrogressive return of American liberal arts colleges to their 19th-century roles as doctrinal institutions, the difference being that this time the doctrines are secular and political rather than religious.

Of course a large and important sector of our modern research universities has not regressed. The hard sciences—the engines of our technological futures—continue to progress. If one were to walk over to the departments of biology and neuroscience, one would learn that gender differences are not "socially constructed" but hard-wired as part of our genetic makeup. We can already see the next academic reformation coming as the new progressive religions increasingly clash with empirical discoveries in the biological sciences. *Plus ça change.*

While some changes add up to less than meets the eye, others have led to consequences that are nothing short of catastrophic. The last fifty years have witnessed the growth of a new environmental consciousness, for example, whose modest goal is to "save the planet." Talk about *hubris*! Shortly after we graduated Columbia, Rachel Carson published a book that is regarded as a founding document of the environmental crusade. Her tract warned that the continued use of DDT pesticides would kill the world's bird population and create a "silent spring." A little over a decade later, because of the influence of her book, DDT pesticides were globally banned.

As it happens, at the time Carson wrote, the world had been recently freed from the scourge of malaria, which had previously accounted for three million deaths a year. This was thanks to the Rockefeller Foundation[1] and its funding of a malaria eradication program, which relied on the pesticide DDT. Soon after the pesticide was banned, malaria reappeared. The resulting epidemics have produced a toll of preventable deaths that already exceeds any other in the grim annals of man-made mortalities.

Since the progressive doctrine of *The Silent Spring* was implemented, three million people have died of malaria every year for more than thirty years, adding up to a total now of nearly 100 million. Ninety-five percent of the victims have been black African children under the age of five. As a footnote to this tragedy, Carson's claim that DDT was harmful to birds has since been discredited.

Of all the battles Americans have fought to advance agendas that are generally regarded as "progressive," the one that appears to have had the most uncontroversial success is the fight against racial discrimination. There was a time not long before we came to Columbia when there were overt and unapologetic bigots in the U.S. Congress, such as Senator Theodore Bilbo, a member of the Ku Klux Klan and an avowed racist. Today no anti-black bigot could stand up in the public square and proclaim his bigotry and survive with a public career. And now we have our first black president.

---

[1] http://www.discoverthenetworks.org/funderprofile.asp?fndid=5210&category=79

At Columbia last year a noose was posted anonymously on an African American professor's office door.[2] The entire university—administrators, faculty and students—recoiled in horror and came to the defense of the target. We have come so far that no one could be surprised at that.

But it is only half the story. At the same time that anti-black prejudice has retreated from the public square, other forms of prejudice using other groups as targets have become acceptable, even normal, and particularly in the most "progressive" circles. At Duke University not too long ago a drug-addicted prostitute who was black accused three white students of a crime they did not commit.[3]

There was not a shred of evidence to sustain the charge, and much to contradict it. Yet the prosecutor, seeking the support of the black vote in Durham was not deterred. So reckless and racially motivated was his prosecution of the innocent students that he was subsequently disbarred for his actions, which included suppressing evidence that proved conclusively that they had not committed the crime.

Yet because they were white and the alleged victim was black, the public lynching of their reputations continued for a year. The president of Duke, an Ivy League scholar, expelled them in advance of any trial, terminated the athletic season of their team, and fired their coach.

Eighty-eight professors[4] condemned them as racists, associating them with slave owners and white rapists of the past. While the press protected the name of their accuser, it paraded their images before a mass audience and made them national pariahs.

This is a particularly ugly case, but the new racism reflected in its details has become institutionalized. At colleges and profes-

---

[2]http://articles.cnn.com/2008-02-21/us/columbia.noose_1_plagiarism-teachers-college-noose?_s=PM:US
[3]http://en.wikipedia.org/wiki/Duke_lacrosse_case
[4]http://www.discoverthenetworks.org/Articles/List percent20of percent20Gang percent20of percent2088 percent20Duke percent20Professors3.html

sional schools across the country, privileges are routinely granted to individuals officially designated as members of so-called "under-represented minorities" and withheld from others who belong to so-called "over-represented minorities."

The result is that if you are an impoverished and discriminated-against Asian student, universities will deny you financial aid available to wealthy African Americans and you will have to score much higher on your graduate achievement tests just to be able to apply to medical and law schools.

Forty-five years after the civil rights revolution, we have taken a giant step backwards in our efforts to create a society where the rules are color-blind and individuals are rewarded on their merit.

Taking a personal view of these developments, I note that when we entered Columbia in 1955 we understood that there was a quota system for Jewish applicants. It was masked as a geographical diversity program, as deceptive as the one I've just described, and rationalized as an attempt to create a student body drawn from all parts of the country. Its architects had figured out that that the pool of Jews in states such as Arkansas and Nebraska was likely to be small.

Still, the overall quota was rumored to be 48 percent of the entering class, which seemed generous to us then. The Nazis' "Final Solution" had recently (but only recently) given anti-Semitism a bad name, and it seemed as though things were changing for the better for the Jews. I was privileged, for example, to have taken a class with Lionel Trilling, the first Jew ever to be hired by an Ivy League English Department. From this perspective, a 48 percent quota persuaded us we were making real progress.

Today, even though there are many Jews on the Columbia faculty and Jews even sit on the board of trustees, there are also overt and unapologetic anti-Semites lecturing in Columbia classrooms, which would have been unheard-of in our day. There are now tenured bigots on the Columbia faculty whose classes are an assault on the only existing Jewish state—a tiny nation under continuous attack from an Arab world determined to extinguish it from the day of its creation more than 60 years ago.

More than six decades after Hitler's demise, an Islamic death-cult in the Arab world has made very clear—and in so many words—that it is determined to finish the job he started. A state leader of this cult whose government is about to become a nuclear power and who has declared his intention to wipe both Israel and America from the face of the earth was not too long ago invited to speak to students by Columbia's president.

It is true that President Bollinger was rude to the dictator when he came, and criticized him as a tyrant—an act of minimum decency (which notwithstanding elicited protest from Columbia's radical faculty). But why was a genocidal maniac whose declared goal is to kill the Jews so honored in the first place?

When we arrived at Columbia 54 years ago, America was engaged in a world war with another totalitarian ideology seeking to put an end to the West. Today we are faced with yet another that seeks our extinction. *Plus ça change, plus c'est la même chose.*

What is this *chose* anyway, this thing that doesn't change? It is the human desire to fill the emptiness that is our fate, which is unchanging and unchangeable: that we are born alone and we die alone and we are forgotten. Over this emptiness human beings drape their mythic causes and impossible dreams, their hopes for an earthly redemption—for a change that will fill the emptiness by creating a world that is holy or just. It is this hope that allows us to forget who we are. It is this vision that inspired the ideologues of communism; and it is this vision that drives the Islamic radicals who believe they are making the world safe for Allah by purging it of infidels, and the unfaithful, and especially Jews.

In these visions we Americans are seen as the party of Satan, as the unbelievers who stand in their way with our pragmatism and tolerance, our devotion to enterprises and pleasures that are *bour-geois* and mundane; and our hope that is reserved for individual lives and not for grandiose social collectives and schemes.

2

Reflections of a Diaspora Jew on Zionism, Israel and America

L et me begin by saying how honored I am to be invited to this podium by the Zionist Organization of America and Mort Klein, its courageous leader. For decades Mort Klein and the ZOA have stood on the frontline defending the state of Israel and American Jews, and they are doing it now in what is certainly one of the darker periods for the Jewish people—darker all over the world—in our 5,000-year history. I applaud you for supporting Mort Klein and his team. I am touched by the recognition of an organization like this for the modest work I have done in behalf of Israel and the Jewish people.

Still, there is a paradox at the heart of this honor awarded me by the Zionist Organization of America, which will take me a moment to explain. It is true that I am widely attacked by anti-Semites and Jew-haters and the enemies of Israel as a Zionist—and an arch Zionist at that. I have been called variously a Zionist Jew, an "Israel Firster Zionist Jew," "a rabid Zionist" (by Julian Assange no less), a "radical right-wing Zionist," an "extreme Zionist," an "extremist Zionist stalwart," an "un-repentant Zionist," an "ultra Zionist" and, inevitably, "a Nazi with a Zionist face."

Today, anti-Zionism is the cause of Jew-haters and anti-Semites the world over, and for Jews embarrassed by the fact that they *are* Jews and that others fear and despise them for that reason. Even the rare Jewish magazine of the left that is actually a sup-

Speech given before the Zionist Organization of America, September 6, 2012

porter of Israel, is uncomfortable with the connotations of the Zionist label, and with what it means for Jews to defend themselves. In a recent unflattering profile, *Tablet* magazine described me as touring the country "making the case for a *muscular Zionism.*"

I plead guilty to this charge. I plead guilty though I have never actually been a Zionist, or made a case for Zionism in the sense that Herzl and traditional Zionists understand it. Yes, I want muscular Jews and a muscular Israel. I want Jews proud of the extraordinary nation-state Jews created in 1948 out of the ruins of the Ottoman Empire. I want Jews who are armed, and Jews who will defend themselves with arms if necessary. Muscular in every way. Yes.

I want more than just *individual* Jews armed. I want a Jewish nation-state possessing in its arsenal the most advanced modern weapons available, a state that can be counted on to defend Jews from their global enemies, and particularly from their enemies in the Muslim world who are legion and who have sworn our destruction, and who are openly planning to complete the job that Hitler started. I want a Jewish state, armed to the teeth, because Islamic Nazis, who are the storm troopers of a second Holocaust, are already mobilized, and because—as we discovered during the first Holocaust—there are not enough non-Jews in the world who are willing and prepared to defend us.

I am glad that Israel exists. I am glad that there is a country that will preserve Jewish culture, and be a model to the world of what Jews can do when they are given the chance. Today Israel is per capita the world's leading scientific and technological innovator and contributor to human advancement. As a Jew I am proud of that.

I am also thrilled that in the creation of Israel Jews have regained their birthright. After 2,000 years of exile, the oldest surviving indigenous people in the world has won the right to some of its stolen homeland. I look forward to the day when Judea and Samaria, the historic centers of Judaism become part of the Jewish homeland as well.

That homeland is now occupied by Palestinian Arabs who are at war with Israel, who have proclaimed their Jew-hatred to the world, and who have forfeited any right to the territories by conducting five unprovoked, armed aggressions against the Jewish state. The official policy of the Palestinian Authority in the West Bank is to make Jerusalem and the entire region of Palestine *Judenrein*. No other country in the world is expected to suffer such genocidal assaults without securing borders that are defensible, and Israel should not be expected to either.

Nonetheless, there is a paradox in this honor given to me, a Jew who has never been to Israel and who has never considered himself a Zionist in the sense that its founders intended. Theodore Herzl and his followers embraced the Zionist idea because they believed that the creation of a Jewish nation would provide a solution to the "Jewish Question"—the fact that Jews had been a homeless people for nearly two thousand years and were ghettoized and persecuted in the alien lands to which they were driven.

Herzl's Zionist idea was grounded in the belief that the establishment of a Jewish state on Jewish land would finally "normalize" the Jewish people and end their persecution. The Zionist idea was that by including Jews among the nations, Jews would become like other peoples—that their inclusion would finally "solve" the Jewish problem. That was the meaning of Zionism as Herzl understood it, and indeed as it was understood until the Holocaust and the actual creation of the Jewish state.

But Herzl's dream proved to be a fairy tale, as delusional in its way as the dreams of socialism, communism and progressivism, whose believers hoped would provide solutions to the conflicts and sufferings that blight our human state. All these isms took hold in the 19th century, and became forms of modern faith. The traditional religions they supplanted had trusted in a Divinity for such a solution, but were forced into retreat before the advance of Darwinian theory and modern scientific developments. All the messianic visions of the modern age were driven by the desire for an earthly redemption that would resolve our human dilemmas and achieve what the heavenly redemption could no longer convincingly offer.[1]

Among these fantasies of a better world than the one we inherited, Zionism was the most conservative, and the most practical. The quest for a socially just future is based on no human reality but on the expectation of a human miracle, a transformation of who we are and what we have been into something wonderfully different. Zionism by contrast was based on the experience of actual peoples who had already taken their place among the nations. It was a quest for normality. Not for a world transformation but for an integration into the existing world of others.

But even this modest hope of the Jews has proved an impossible dream. It is true that half of Herzl's goal has been realized, and in an astounding way. Yet its very realization has proved the hope that inspired it to be a folly. By all standards of civilization and modernity Israel should be admired and emulated by the rest of the world. Instead, the Jewish state is hated and is a pariah among the nations, just as Jews themselves are pariahs in most of the world outside America today.

Far from creating a refuge, Israel has become the focal point of all the genocidal intentions against the Jews, which have never been more overt or more global. Today Israel is the site of a Holocaust for which the Islamic world openly yearns, and which the rest of the world—with the possible exceptions of America and Canada—will not lift a finger to prevent. This sobering reality has changed the meaning of Zionism, and has made it a more comfortable fit for me. Call it the Zionism of Survival.

In the household I grew up in, I was not brought up to be a Zionist because my parents were Marxist progressives who looked to a socialist future to provide an earthly salvation, and an end to the persecution of the Jews. My parents and their comrades believed that mankind's conflicts would be resolved by a universal

---

[1]This is the subject of my book, *A Point in Time: The Search for Redemption in This Life and the Next,* 2011.

class whose revolution would abolish all nations and unite all peoples, and thus remove the distinctions that made them Jews.

My realization that this was not going to happen occurred through my relationship with a Marxist mentor named Isaac Deutscher. Deutscher had written a book called *The Non-Jewish Jew*, by which he meant Marxists like us—Jews who were of Judaism but not in it. By the time I came under his influence in the 1960s, he had become a defender of Israel and had been one since the Second World War. Deutscher viewed Israel as a "raft-state"— a refuge that Jews could cling to after they had been shipwrecked in the storms that periodically engulfed them. The particular storm he was referring to was Hitler's "Final Solution."

During the interwar years, a debate had raged in Europe's left-wing circles, which carried momentous consequences for those who participated in it. The debate was about how Jews should respond to the looming fascist threat. The Zionists were urging Jews to flee the continent and take refuge in the Palestine Mandate. Marxists like Deutscher argued that the Jews should stay in Europe and fight for the socialist revolution. But as Deutscher ruefully acknowledged later, the Jews who listened to the Zionists were still alive, while those who listened to Marxists like him were dead.

Under Deutscher's influence, I became a quasi-Zionist, a believer in the raft state. Israel should exist and be defended until the socialist transformation abolished nation-states and solved the problem of the Jews once and for all.

Don't think for a moment that this is some quaint Marxist delusion now consigned to the historical dustbin. The idea of a world without borders is alive and well in the international left and among liberals and progressives in America. It is the idea that animates the Democratic Party's attacks on American sovereignty, and it is a vision whose intellectual leaders are Jews.

One of its canonical articles is called "Patriotism and Cosmopolitanism"—*for* the latter and against the former. It was written by Harvard philosopher Martha Nussbaum. According to

Nussbaum, the cosmopolitan ideal which progressive people should aspire to is "the person whose primary allegiance is to the community of human beings in the entire world." This attitude— that we are not Jews or Americans but "citizens of the world"— explains why people on the left are so uncomfortable with—or simply hostile to—issues of national security and patriotism. It explains why progressive Jews can be indifferent to the survival of the Jewish state.

Even as I absorbed Deutscher's lesson about the raft state, my belief in the progressive fantasy was rapidly eroding. I had begun to doubt the possibility of a redeemed future, a future fundamentally different from those with which we were historically familiar. As these doubts grew, they were changing my view of the unredeemed present. By the middle of the next decade I no longer believed in a new world order. This had immediate and profound consequences for my attitude towards Israel and my identity as a Jew, and as an American as well.

There was not going to be a future in which there were no longer nations or peoples in conflict; there was not going to be a future in which Jews would cease to be the objects of envy and resentment, and virulent hatred. There was not going to be a future in which a refuge—a raft-state—was no longer useful.

Then came 9/11 and the Islamic attack on the World Trade Center. It was an event that made millions of people aware of the Islamist movement in the Muslim world and the fact that they were conducting a holy war against infidels in general, and Jews in particular. The incubator and leading force of this holy war is the Muslim Brotherhood, an organization founded by an admirer of Hitler and a godfather of the call to push the Jews of Palestine into the sea. Today, the spiritual leader of the Brotherhood is the Egyptian imam, Yusef al-Qaradawi, who has publicly prayed that the Muslim believers will finish the job that Hitler started.

Millions of Jews are in denial when it comes to the determination of Islamists to kill them. In part, this denial is psychological and familiar as when people face a prospect that is too terrible to contemplate. There are a billion-and-a-half Muslims in the world today who worship a prophet who has told them that "the day of redemption will only come when Muslims fight the Jews and kill them, when the Jews hide behind the rocks and the trees, and the rocks and the trees cry out, 'Oh Muslim, there is a Jew hiding behind me. Come and kill him.'" For a billion-and-a-half Muslims that is the word of God. Denial is one convenient way of dealing with this fact.

This particular death-warrant for the Jews can be found on the official website of the University of Southern California, where it was placed by the Muslim Students Union, which is a front for the Muslim Brotherhood. When I asked a leader at the Wiesenthal Center to demand that this genocidal incitement be removed, his initial response was, "But it's a religious statement." Well, yes, but it is also a summons to kill the Jews. Such is the force of denial.

One of the chief instruments of the Muslim Brotherhood is the Muslim Students Association, which sponsors "Israeli Apartheid Weeks" at universities across America and throughout the western world calling for Israel's destruction. Muslim Students Association members chant "Palestine will be free from the river to the sea"—that is from the eastern boundary of Israel to the western one. It is a call for the liquidation of the Jewish state *because* it is Jewish. Yet all across America, campus rabbis hold ecumenical dialogues with the Muslim Students Association, and defend it against its critics.

I have traveled to many universities to oppose these Jew-haters, and everywhere I go I am protested against and defamed by the Muslim Students Association and by their Jewish enablers. I have met with numerous campus rabbis and asked them to set conditions for their ecumenical outreach: first, that their Muslim counterparts desist from sponsoring Israeli Apartheid Weeks, and denounce those who conduct them; and second, that they only hold dialogues with people who publicly support the right of a Jewish state to exist in the Middle East.

For these efforts I have been attacked by Hillel rabbis at Yale, the University of North Carolina, the University of California

Santa Barbara, and the University of Florida, and by Hillel student leaders at the University of Pennsylvania and other schools. For voicing these concerns, I have been called a bigot, a racist and an "Islamophobe," which is a smear invented by the Muslim Brotherhood to silence its critics.

Last year I published a full-page ad in the *Yale Daily News* whose headline read: "The Palestinian Case Against Israel Is Based on a Genocidal Lie." The genocidal lie is the claim that all of Israel—or any of Israel—is occupied Arab land. It is a claim used to justify all of the murderous acts committed against the Jews of Israel. In fact, Israel was created out of the ruins of the Turkish Empire, as were Jordan, Syria, Lebanon and Iraq. The Turks are not Arabs, and Israel does not occupy any Arab land.

The Middle East conflict is not about land or a Palestinian state. It is a 60-year war of aggression first by the Arab League and then by Sunni and Shi'ite Muslims to destroy the Jewish state and push the Jews into the sea. This war is now a religious war, an expression of Islamic Nazism.

To be perfectly clear, I am not referring to all Muslims as Nazis. I am referring to the Muslim Brotherhood and the Islamic forces now ascendant in Egypt and the Middle East who are actively promoting a second genocide of the Jews, along with their supporters in America and their secular allies on the political left.

When my ad about the Palestinian lie appeared in the Yale paper, the Slifka Center, the focus of Jewish life on campus, was outraged. They were *not* outraged by the Palestinian lie but by my ad, which told the truth. They were outraged because the truth offended the Muslim Students Association, with whom they wished to be friends. To counter my ad the Slifka Center published its own full-page statement. It affirmed the Slifka Center's "respect"—and I quote their words—"for the Muslim Students Association, which does not spread hateful lies about Israel."

The Slifka statement then attacked my ad as the purveyor of "hateful ideas," which it said would "lead to tragic rifts between the Jewish and Muslim communities," as though campuses across the country were not already reverberating to the chants of "Palestine will be free from the river to the sea," or as though Muslim masses were not already chanting "death to Israel" at the call of Hizbollah and Hamas and the Islamic Republic of Iran. Having made its commitments clear, the Slifka ad then invited students to an evening with the Ground Zero Mosque imam, Feisal Abdul Rauf, hosted by Slifka Center director James Ponet, the celebrity rabbi who officiated at Chelsea Clinton's wedding.

The suicidal tendencies of the intended victims of Islamic supremacy are tragically familiar. They recall the sad delusions of members of the *Judenräte*—the Jewish Councils in the Nazi ghettos—who organized the Jews for Hitler's death camps, while pretending to themselves that the Germans were too civilized to kill them.

Delusions about Islamic Nazis are hardly confined to Jews, however. In the eyes of the Islamic fanatics, Israel may be the "Little Satan" but America is "The Great Satan," the arch demon that must be destroyed in the name of Allah. In his *fatwas* Osama bin Laden identified Islam's enemies as "Jews and Crusaders," America being Christian and therefore the "Crusader Nation." Every Islamist leader and organization from Ahmadinejad to Qaradawi, from the Muslim Brotherhood to Hizbollah and Hamas has promised death to Israel *and* America as the necessary means to their malignant ends.

Meanwhile, the Crusaders—like the Jews—are asleep. It is an old story. Just before the Second World War, Whittaker Chambers, a Communist defector, attempted to warn Roosevelt that a White House advisor named Alger Hiss was a Soviet agent and that his administration had been penetrated by Communist operatives. When Roosevelt was informed of Chambers' charges he laughed and dismissed them. Hiss then accompanied Roosevelt to Yalta where he helped conclude the deal that delivered Eastern Europe to the Soviet Empire and triggered the Cold War.

Here is a story that may prove worse than that of Alger Hiss. In a series of foreign-policy disasters the Obama Administration has assisted the Muslim Brotherhood in transforming the Arab Spring in the Middle East into an Islamist winter; beginning with the toppling of an allied regime in Egypt and the accession to power of the Muslim Brotherhood, and its expansion throughout the region. In August, the new Egyptian president sacked his military commanders, abrogated the Constitution, and assumed dictatorial powers greater than those possessed by his predecessor, transforming Egypt into an Islamist state. Opponents of the dictatorship were crucified—literally nailed to crosses—in front of the government headquarters. It was the Brotherhood's way of dramatizing its intentions to turn Egypt into a medieval totalitarian state.

This was exactly what the American State Department had assured the world the Muslim Brotherhood would not do as it paved the way for the Brotherhood's accession to power. The intelligence chief of the Obama White House had officially described the Muslim Brotherhood as a "moderate" and "secular" organization, which had embraced democratic and constitutional government.

The betrayal of these promises, and the violation of every principle the American government claimed to be supporting in the Middle East's most important state, took place without a word of protest from the American government or the American Secretary of State.

As it happens the chief adviser on Muslim affairs to the American Secretary of State is Huma Abedin, one of whose mentors was the Nazi imam, Yusef Qaradawi. Abedin is an operative for the Muslim Brotherhood and a lifelong servant of its agendas. In the twelve years directly proceeding her hiring by the U.S. Government, where she became deputy chief of staff to Hillary Clinton, Abedin worked for Abdullah Omar Naseef, one of the principal financiers of Osama bin Laden and al-Qaeda, and a Muslim Brotherhood eminence. Huma Abedin's mother and brother are Muslim Brotherhood leaders, as was Huma's father.

In its work for the Brotherhood, the Abedin family was specifically tasked with running Abdullah Omar Naseef's *jihad* operation, the Institute of Muslim Minority Affairs. The title sounds innocuous enough until you understand that the express goal of the Institute is to transform the Muslim minorities in non-Muslim countries into Muslim majorities as part of the Islamic *jihad*, with the express intent of creating Islamic states—in short, to conquer those countries for totalitarian Islam. To accomplish this goal Muslim minorities must be prevented from assimilating into non-Muslim societies and also be indoctrinated in Islamic supremacist ideas. That was and is the mission of the Abedin family. In addition to the network of Saudi-funded mosques in target countries like the United States, the chief organizations for accomplishing this goal are the Muslim Students Association, on whose Executive Board Huma Abedin served, and its offshoot, the Islamic Society of North America, which is now the principal source of advice on Muslim affairs for the Obama administration.

In other words, at the right hand of the American Secretary of State and the center of American foreign policy, is a woman whose family-members are leaders of what the Muslim Brotherhood calls its "grand jihad"—its plan to infiltrate non-Muslim societies and "destroy the Western civilization from within"—in those exact words. And what people do these *jihadists* regard as the chief obstacle to their sinister designs? The Jews.

In the words of their own manifesto: "The greatest challenge that faces Muslims in America and Canada are the Jews, who take advantage of their material ability and their media to distort the image of Islam and Muslims thereby spreading lies in the minds of the people of these countries." The Jews also "serve Zionist interests in the Arab regions."

In the hands of the Islamists and their allies, Zionism has become the name of all the opponents of Islamist supremacy and its holy war against infidels, against Jews and Christians, Israel and the United States. Americans and Israelis, Jews and Christians have their backs to the same wall. One cannot be defended without defending the other. Supporters of freedom are all Zionists now. And that includes me. That is the way this war of the civilizations, or—as I prefer it—this war between Islamist barbarism and civilization, will continue until it is finally concluded, and the next conflict begins.

I say this because, as a conservative, I understand that conflicts are endless and these battles are without end. To be a conservative is first to understand that there is no solution to the dilemmas of the human condition. Second, it is to understand that to escape these dilemmas, human beings will inevitably embark on desperate quests for redemptions in this life. These redemptions, in turn, will require holy wars to purge the world of demons—of those who do not share their faith, and who stand in their way. In this regard, totalitarian Islam is really no different in its heart from totalitarian socialism or progressivism, even though the latter are secular and the former is pursued in the name of a vengeful and malignant God. Both seek to cleanse mankind of its irreparable imperfections.

To remain free beings, we are continually forced to defend ourselves and our breathing space, against the efforts of the redeemers to perfect us—against the armies of the saints who are determined to make the world a better place than it can ever be. That is how I see the political wars we face, and why they will never end.

On a personal level, and to answer the question I raised at the beginning of this talk about my identity: I am comfortable being a Diaspora Jew, both in this present struggle with the enemies of America and Israel, and beyond. Diaspora is the name of our Jewish exile, but exile is also the name of our human condition. We are thrust into this life, and remain here for a while, and then we are gone. If there is a home for us that is truly permanent, it is not of this time or of this place.

My country, America, and the country of my people, Israel, share a common destiny. They are the gathering-places of exiles, of those who understand better than others that we have no permanent abode in this world. It is because of this that we cherish the freedoms and the homes we do have, and we are not afraid to fight for them.